Physics, Patents, and Politics:
A Biography of Charles Grafton Page

PHYSICS, PATENTS,

AND

POLITICS

A Biography

OF

Charles Grafton Page

ROBERT C. POST

SCIENCE HISTORY PUBLICATIONS
NEW YORK • 1976

Science History Publications
a division of
Neale Watson Academic Publications, Inc.
156 Fifth Avenue, New York 10010

© Science History Publications 1976

First Edition 1976
Designed and manufactured in the U.S.A.

Library of Congress Cataloging in Publication Data

Post, Robert C
   Physics, patents, and politics.

   Bibliography: p. 206
   Includes index.
   1. Page, Charles Grafton, 1812-1868. 2. United
States. Patent Office--History. I. Title.
TK140.P3P67   621.3'092'4 [B]   75-44017
ISBN 0-88202-046-3

Contents

Prologue:

Franklin, Henry, and Page

> In pure science we think that we have no reason to be abashed. Franklin, Henry, and Page, not to mention others, certainly may be regarded as exponents of pure science of whom any country should be proud.
>
> Journal of the Telegraph, *June 16, 1878*

This is a book about a man famous in his own time but since forgotten. Never was he as famous as Benjamin Franklin, the archetype of all American culture heroes. Nor did his repute match that of his contemporary, Joseph Henry. Nevertheless, a century ago his name could come readily to the mind of a journalist seeking exemplars of "pure science" in America. The *Journal of the Telegraph,* the leading periodical of its kind, was not posing a deliberate anomaly for future generations to puzzle over. Nor was it by any means alone in assigning Page lofty rank. A year later a prominent Washingtonian named Peter Parker wrote that Page was somebody "of similar intellect and virtue" to Professor Henry.[1] Parker was speaking as the head of a committee (the other members were Spencer Baird and Asa Gray) charged with compiling a volume of "obsequies" to Henry, who died in May 1878 after 32 years as secretary of the Smithsonian Institution. Charles Page had died exactly a decade earlier after almost as long in the capital himself, most of it in association with the United States Patent Office. Numerous obituaries recalled his "eminent scientific attainments," and *Silliman's American Journal of Science* published a 17-page memorial.[2]

Page's obituary in *Silliman's* was laudatory but not quite so effusive as those in the press or in technical periodicals. His strongest encomiums came from quarters peripheral to the mainstream of professional science. There was a reason for this, which I shall examine in due course. While Page and Henry had once projected similar images in the scientific world, by the time of Page's death he generally was not afforded the same degree of status. The *Journal of the Telegraph* was obviously not a scientific periodical, nor was Peter Parker, who linked Page's "intellect" with Henry's (and with that of Louis Agassiz), a scientific man. He had made his reputation as a surgeon, missionary, and diplomat in China. Moreover, he had been Page's brother-in-law and a close family friend for many years. Parker, nevertheless, moved in the same circles as Washington's most eminent scientists and had come to know many of them intimately. Like Jonathan Homer Lane, who wrote Page's obituary for *Silliman's*, he had been present at the creation of such elites as the Scientific Club in the early 1860s and the Philosophical Society of Washington in the early 1870s. And for more than ten years he had been a regent of the Smithsonian Institution and a confidant of Joseph Henry.

The question, therefore, is why posterity has not shared the judgement of a significant number of Page's contemporaries. Were Peter Parker's perceptions simply all awry? Or do they illustrate Page Smith's dictum on the advantages possessed by "an intelligent contemporary:"

> He was there. He saw it happen, felt it, experienced it on many levels. It was part of the complex fabric of his life. Like a seismograph, he recorded through the channels of his nervous system and stored in his brain (rather than in a filing cabinet or archive) the emotions, ideas, realities of his era. And he recorded these, if he was a person of sensitivity and judgement, in roughly the proportion in which they were present in his environment.[3]

Dr. Parker was certainly a person of sensitivity and judgement, but he was no more a deliberative historian than he was a scientist. Of course, the truth lies somewhere in the middle— between the perception of those who rank Page with the best, and the assessment of those who dismiss him as scarcely worth mentioning. His strangely mixed repute, indeed, is one reason why I think Page clearly merits a biography. I also hope to show that among other things he *was* a noteworthy exponent of "pure science"—or, at least, that he should not be consigned to a realm altogether different from that of Franklin and Henry.

A very grand man once wrote, "The author of every book must feel surprised that his subject has waited for him."[4] With Page there is reason both to be surprised and not to be. I shall not elaborate much on that here, since all that follows is essentially aimed at unraveling this apparent paradox. Still, I ought to emphasize a couple of points. First, there exists no extensive body of secondary literature relevant to any of the major facets of Page's professional career. For the history of federal administration and science policy, the writings of Leonard White and Hunter Dupree are genuine landmarks. But they have not yet spawned many progeny. The history of American technology has quite accurately been depicted by Edwin Layton as being in its "Jared Sparks" stage of development.[5] The overall picture of the internal development of science in 19th-century America remains sketchy in spite of the productivity of more than a dozen first-rate scholars. How peripheral the subject still is to *general* American historiography is suggested by the lacunae in the recent *Encyclopedia of American Biography*. Some of the very best specialists in the field, such as Dupree, Edward Lurie, and Carroll Pursell, wrote essays for that volume, yet the editors omitted Alexander Bache (while including John Barrymore), Robert Hare and Eben Horsford (while including Dashiell Hammett and George Halas), and Charles Henry Davis (while including Elmer Davis). Which is not to say that important actors, writers, sportsmen, and commentators do not merit attention. Yet, so do the preeminent figures in American science. I think there is cause for optimism, however, since it is scarcely conceivable that general historians will ignore the splendid books published recently by Bruce Sinclair, Margaret Rossiter, and Sally Kohlstedt.[6]

Second, with reference to some grand scheme of things, it would perhaps have been more fitting to tackle Bache, or Davis, or even Joseph Henry, all of whose existing biographies leave something to be desired. It so happens that Page provides a fine focal point for studying subjects whose import far transcends the history of science or technology per se, but the same is true of the others. When it comes to why historians choose to write about what they do, I am somewhat inclined toward mystical explanations. Given the apparent *raison d'être* of much ordinary political biography—easy availability of source material—Page is not an obvious choice. I have frankly had to guess about some important matters, simply because there is no collection of *Page Papers* to consult. At the time of his death in 1868, his correspondence was described as "voluminous" by a personal friend whose word on the subject may safely be taken literally.[7] I know of the whereabouts of only a small amount, and, while it is not inconceivable that a substantial cache still exists in some proverbial old attic, the likelihood seems remote.

That being the case, it *is* a bit distressing to realize that determinations of individual historical stature rest in part simply on the survival of manuscript resources—that is, often on sheer accident. To shift the focus briefly, take Leonard Gale, a scientist close to Page and even closer to that most renowned of American inventors, Samuel F. B. Morse. As the best of Morse's biographers suggests, Professor Gale was by no means the least noteworthy of Morse's associates. Yet he is surely the least known—no doubt because he "did not leave a mass of papers for the benefit of prying historians." [8]

Of course, the mere existence of a body of personal papers hardly guarantees that historians will do their "prying," no matter how deserving the subject: Lane, for years Page's best friend, and a bona fide mathematical physicist from an era when nonesuch was thought to exist in America, has attracted the attention of only one scholar, while Moses Farmer, the most prolific American electrical inventor prior to Edison, remains almost totally neglected. Nevertheless, the absence of manuscripts is usually sufficient to relegate significant figures, particularly scientists, to the nether lands of our historiographical panorama. The irony is that with many people their most revealing correspondence is going to turn up in the papers of others *anyway*. There is a substantial body of "Gale Papers," for instance, both in the Morse and Alfred Vail collections in Washington. By the same token, Page manuscripts are not at all difficult to come by in the papers of at least a dozen of his contemporaries. They also exist in great profusion in the records of the Patent Office. That practically all of this is stilted and official prose by no means renders it useless—indeed, examiners' comments are extremely valuable as source material for the history of technology—but it does greatly diminish its value as an avenue of insight into personal motivation or as a means of filling narrative gaps.

On the other hand, I am willing to accept Mr. Gibbon's presumption that "conjecture" is a legitimate historical technique and that "the knowledge of human nature . . . might, on some occasions, supply the want of historical materials." I may as well admit in advance that here and there—solid documentation being absent—I have fallen back on introspection. Certainly the number of unambiguous discrete "facts" available about Page is tiny compared to those on Franklin or Henry (whose papers have provided material for two of the most important editorial projects of our time). I am not greatly concerned, nor have I tried to elevate him to their level in a pantheonic sense. I do presume, however, that his life has an intrinsic interest; and, beyond that, I propose to use him to look at some neglected aspects of science and technology, and at some of the interrelationships between scientists, inventors, politicians, and bureaucrats in mid-19th-century America.

I hope not to distress anybody unduly by occasionally throwing in the much-maligned dichotomy, *internal* and *external*. For better or worse, I use these words as a convenient shorthand in the most simplistic sense possible: the one to signify science (or technology) per se, the other institutional superstructure. They still identify two hostile historiographical camps, I know, but on that score I stand nonaligned. I can see only limited virtue in deliberately divorcing science from its socio-cultural context. On the other hand, to ignore the fact that 19th-century American science did have an identifiable and sometimes significant internal substance is to play into the hands of those who contend that a specialist in this subject really has nothing important to deal with *except* externals. That I simply cannot admit.

The scholars responsible for our two most exemplary biographies of American men of science, Edward Lurie (Louis Agassiz) and Hunter Dupree (Asa Gray), each did me the great honor of reading and commenting upon earlier versions of my manuscript. While neither will agree fully with everything I have written, each will see ideas of his own reflected and sometimes even his very words. Professor Dupree's *Science in the Federal Government* is a book I found literally indispensible. I also appreciate all that I have learned, face-to-face and in print, from Nathan Reingold, P. J. Federico, James E. Brittain, and many of my colleagues at the National Museum of History and Technology. From two others I learned much more than just data and interpretations, I learned most of what I regard as important about history as a craft. Those two are Professor John W. Caughey and Dean John G. Burke of UCLA.

To Professor Caughey and his good wife LaRee, and to the Smithsonian Research Foundation, I owe financial sponsorship during many long months of data grubbing. While attempting to breathe some life into my stacks of facts, I had the opportunity to try out ideas in a variety of settings: annual meetings of the Society for the History of Technology, Dr. Reingold's Nineteenth Century Seminar—an institution in the Smithsonian castle, informal reports to the National Museum's Department of Science and Technology, and formal lectures at UCLA, the University of Minnesota, and the University of Delaware. I appreciate the feedback of each of these occasions. Portions of what follow were originally published in the April 1972 and January 1976 issues of *Technology and Culture,* and to the worthy editor of that worthy journal, Dr. Melvin Kranzberg, I say thanks. Thanks also to Mrs. Joseph W. Hazell, Page's grand-daughter, for prints of portraits and daguerreotypes she owns; and to her son, Dr. William Hazell, for copies of family correspondence from his collection, which includes both the first and last extant writings in Page's hand.

Finally, a dedication: I could dedicate this book to Professor Page, whom I consider a good friend and a good man, if not perfect—for obviously *it* could not exist had *he* not, or had he, say, managed to electrocute himself at a young age (something easily conceivable). But then I perhaps could have written about someone else. Not alone, though. I couldn't have written *any* book at all without the help, encouragement, and understanding of my wife, Dian—and so it is to her that this is dedicated with gratitude and affection.

Robert Charles Post
Washington, D.C.
January 12, 1976

Chapter One

Career of Science

> . . . it would be difficult to name a philosopher, either in this country or Europe, whose discoveries and inventions in this department of science [electromagnetism] have, within the last two or three years, been more numerous or valuable than those of Dr. Page.
>
> Report of the Second Exhibition
> of the Massachusetts Charitable
> Mechanic Association, *1839*

> I know of no philosopher more capable of close reasoning on electro-magnetic and magnetic electrical physics than Professor Page.
>
> *William Sturgeon, 1850*

> . . . if the achievements of mind are to terminate only with the exhaustion of its resources and capabilities, then *'the end is not by and by.'* . . . Part of man's duty and destiny is to comprehend and know all that the GREAT CREATOR has put under his dominion, and he is yet hardly aroused to the task.
>
> *Charles Grafton Page,*
> *"Career of Science," 1853*

In the spring of 1838, a veteran Salem shipmaster dropped anchor for the final time, closed his accounts, and headed south to settle down beyond sight or sound of ocean waters. During nearly 40 years in the East India trade Captain Jere Lee Page had shared ownership in more than a dozen vessels, his personal commands ranging from the *Sally*, a 56-foot schooner, to the *Betsey*, a ship of 207 tons. Having seen his fortune ebb and flow, he quit the sea at 59 with less than he might have at another time, but with a nice profit still—enough, first of all, to pay $4,000 for a handsome half-section on the Leesburg and Alexandria Road in Fairfax County, Virginia, five miles from Washington City.

Right off, he christened his new plantation "Pageville." Joining him there were Lucy Lang Page, his wife for 34 years, and seven unmarried children, four daughters and three sons. Hardly a year later the youngest, 16 year-old George Derby Page, was dead of typhoid. With their boys, the rude instrusion of tragedy was something all too familiar to Jere and Lucy Page.

One had died in infancy; another, his father's namesake and a sea-captain too, perished in the Caribbean at age 25. Yet another, Henry Lawrence Page, was crippled by poliomyelitis and forever dependent.

There was one more son, Charles Grafton Page, at 26 now the eldest. In the eyes of his mother and father, Charles made up for an enormity of heartache. He was strong, quick, cultured, and altogether brilliant. Henry Wheatland, a schoolmate who became head of the Essex Institute in Salem, recalled him as "a leader among the gymnasts, a famous skater, a loved companion, and a very great favorite with all."[1] He could hold himself at arms' length from a vertical pole, vault a fence higher than his head, throw his voice, do uproarious impersonations, and perform wonderful tricks of magic. He excelled at rhetoric. He sang and played the flute exquisitely. He wrote with consummate grace.

But most impressive about Charles Page were his learning and intellect. He read everything. Not long since, he had earned a Harvard M.D. degree, America's most respected academic credential. Everyone who knew him well, even as a boy, could see he was special. Elder brother Jery might follow his father to sea when not yet 21, but that was not the life for Charles. Indeed Jery had written him from Havana in 1828:

> You are the only classical Page in our book, and take care you do not disgrace any of its meaner leaves. If you do I'll heave you overboard [even] if you are expert at gymnastics. Be aware that you now stand at the head of the Page and mind keep there or I will log you and stop your grog.

A day or two later, Jery cleared port and sailed into the eye of an uncharted late-summer hurricane, never to be seen again. He had felt a premonition: in his final letter he mused that "only a pine plank is the barrier between us and eternity," and then closed by telling Charles, "May God bless you, may you have a long and happy life, and may the promising appearance of your early younger years never be blasted by any of the storms of this frail life."[2]

Charles would have made his brother proud. Between the founding of the Republic and the War of 1812, Salem produced a remarkable generation of men who attained preeminence in letters and science, among them William Hickling Prescott, Josiah Willard Gibbs, Nathaniel Hawthorne, Benjamin Peirce, and Henry Wheatland. Historian, scholar, novelist, mathematician, naturalist—Charles Page might have made his mark in any of these ways. Like Prescott, born in 1796 and 16 years older, he had a fine sensitivity to the vitality of things past; like Wheatland, just his own age, he was insatiably curious about every facet of his own environment. He loved natural philosophy in each of its branches, but the one whose attraction proved strongest was the most abstruse of all. It was an enthusiasm which made him—all his congeniality notwithstanding—a rather awesome figure among his peers. For Charles was interested in electricity.

Tales of his youthful Franklinesque exploits abound. In 1821, at the age of nine, he carried a fire-shovel to the roof of his father's house at 15 Chestnut Street amidst a roaring thunderstorm, determined to catch a shock from a surcharged cloud. "What a merciful providence that shielded the future genius from instant annihilation," a close friend later remarked.[3] At ten, he fixed up an electrostatic machine using a lamp-glass and took utmost delight in shocking unwary visitors. In 1828 he made another such machine, a rather novel one he called a "portable electrophorus." A few years later—on the day of Andrew Jackson's reinauguration in 1833 as it so happened—he sent a description of it to Benjamin Silliman at Yale. This became Page's initial article in Silliman's *American Journal of Science*, the first of more than 40.[4] The device was, besides, the first of dozens he conceived that Daniel Davis, Jr., subsequently manufactured and marketed as laboratory equipment.

It was in 1828 that another American turned to the study of electricity, Joseph Henry of the Albany Academy. Over the next four years Henry made experiments which, if not so dazzling as the contemporaneous researches of Michael Faraday at the Royal Institution, were remarkable nonetheless. Inspired by Henry's presence so close by, Page was bound to focus his own attention on electromagnetism. He was 19 and a junior in Cambridge in 1831 when Faraday and then Henry discovered electromagnetic induction; five years later he himself began a series of experiments that significantly extended scientific knowledge relating to this phenomenon. For some of these he designed an instrument for augmenting voltage that constituted the prototype of the 19th-century's most important tool for basic research in physics, the induction coil.

By the time Page left Salem in 1838 nearly a dozen of his research papers had appeared in print. These had caught the attention of William Sturgeon in London, an electrician whose experimental finesse was second only to Faraday's. Sturgeon had just launched a periodical he called *Annals of Electricity, Magnetism, and Chemistry*, which was then unique for its specialized purview. Not the least significant contribution of Sturgeon's *Annals* was to broadcast in Britain the work of both Page and Henry. He began reprinting "Dr. Page's interesting papers" in his initial volume, often appending remarks about this discovery being "very important" or that apparatus "exceedingly ingenious."[5] Later, James P. Joule, confronted with an anomaly in his youthful experiments with electromagnets, saw how it could be resolved on the basis of Page's research. At home, promising youngsters like Oliver Wolcott Gibbs had been expressing unabashed admiration for the elegance of his apparatus. And Joseph Henry himself had begun to repeat Page's experiments. Soon he would get in touch, addressing Page in a tone of high regard.

A few years hence, Professor Henry would be coming south himself, to take in hand the infant Smithsonian Institution and there build a reputation assuring his place as the most honored American scientific figure of the century. In the late 1830s, however, the Smithsonian Institution remained without form, and void, an object of perhaps irreconcilable controversy about the meaning of James Smithson's enigmatic phrase "for the increase and diffusion of knowledge." To contrast the ideas of two scientific men who later became close associates of Page, Walter R. Johnson wanted an institution for experimental physics on the order of the École Polytechnique in Paris, but Charles L. Fleischmann envisioned a Germanic sort of school of agronomy and agricultural chemistry. Joseph Henry was nowhere in the picture, especially since there was really no reason to presume that the Smithsonian should be a *scientific* institution at all.

Moreover, in some quarters it appeared as if Henry was losing his preeminence in electrical science. Refer, for example, to the first comment on Page quoted at the head of this chapter. In 1838, Sturgeon told his fellow editor, Benjamin Silliman, of his "very great respect for [Page's] high talent as an Experimental Philosopher," then added—seemingly as an afterthought—that Henry was "another esteemed worthy in Experimental Science."[6] Six years later, Senator Robert Walker, an astute amateur, looked back and concluded that the outstanding pieces of electromagnetic apparatus developed in America had been the "machine for producing shocks, invented by Page, and the powerful galvanic magnet of Henry."[7] Even in 1846, the year of Henry's decision to

10

move to Washington, a new periodical called *Scientific American* could toss off a remark about "the [electromagnetic] discoveries of Professors Page, Henry, and others."[8]

Rarely if ever since 1846 has anybody else seen fit to assign Page and Henry that order of billing. From the perspective we now have on the half-century spanning the 1830s and the 1870s, Henry clearly looms first as the premier scientific practitioner in America, then as an institutional figure virtually without peer. While there can be no question about Henry meriting his stardom, Page had very much more than a bit part. Nevertheless, subsequent generations tended to forget what his contemporaries knew, that he, too, was a scientist of "high talent."

Page even played an institutional role of some consequence. Before Henry arrived in the capital—even before the man who became the great sultan of science in the federal government, Alexander Bache—he had made himself a fixture on the Washington scene, learned the more recondite aspects of its power structure, and established an important professional affiliation with the Patent Office. The antebellum Patent Office constituted one of the few places outside academia that employed men on the basis of their scientific competence. Moreover, it paid them extremely well and allowed them remarkable latitude, at least in its formative years. By the time Page died, after the Civil War, the office had 20 principal examiners plus a swarm of assistants and showed signs of bureaucratic stagnation; but when he arrived in 1842 he was one of just *two* and policy remained exceedingly fluid. Examiners were officially subordinate to the commissioner, of course, yet in the day-to-day run of things much depended on individual personalities. Men of exceptional prestige like Page often attained a virtually unchecked autonomy. For a time the office was dominated by examiners who had a very stringent concept of novelty. Initially Page was their philosophical leader, but he later switched his precepts completely—with quite profound consequences both for himself and for the operation of the patent system.

An analysis of Page's position *vis-à-vis* the Patent Office and its constituency helps shed light on various conflicts attendant upon the professionalization of American science in the mid-19th century. Still, there is absolutely nothing to be said about Page— not even had he been the most extraordinarily autonomous patent examiner, or the most influential proponent of patent reform (for he was that too)—which from an institutional standpoint could

11

make him appear very large next to Joseph Henry. In electrical science *qua* science, however, the two men do not seem so mismatched. It is true that Page neither made a discovery as seminal as Henry's "extra current" (self-induction), nor pursued any investigation with the thoroughness of Henry's five-part "Contributions to Electricity and Magnetism." There are, nevertheless, intriguing comparisons to be made.

Page's publications on electricity and magnetism between 1836 and 1839 roughly equaled Henry's total for the whole decade, and in the 1800–1863 volume of the *Royal Society Catalogue of Scientific Papers* each man has precisely the same number of citations, 41. Page's all date between 1834 and 1854, whereas Henry's span a considerably longer time. Both ultimately shifted their research to fields other than electromagnetism. What was unusual about Page in the beginning, however, was his high level of specialization. This was in contrast to Henry, or to any other American scientist, for that matter. Henry's first major paper dealt with the topography of New York State. Robert Hare of Philadelphia did significant work in electromagnetism, but traditional chemical pursuits always commanded his fundamental loyalties. The electrical experiments of other chemists such as John White Webster of Harvard were prompted simply by a transient curiosity. Chemistry was the science in which Page was best trained formally—the professor who influenced him the most was Dr. Webster—and as an undergraduate he may well have regarded electromagnetic effects "as a subspecies of chemical phenomena," a common contemporary assumption.[9] For years afterward he was sought out because of his expertise in chemistry; for example, he served as a formal consultant to committees charged with ascertaining the most suitable stone for constructing both the Smithsonian Institution and the Washington Monument. Nevertheless, his comprehension of electricity as a branch of physics could be matched by few of his contemporaries.

Consider an assessment by a great electrician of a later generation, John Ambrose Fleming. In Fleming's opinion, by the late 1830s Page "had acquired a strong grasp of the true principles of electro-magnetism."[10] In view of the Whiggish propensities of such a scientist *cum* amateur historian, one must assume that Fleming meant the "true principles" as *he* understood them in the 1890s.

Another *fin de siècle* historian of electrical science, very much impressed with Page's "reasonings" on magnetism, implicitly

12

ranked him with Joule, Arago, Foucault, and Faraday.[11] Others elevated him to comparably lofty realms. They exaggerated, of course, yet it does seem ironic that in our own time historians have often consigned Page to their pigeonhole for "ingenious mechanics," along with Thomas Davenport, thereby denying that he was any scientist at all. Davenport surely has an impressive claim to credit for inventing the electric motor, yet as late as 1833 he was under the impression that a galvanic battery "possessed powerful magnetic properties."[12] Page's "achievements of mind" were simply of an altogether different order.

As for Page, the man, it is clear that he was a complex individual whose values, needs, and aspirations changed materially as he grew older. While his pursuits after mid-century were remarkably diverse and sometimes mundane or even selfish, he channeled the substantial imaginative talent of his prime years—particularly his mid-20s, but to some extent on through his 30s—into the pursuit of knowledge about electrical physics. Professional historians looking at American science in the 1830s and 40s have generally treated physics as the exclusive province of Joseph Henry. The misapprehension this entails should be apparent to anyone willing to accept as "scientific" those "inquiries defined by curiosity and by the aesthetics of inquiry itself; by the pleasures of just finding more knowledge. . . . rather than some other human need."[13] When the leading authority on Henry writes that his study of electromagnetism in America in the 1830s marked him as "almost unique,"[14] it is because of Page that the qualifying adverb cannot be omitted.

By taste and training Page was splendidly primed for a "career of science."[15] The Salem in which he grew up was a place where "interest in science and the mechanic arts abounded."[16] It could boast one of the finest scientific libraries in America, the Salem Athenæum, and Page used its resources to full advantage. Because his early enthusiasms included botany, entomology, and floriculture, he was instrumental in founding the Essex County Natural History Society, forerunner of the Essex Institute.

And mathematics—every bright lad in Salem must have had some special feelings about mathematics. Young Page often saw Nathaniel Bowditch, a legend in his own time, going about his business amid the commercial bustle downtown, or near home on Essex Street, a few blocks from his own on Chestnut. Bowditch was acquainted with Page's father, and perhaps, on occasion, he even spoke to Charles. A pal as well as a hero was Benjamin

Peirce, who succeeded Bowditch as America's most illustrious mathematician. And the master of Salem's English High School, Henry Kemble Oliver, was something of a mathematician too. Among his writings was a book on mathematical instruments, and as a senior exercise he had Charles compute every eclipse through the end of the century. This had once been the ultimate test of competence for upperclassmen at Harvard College.

Charles chose Harvard against the advice of Jery, who was full of big-brotherly advice and thought he had better attend Amherst in order to "be more out of the way of dissipated life."[17] Although the record is moot as to how much he may have "dissipated," he did possess "ample facilities for the gratification of his tastes as well as for the pursuit of knowledge," and he enjoyed his Harvard years immensely.[18] He had always been gregarious—one finds him on the rolls of organizations ranging from the Salem Glee Club to the Salem Light Infantry—and his extracurricular activities included membership in Hasty Pudding and the presidency of Med-Fac, a society that spoofed "learned bodies in general and the College government in particular."[19]

Nevertheless, Page took his formal course-work seriously, especially a term of lectures and experiments based on Volume II of the Cambridge Natural Philosophy, *Electricity and Magnetism*, and his study of chemistry with Dr. Webster. His courses also included mineralogy, anatomy, astronomy and optics, mechanics, and mathematics through calculus. The scientific training of an undergraduate was surprisingly thorough. Both physics and chemistry included laboratory demonstrations, and Webster, in particular, took care to keep his material up to date. So intriguing did Page find chemistry that he persuaded his father to buy him a vacuum pump and other expensive experimental apparatus. He helped charter the campus chemistry club, and at commencement in 1832 he delivered an oration on his current idol, Sir Humphry Davy.

Page's graduating class of more than 70 was the largest between 1818 and 1849; more than two-thirds went on to earn higher degrees, and nearly one in five became M.D.s. While in medical school in Boston he presented evening lectures on galvanism at the Salem Lyceum, and by the time he graduated and finished his residency at Massachusetts General Hospital his consuming interest had become what he termed "the physics of chemistry." So, even though he set up practice in 1836, he apparently pursued this halfheartedly, if at all.

14

What Henry Oliver—his early mentor who became a lifelong friend—recalled most vividly about Page's Salem office was nothing related to medicine at all but rather "a miniature railway, an elliptic curve of about twelve feet long and six wide, around which travelled a miniature magnetic engine drawing at high speed a miniature car."[20] This, Oliver must have seen shortly before Page took leave for Virginia. By then he had been working with electromagnetic apparatus for more than two years and had made his name familiar to all readers of *Silliman's Journal* and Sturgeon's *Annals*.

Page's publications, approximately 100 all told, are concentrated in three discrete periods, the late 1830s, the mid-40s, and the early 50s. Each period is marked by a distinctive orientation; in the first he emerged as an experimentalist concerned foremost with novel phenomena. He set the motif in a paper sent to Silliman on May 12, 1836: "Method of increasing shocks, and experiments, with Prof. Henry's apparatus for obtaining sparks and shocks from the Calorimotor."[21] Page went on to publish nearly a score of articles during the ensuing three years, in the course of which his analytical powers clearly became more acute. Yet, what he described in his 1836 paper constituted his single most heuristic experimental discovery. He had a nice sense of propriety. His title acknowledged his debt both to America's foremost electrochemist (the Calorimotor was Robert Hare's low resistance copper-zinc voltaic cell), and to its leading electrician.

In 1835, while going over experiments from Faraday's Ninth Series, Henry had resumed investigating self-induction, a phenomenon he himself had discovered in 1832. By winding a piece of insulated copper ribbon into a helix, connecting an end of it to one pole of a Calorimotor, and drawing the other end across a piece of rough metal wired to the other pole, he got electrostatic effects—sparks and shocks—due to momentary interruptions of the circuit.

In England, Sturgeon read about Henry's experiments and repeated them with minor embellishments; in New England, Page repeated them too, but Page discovered something as noteworthy as Henry's initial discovery. He started with considerably more coiled copper ribbon than Henry had utilized, 220 feet, and he wired contacts not only to the extremities but also at several intermediate points (Fig. 1). He had set for himself a seemingly simple problem: to determine whether the intensity of the sparks and shocks increased in a fixed relation to each other

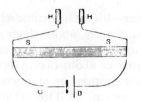

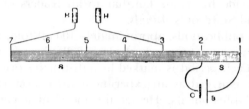

Fig. 1. Schematic diagram of Henry's coil and Page's. With Page's, different segments of a conductor act as primary and secondary circuits to each other. (From J.A. Fleming, THE ALTERNATE CURRENT TRANS-FORMER IN THEORY AND PRACTICE, II, p. 6.)

and proportionately to the length of the circuit. However, he encountered something entirely unanticipated: shocks could be detected from contacts "entirely without the actual circuit."[22] When a battery circuit made through terminals 1 and 2 was broken, for example, a shock was perceptible from any pair of external terminals, the strongest when the human circuit (as it were) was twice as long as the electric circuit. Page did not fully perceive the import of this, at least he did not stress it in his publication. With regard to shocks taken from the *entire* coil while only half was in the battery circuit, he properly inferred a "lateral cooperation." But he ventured no explanation for the shocks from wholly outside the circuit. Sturgeon immediately saw, however, that "Mr. Page's variations of Professor Henry's original experiments are very important." He reprinted the paper verbatim in his *Annals*, then correctly postulated that a segment of the coil exterior to the battery circuit could act as a secondary to a segment within it.[23] What Page had done was to correlate two theretofore disparate phenomena discovered by Faraday and Henry, respectively—induction between two separate conductors and induction in a single helical conductor (Fig. 2).

Having created a rudimentary form of the device later known as the autotransformer—his term was "Dynamic Multiplier"—

16

Page followed suit with a series of experiments.[24] First he built a more elaborate and refined piece of apparatus. Meantime, he had been reading Ampère and Claude Pouillet and had familiarized himself with the substance of Ohm's Law. By ascertaining the optimum relationship between such variables as the number of battery plates and the length and thickness of the primary and secondary circuits, he induced a spark discharge between charcoal points and also succeeded in charging a Leyden jar. These were phenomena, a fellow electrician later pointed out, "belonging to that class of facts which warrants the use of the term *current* as correctly expressive of the actual relation existing between statical electricity and voltaic, or dynamic electricity."[25]

Page even induced sparks and shocks (the latter by "acupuncture") after replacing his galvanic battery with various thermoelectric elements. For the moment at least, this was merely an amusing diversion, because the main thrust of his experimentation now posed a problem that was largely mechanical. Certain electrostatic effects—the decomposition of water, say, or a continuous arc—required a very rapid interruption of the primary. Theretofore Page had used a hand-rotated spur wheel (Fig. 3). This was a novel invention, but now he reviewed the state of the art in electromechanics and then designed more than a dozen diverse sorts of automatic circuit breakers. Most were rotational, although one consisted of a straight electromagnet wound from

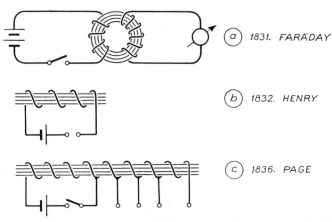

(a) 1831. FARADAY

(b) 1832. HENRY

(c) 1836. PAGE

Fig. 2. Page's induction apparatus contrasted to Faraday's and Henry's. Faraday and Henry utilized a solid core; Page discovered the advantage of a divided core in 1838. (From MTA MÜSZAKI TUDOMÁNYOK OSZY-ÁLYANAK KÖZLEMENYEI 32 [1963]: 469.)

17

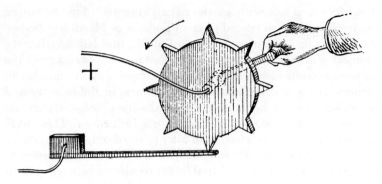

Fig. 3. *Page's manual interrupter, a spur-wheel rotated in a trough filled with mercury. (From A. Frederick Collins, THE DESIGN AND CONSTRUCTION OF INDUCTION COILS, p. 8.)*

the center in opposite directions and pivoted so that it vibrated between the poles of a permanent magnet, as a feedback system reversed the polarity during each oscillation. A modified form of this was manufactured by Daniel Davis (see plates). Like the Dynamic Multiplier, the inspiration for such a device may be traced to an invention of Henry's, in this instance his beam motor of 1831. With an eye to Page's future, it is significant that each of his circuit breakers *was*, incidentally, a tiny motor. Later, electric motors became a primary object of his attention and his experiments assumed a distinct utilitarian cast. It should be stressed, however, that this contrasted strongly to his earlier work.

In the 1830s, what he was most concerned with was apparatus for demonstrating new electromagnetic phenomena. Perhaps it might prove useful in ways as yet unforeseen, perhaps not. Nowhere is premeditated utilitarianism more conspicuous by its absence than in Page's experiments with sound, which constituted the genesis of a new science, electroacoustics. This was recognized by several contemporaries, and later by pioneers of telephonic communication including Alexander Graham Bell himself.[26] Page called his discovery "Galvanic Music." The instrument from which it emanated had two principal components, a coil of copper wire cemented into a rigid unit and mounted between two upright supports, and a horseshoe magnet hung astride the coil. The ends of the wire were connected to the zinc and lead electrodes of a small galvanic cell; breaking the circuit caused the magnet to give off "a distinct ringing." The

18

pitch and overtones changed according to the dimensions of the magnet, and when Page incorporated a rapid-action circuit breaker he got continuous tones of high audibility.[27] He made no attempt to *transmit* this sound. But he did perceive that it evidenced a "disturbance of molecular forces."[28] Moreover, he explained things quite clearly from the standpoint of harmonics, for the theory of sound was something he knew intimately.

While many of Page's previous experiments bore a direct impetus from Henry's work, with this one the influence went the other way: Henry's laboratory records show him repeating "The exp. of Dr. Page for producing musical sounds from a magnet."[29] Page *could* have tried to quantify his discovery. There were instrument makers in America sufficiently skilled to have built apparatus of the sort later used to measure magnetostriction. But all-told he published only a few hundred words about "musical tones in magnets." As was typical, he seemed satisfied just to describe an interesting new effect, then press on to other things.

Indeed, in the very paper concluding his remarks on Galvanic Music, he also dealt with battery powered motors—his eventual nemesis. Around mid-century, after several years of painstaking research and development, he designed motors that were not equaled in sheer power until the 1870s. Technically, these were remarkable; economically, they made no sense. Page was most reluctant to concede this, however, and consequently found himself waging a quixotic battle against the "discouraging limitation of mathematical reasoning."[30] By remaining dedicated to empiricism even with respect to problems for which mathematics could provide the only satisfactory answers, he ultimately isolated himself from the mainstream of electrical science. Still, it is worth remembering that even the formidable C. P. Steinmetz, long after, could disparage "mere theoretical reasoning"[31]—and that in the 1830s empiricism was indisputably the most fruitful way of investigating electrical phenomena. As for electric motors, these were a matter of intense interest even to scientists of immense theoretical—not to say mathematical—sophistication.

From time to time throughout the rest of this first series of papers, Page outlined his progress with "the application of electro-magnetism as a moving power." By and large he appears to have been more interested in form than function, though he did occasionally suggest possible applications for motors and even applied for a patent. What seems most important in retrospect about his motor experiments, however, is extrinsic—

principally, the notice they drew to his work as a whole. For instance, because Sturgeon was then working along the same lines, he naturally kept close track of what Page was doing with his "beautiful pieces of electro-magnetic apparatus." [32] Although Page and Sturgeon never met, they came to hold each other in highest mutual regard. Page spoke reverently about the "distinguished philosopher of England," [33] and as late as mid-century Sturgeon could pay Page the extravagant compliment quoted at the beginning of this chapter. [34]

Such rapport is partly explicable in light of Sturgeon's exemplification of a group "who sought means of exhibiting electrical science in graphic and exciting ways," [35] for Page surely belonged to that group. Yet, this was something about which *many* scientists were enthusiastic, certainly not excluding Faraday and Henry. His biographer writes that Henry "never lost his zest for creating apparatus that could not fail to impress on a student's mind an understanding of the principle it was designed to demonstrate." [36] Unquestionably, Henry owed much of his scientific reputation to his "great electromagnets," well said to be "the equivalents of our atom smashers, computers, and rockets—new, exciting extensions of human control of the unknown." [37] What Henry had done was show that the power of Sturgeon's rudimentary electromagnet was amenable to enormous, perhaps unlimited, augmentation. Ultimately, the same sort of impulse motivated Page with his motors.

What greater challenge than determining how to arrange a system of magnets and armatures so as to exert a dynamic power comparable to the stupendous static power of an electromagnet? Thomas Davenport and others were seeking to transform existing philosophical toys, but with only modest success. More power remained to be unlocked—no telling how much more. Page wanted to know. It was one thing to have persisted after mid-century in regarding the decomposition of zinc in a galvanic cell as a "substitute" for the combustion of wood or coal in a steam engine. It was something else in the 1830s, before anyone had begun the calculations and comparisons from which was derived the law of conservation of energy. Even James P. Joule, one of the key figures in formulating this, "the greatest generalization in physics of the nineteenth century," [38] had once held high hopes for battery powered motors.

And Joseph Henry: here was Henry, in 1839, advocating the construction of a large electric motor to "be submitted to the

20

experiments of a committee of distinguished men of science." [39] Indeed, when it comes to utilitarianism, it was none other than Henry who designed the first motor clearly "capable of further mechanical development," [40] and whose principle he himself suggested might "hereafter be applied to some useful purpose." [41]

As it turned out, it was Page's inadvertant failure to assign Henry due credit in this regard that led to their becoming acquainted. Late in 1838 Page published a paper in which he speculated on the practical application of motors, a possibility he earnestly welcomed but by no means felt to be certain. (By expressing regret "that in our country the invention should be a subject of mercenary speculation, when in reality it has no value except as an experiment," [42] he inadvertantly fueled a feud with Davenport.) In addition, he sketched a brief history of electric motors, in which he credited "the first successful step" toward rendering electromagnetism "available as a mechanical agent" to Sturgeon, the second to Henry. [43] Page was clearly in error, and in October 1838 Professor Henry addressed him a letter from New Jersey:

> I have all ways supposed myself to be the first in this invention. The affare is not one of much consequence and is scarcely worth the correcting since time settles with perfect impartiality all matters of this nature. You may however have some information on the subject with which I am unacquainted and you will therefore confer a favor by giving me a refferance to the source.

Henry knew full well that Page could provide no such "refferance." Indeed, it appears that he had simply taken advantage of Page's misapprehension to begin corresponding. Read his concluding words:

> The circumstance which has called forth this letter will probably be considered as an apology for my addressing you with out an introduction and the fact that we are fellow labourers in the cause of American Science would as I have presumed render any formality of the kind unne[ce]ssary.
> With much respect
Yours
Joseph Henry [44]

The whole tone here suggests that the complimentary close was something more than just an empty formalism. Henry's other correspondence leaves it unclear as to how impressed he was with Page's work generally. But in any case nobody then pursuing electrical science in America more closely approached his own attainments. Henry himself had not begun to make his mark in science until he was in his 30s; Page's first paper on his Dynamic Multiplier had appeared when he was only 24. Furthermore, Page was fortified with superior formal training, blessed with great imagination and experimental skill, and was "a ready and spirited writer." And Page knew he was good: his reply betrayed not the faintest suggestion of a humble *mea culpa* from the foot of Olympus. He politely thanked Henry for his letter, but conceded only that if he had "committed an error in reference to the claim of individuals to discoveries or inventions," he would "most readily make reparation in a future communication."

> I am always desirous that credit shall be given where it is due [he concluded], and if I should fail in so doing that it should be imputed to ignorance on my part rather than to any interested motive. It will give me pleasure to consider this accidental correspondence as an introduction to a good understanding between us, and better feeling than exists generally among the labourers in the cause of science.[45]

Page soon sent Silliman a note in which he publicly apologized for failing to credit Henry with having "laid the foundation of a new branch of science,"[46] and a "good understanding" was indeed established. Page and Henry subsequently corresponded not just about scientific questions, but about Smithsonian politics, jobs for mutual friends, and much else. When Henry came to Washington their friendship acquired a social as well as a professional dimension. Page helped introduce Henry around, then threw his weight against those who envisioned a Smithsonian different from Henry's vision. In turn, when Page started waging political battles of his own, Henry stood with him as an invaluable ally.

After mid-century something more profound than simply a 15-minute walk along Seventh Street began to separate the Smithsonian from the Patent Office, and the two men ceased to move much in the same circles. Yet almost the last surviving piece of Page's correspondence, sent less than a month before his death in May 1868, is addressed to Henry. That letter is terribly pathetic: bedridden for weeks with an extremely painful and no doubt terminal malady, Page wanted to know if Henry could suggest a

22

buyer for an electrical machine he owned. Badly needing money to defray the expenses of his illness, he was willing to let it go for one-fifth its original cost of $150.[47] Henry wrote "attended to" at the top of Page's letter, and perhaps he located a purchaser, since the postmortem inventory of his possessions included no specific mention of this item.

Even in 1868, however, numerous pieces of Page-designed apparatus remained extant, particularly in school laboratories— motors of many kinds, magnetos, and, most common, induction coils. Indeed, the coil represents both the alpha and the omega of Page's scientific career. A spiteful wrangle over patent rights kept his name in the news for years after his death. Allegations of fraud and deceit eventually tended to obscure the reality of Page's primary role in its conception and development. Nevertheless, that device epitomizes the quest which most strongly motivated him as a young man. Because it was both "man's duty and destiny" to "know all that the GREAT CREATOR has put under his dominion," Page sought first and foremost to elucidate untracked phenomena. This might, incidentally, open up possibilities for application. Today, scientists invent a machine capable of, let us say, amplifying light by stimulated emission of radiation. Next they try to figure out what to do with this thing, their *laser*. These scientists are said to be engaged in "basic research." How can one distinguish such research from Page's, intent upon producing electrostatic effects from galvanism?

As historians of science characteristically define the term, Page's approach was the very soul of Baconianism. A French historian who was also a physicist, and who also took a very dim view of inductive science, once described Baconianism thus: "Experiments will be made without any preconceived idea, observations will be made by chance, results will be presented in crude form as they happen to present themselves. . . ."[48] This is not an inaccurate characterization of the majority of Page's scientific papers. Scarcely ever did he quantify, formulate an abstraction, or speculate on the fundamental nature of things. His method entailed an abiding concern for "observations made by chance" and an emphasis on phenomenological comparison, especially comparisons of intensity. Very Baconian. So it also was with Henry. Henry sometimes generalized and proceeded deductively, yet that was in no sense his standard methodology. As his biographer states, he was stamped "irredeemably as a scientist who was satisfied with qualitative knowledge," and whose

23

"strength was always with experimental rather than theoretical science."[49]

Whatever else one may say about Page's method, it was not that of someone who seeks applications of science before understanding. Take the induction coil: we live in an age when coils comprise part of the hardware of tens of millions of workaday machines—yet the coil as Page conceived it belonged to *science*, not technology. To be sure, coils whose induced tension was small had a hypothetical utility as therapeutic devices. But Page was happiest with a coil "entirely too powerful" for medical use, one he considered "an instrument for scientific observation upon the electrostatic powers of the secondary current, rather than for any other purpose."[50] Prior to the 1850s the range of observable effects was severely limited, one factor being the absence of important ancillary devices. When William Crookes came along with his vacuum tubes he rendered Page's invention immeasurably more useful to science. Yet the fact that the coil long antedated even the Crookes Tube is, in itself, convincing evidence of how little Page was motivated by utilitarianism.

Just before he left Salem, Page completed an instrument he called a "Compound Magnet and Electrotome," a permutation of his Dynamic Multiplier embodying separate primary and secondary windings and an integral self-acting circuit breaker (see plates). That was in April 1838, more than a dozen years before H. D. Ruhmkorff unveiled his first coil in Paris. Although Ruhmkorff's name became a generic designation, Page's coil of 1838 was truly the prototype of the device that eventually found its way into every physics lab—and, in key respects, the one that is still accessory to any internal combustion engine with a battery ignition system. Technology, now, yes, but then, "an instrument for scientific observation."

Initially Page used the term "compound magnet" simply to describe an electromagnet with a core of annealed iron wires rather than a solid bar. This so-called divided core was essential to intensifying voltage in the induction circuit. It was developed independently by Page, and in England by both Sturgeon and George Bachhoffner; it was Page, however, who best comprehended its whys and wherefores. He saw that large iron bars could neither be magnetized as intensely as small ones, nor could they be de-magnetized as quickly. This was important because the more rapid and complete the neutralization of the primary, the more potent the current through the secondary. Yet the effective-

24

ness of the divided core was only partly due to the reduced size of the bars. Chiefly, it was due "to the action of their similar poles on each other, when the exciting cause is withdrawn."[51]

Now, this appears simple, but it is in fact quite subtle and suggests that Page was acquiring a considerable degree of theoretical sophistication. In the following issue of *Silliman's* he enumerated experiments with many different kinds of magnetic cores. The most effective arrangement yielded shocks so strong "as to render it difficult to keep even the tips of the fingers upon the wires." Even after the substitution of a thermoelectric cell for a galvanic battery he could still get a bright spark and a shock "which could be felt as far as the wrist."[52] That sounded like typical Page—arch-empirical, purely descriptive. But then he suddenly launched into a veritable *tour de force* of theorizing, beginning with an analysis of a battery's function in determining the quality of secondary electrostatic effects. With any number of cells up to a dozen, a series arrangement proved better. This, he deduced, was because the battery current itself possessed the capability of

passing through perceptible space, with appreciable duration, and as the secondary current, (which is the natural electricity of the wire, set in motion by magnetic forces,) returns to its equilibrium through the medium of the battery plates and its liquid, the two currents must here move in conjunction, and enhance the combustion of the metals used.

Because "the power of the pure secondary developed in this way" never exceeded "the secondary from the same pairs arranged as an elementary series," not only did the magnetizing strength of a compound battery begin to diminish as the series was extended, but also the secondary power. Moreover, Page continued, induced electrostatic effects were not really secondary phenomena at all, but *tertiary*, "the secondary production being the development or neutralization of magnetic forces."

All this was pushing Page toward a commitment to some *metaphysical* position *vis-à-vis* electromagnetism. Once, he would have drawn up short, but now he felt bold enough to go on. "In the present state of our knowledge," he wrote,

it is indispensible to the explication of the reciprocal action of magnetism and electricity to *suppose* the existence of a

25

secondary intervening medium, whether the coiled connectors act with or without the co-operation of ferruginous bodies.[53]

For Dr. Page this took more daring than the self-infliction of nearly lethal shocks. His charge as a scientist was to observe and record, not suppose. While he never doubted his first duty, ultimately he had too fine an imagination to remain a pure inductivist always and forever. As the basis for his supposition regarding "the existence of a secondary intervening medium" Page cited Sturgeon's "beautiful theory of electro-magnetic lines." In the paper to which he was referring, Sturgeon had included a comment which suggests how Page knew that his first duty was *not* to fabricate hypotheses: such suppositions, Sturgeon wrote, "however curious they may appear in themselves, are perhaps not of much interest in the present state of our knowledge of physical operations."[54]

While Page seems to have been rather fond of philosophical speculation, in private, he characteristically avoided it in print. This simply reflects his feeling that "in the present stage of knowledge" speculation had best not be mixed indiscriminately with clear-cut, discrete *facts,* experimentally observable and unambiguously describable. The scientist's calling was to cut down metaphysical webs, not spin more of them. Clear as this rationale may be, however, historians of science still tend to assume that Americans of Page's generation were afflicted with some peculiar intellectual infirmity conducive to "the defeatist position that the 'facts' were all of science."[55] It is true that they sometimes seemed to confuse speculation with *generalization.* Yet it is a gross sin of the positivist mentality to condemn them even on that score. Worth repeating, I think, is a suggestion made many years ago by a couple who ought to be better remembered for their insight on American science, Charles and Mary Beard. Commenting on Alexis de Tocqueville's classic critique, they wrote:

> Absence of generalization may be due to ignorance or to a failure of supreme imaginative qualities—or to a recognition of the baffling complexity of things. Generalizations themselves are nearly always subject to later modifications and rejections; few of them escape the impress of continuous research. . . . In any case, American men of science were not

ignorant; if they did not find what Emerson called the 'electric word,' they certainly helped to prepare the way for new explanations. . . .[56]

Page was acutely aware of "the baffling complexity of things." He was, after all, pursuing a mysterious discipline that had not even existed a few years previously. Nobody could have been more thrilled to spread the "electric word," yet he remained certain that any sort of broad hypothesis concerning electromagnetism had to await a vast amount of inductive spade-work. Scientists needed first to determine its essential range of qualities, properties, and effects. And the way to do that was clear—apply all possible ingenuity to developing experimental apparatus. Herein, no doubt, lies the thinking that went into Page's ultimate instrument, his Magneto-Electric Multiplier (Fig. 4).

What was most noteworthy about the Magneto-Electric Multiplier was that it incorporated a means of making and breaking the *magnetic* circuit in the core as well as the electric circuit in the primary winding. Page had found still another method of expediting the collapse of the field—which was, to repeat, the key to boosting secondary tension. Employing a divided core was one way. Yet another was overlaying the mercury at the break-point with some non-conducting liquid to prevent any residual flow of current through mercury vapor— Page's innovation too, though it is usually attributed to Léon Foucault. He was even close to another significant possibility, a

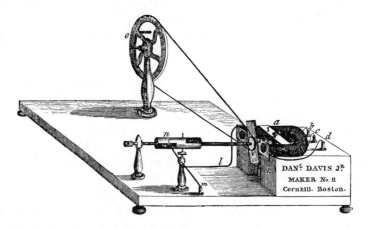

Fig. 4. Magneto-Electric Multiplier. (From AJS 34 [1838]: 371.)

27

condenser in the primary, but never followed through as Armand Fizeau finally did in 1853 with a Ruhmkorff coil.

On the other hand, the Magneto-Electric Multiplier was the first closed-core transformer, an innovation usually ascribed to Cromwell F. Varley in 1856. Let Fleming describe its mode of operation:

> . . . It occurred to [Page] that if he could first of all make his iron core a closed magnetic circuit *before* starting the primary current, and then break the primary circuit and open the magnetic circuit by detaching the armature directly afterwards, the combination of these two actions would put in and take out of the secondary circuit many more lines of force in the same time, and hence produce a greater electromotive force in the secondary circuit than if the primary circuit of a straight coil were simply opened and closed.[57]

Since both the armature and circuit breaker rotated on the same shaft, their relative angular position could be readily shifted. With the primary circuit set to open either in unison with the magnetic circuit or just after it, the secondary would pass brilliant sparks and produce shocks so powerful that they were "sometimes felt by bystanders through the floor."[58] If the armature was rotated ever so slightly back and forth, shocks could be felt even when the primary circuit remained closed—the result of simple magnetic disturbance in the core. (Here was the principle of self-excitation which underlay the development of the dynamo.) Finally, if the circuit breaker was timed to cut the primary *before* the armature was in apposition to the magnetic poles, the armature revolved by itself—slowly if the secondary circuit was left open, rapidly if it was closed.

The Magneto-Electric Multiplier thus embodied elements of an electromagnet, an induction coil, a magneto, and a motor—all at once. Page also designed another form with a straight magnet and a curved armature which proved even better for the sort of experiments he was most interested in. He would later contrive apparatus far more awesome, but never anything quite so subtly ingenious. And its utility? Why, it had none—except, of course, to elucidate further the properties of electromagnetism.

Page believed in this with all the faith he had in the GREAT CREATOR, yet as a purely intellectual quest yielding little return it was not something he could pursue indefinitely. By the time he sent his first description of the Magneto-Electric Multiplier to New Haven in July 1838, he was residing in Virginia, where he possessed only rudimentary laboratory facilities and had no recourse at all to the services of a skilled artisan like Daniel Davis. Quite deliberately he had cast the die anew. He did return to Boston briefly in October to consult with Davis, whose first catalogue of philosophical instruments was about to go to press. At the same time, he tied up a few loose ends in his research. Soon after returning south he sent Silliman a long, discursive paper which epitomized the experimental program he had launched in 1836 with his modification of Henry's coil. Much of it was devoted to apparatus "for exhibiting motion by magnetism." [59] One device, in which a pair of electromagnets alternately attract armatures attached to a rocking beam, he called a Reciprocating Armature Engine. It became an especially popular item of laboratory apparatus, and those that survive confirm Page's praise of Davis's craftsmanship (see plates).

Davis had also built a larger motor, one which suggested to Page that electromagnetism was "susceptible of useful application where only small power is wanted." A manufacturer of gas burners had been able to use it for drilling steel plates, and Page regarded this as "the first instance in which the mechanical application of electro-magnetism has been turned to profitable account." [60] The debatability of this assertion is unimportant. What seems most significant is how uncharacteristic of Page such a utilitarian allusion was. Indeed, throughout this entire series of experimental researches his rare references to potential applications simply provide the exceptions which prove the rule that his fundamental orientation was not utilitarian at all. It was not even goal-directed in any practical sense. While this perhaps lends support to one stereotype—that the prevailing mode of doing science in Jacksonian America entailed a very haphazard sort of methodology—it certainly runs counter to another (with which it is scarcely reconcilable anyway), that "pure" science suffered from almost total neglect.

If I seem to belabor the point about Page's motivation, it demands emphasis simply because the utilitarian theme is so deeply rooted in conventional historiography. Roger Burlingame, for example, probably the most popular writer on 19th-century American technology, notes that "the electric motor became, in America, a focus of attention before the dynamo," and this he regards as demonstrating the 'material' attitude of most Americans of the time. They could see an electromagnet energized by the familiar battery lifting heavy weights. The battery, therefore, a simple thing which any one could make, was capable of producing power to do work. It was natural that minds habituated to manual work rather than to physics books should jump over the theory to its application.[61]

Now, this is very misleading: there was nothing peculiarly "American" about such an attitude, for *nobody* began seriously to investigate the dynamo until the 1860s. As for its relative, the magneto-generator, Burlingame might have considered Page's omnibus paper of 1839, in which the very first subject he took up was the conversion of mechanical energy into electricity. Indeed, he had made some initial observations on this nearly a year previously,[62] when he had published almost nothing about battery-powered electromagnetic motors. His magneto (Fig. 5) was an improved version of the one Joseph Saxton invented in 1834 (and note the presence of *two* Americans in the experimental vanguard of energy conversion). With it he had generated sufficient current to decompose water, and he was brimming with optimism about the future of such apparatus. Since experiments with Faraday's volta-electrometer indicated that a machine with two armatures had double the electrolytic capability of one with a single armature, Page thought that the way to augment power indefinitely was "too obvious to escape notice."[63] This, it happens, was a misapprehension, although magnetos incorporating multiple magnets and armatures did ultimately prove quite useful. Page himself designed such a machine in 1844 with a specific application in mind—telegraphy. In the 1830s, however, he was most intrigued with the possibility of deriving a variety of electrostatic effects from a source of continuous current, rather than from a coil and circuit breaker.

The point is that Page's mind was *not* "habituated to manual work rather than to physics books"—and if he indeed was insufficiently attentive to theory, he was no less unconcerned about application. When he described a device "for exhibiting the magnetic forces of the centre of a helix" (Fig. 6), he was dealing with something that could be put to workaday uses. Yet all he initially emphasized was its capability of resisting "the strength of two stout men pulling by the handles."[64] Here was a way, then, of "exhibiting" science; if he had any ideas about "using" it, he did not say so.

30

On the other hand, he was much less reticent about explicitly addressing matters beyond empirical verification. Perhaps this was attributable to a sense of intimacy with electromagnetism born of hundreds of jolting shocks self-inflicted. He never felt *entirely* comfortable when cut off from empiricism: once, for example, he suggested that a certain acoustical phenomenon might be analogous to the polarization of light and heat, but hastened to add that he would leave the question "in the hands of theoretical philosophers." [65] Nevertheless, this was not the same Page who once had stuck so tenaciously to unembellished report-age of his observations. He was prepared, for example, to advance a very astute hypothesis regarding re-magnetization of the body of a magnet after interruption of the circuit, namely, that "the existence of secondary currents flowing [therein] . . . may be very plausibly inferred." Seeming anomalies in the magnetic core of electrical machines constituted the prime challenge for engineers who set out to rationalize their design at the end of the century. Page, long before, had recognized the importance of this subject. But, while he thought it "well worth pursuing," he himself had to decline the challenge for lack of opportunity. [66]

A little more than three years elapsed between the time Page sent Benjamin Silliman his first paper on the Dynamic Multiplier and his final one on the Magneto-Electric Multiplier. After that, he temporarily retired from the pursuit of science. When he resumed, his orientation had clearly shifted toward a quest for practical applications. He continued to hold pure science in high esteem—as witness the date of the third quote at the beginning of this chapter—and he even published some admirable explications of general laws relating to galvanism and electromagnetism. Nevertheless, by his 40s he presented a different image: no longer was he primarily regarded either as a "philosopher" or as someone gifted with unexcelled powers of "close reasoning." What he *was* reputed for was his cultivation of political favor, and many professional scientists treated him as a backslider from the most sacred tenets of their credo. It became difficult to assess the work he did in the 1830s in isolation from later episodes in which he sometimes appeared injudicious or avaricious.

Still, there is no reason to believe that Robert Walker was voicing a peculiar notion when he ranked Page's coil and Henry's magnet, in that order, as the most noteworthy American contributions to the science of electromagnetism. Walker was, after all, the brother-in-law of Alexander Bache, Henry's intimate cohort. Although it would be foolish to suggest that Page was a greater

31

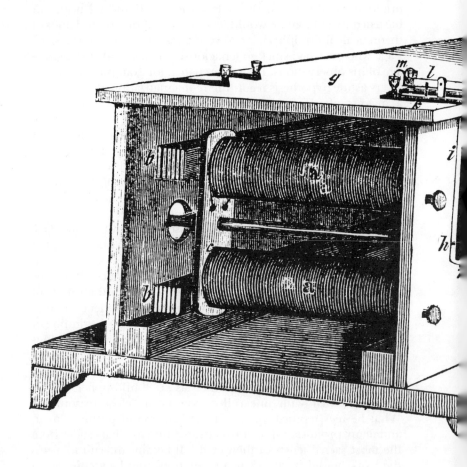

Fig. 5. Page's magneto-generator of 1838. (From AJS 34 [1838]: 164.)

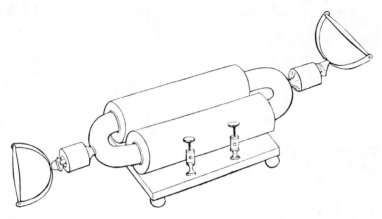

Fig. 6. *Double Helix, precursor of Page's solenoid motors of the 1840s. (From AJS 35 [1839]: 260.)*

electrician than Henry, it is nonetheless true that historians have tended to remain something less than rigorously analytical of the filial-pietistic precedent set by Henry's daughter, Mary. He has been credited with an experimental genius on a par with Faraday's, even though Faraday enjoyed the most propitious institutional position imaginable, while Henry was off in the wilderness, "far from the main stream of scientific thought," a lonely figure of heroic stature.[67]

There is nothing essentially invalid about this. But elements of mythology seem always to be lurking about, ready to insinuate that, with regard to electrical science in America in the 1830s, Henry was unique in his expertise, his methods, his motives, or his aims. First of all, rarely have distinctions between "basic" and "applied" science been less clear-cut than with electricity during that decade. Trying to evaluate "mere differences in the attitude of the researcher's mind"[68] is an exceedingly precarious business. In England, although Faraday dominated the "basic" camp, he was by no means alone, for men like Sturgeon and Charles Wheatstone—both exceptional scientists—seem to have had a foot in each. In America, according to conventional historiography, the situation was different. The "applied" camp was held by resourceful but unschooled Yankee-tinkerer types, while the "basic" was Henry's private domain. One finds, for instance, a popular writer asserting that a lengthy paper on induction which Henry published in 1839 was beyond the comprehension of any of his countrymen, that in America "his fundamental insight into the transformer was entirely missed." [69]

It is with a statement such as this that credibility collapses. Consider the testimony of J. H. Lane, the one electrical scientist who might have assumed the role of America's Kelvin or Helmholtz. Lane was Page's close friend, but would never have described him as "well versed in the theory of electricity" [70] had he not meant exactly that. Or take Théodose Du Moncel, perhaps the most prolific and knowledgeable of all 19th-century historians of electrical science, who rated Page among "les principaux electriciens, constructeurs, et inventeurs du monde entier," right in company with Wheatstone and William R. Grove.[71] No doubt the most noteworthy of all Page's advocates was J. A. Fleming, whose views I have quoted several times. Fleming's description of the electrical researches Page "prosecuted with the greatest zeal and ingenuity" literally abounds in praise. The way Fleming (and his modern-day counterparts) wrote history of science may leave much to be desired, but part of what he sought to do was assess scientific accomplishment in isolation from irrelevancies. It seems that the narrow range of vision of the so-called internalist is simultaneously his Achilles heel and his strongest asset.

By the 1850s Page's major scientific contributions lay behind, as did Henry's. Subsequent developments had the effect of indelibly fixing Henry's image as the nonpareil figure in American science; with Page it was quite otherwise, for events after midcentury seriously undermined his reputation. As far as Fleming was concerned, however, he could not see why things that happened in the 1850s and 1860s should in any way affect his assessment of Page the scientist—any more, say, than Robert Hare deserved a dishonorable discharge from the history of chemistry because he spent his last years in the thrall of spiritualism.

Page's activities during the 1830s are illustrative of another historiographical problem besides the one entailed in making retrospective assessments of scientific accomplishment. Consider some of the apparatus he developed—one for "producing musical tones in magnets," another capable of rotating at "five or six thousand revolutions per minute," yet another for effecting electrolysis from mechanical energy, instruments to demonstrate "the electrostatic powers of the secondary current"—the variety was most impressive. Nearly all of these may now sound like *technology*. But none led to anything beyond the most marginal sorts of applications until long afterward, following the modification of other parameters. None was "useful" except in a didactic sense. Consider, on the other hand, Henry's great magnets. It would have been obvious *a priori* that such a device could be put to practical use. Yet Henry has often gone down in history as the paragon of pure science, Page as a myopic utilitarian. This misapprehension strongly underscores the need for "new terms for describing the relations of theory and practice," [72] not to say a more precise categorical nomenclature for men such as Page and Henry.

If Henry's greatest single claim to scientific immortality is indeed the electromagnet—an opinion I am inclined to accept—then does not this make him appear a utilitarian, lending evidence to the indictment handed down by de Tocqueville? But there is still Page, a man best remembered for his foredoomed attempts to put battery powered electric motors to work at mid-century. *That* sort of activity fits de Tocqueville's portrait, of course. Yet what about those experiments with transformers, acoustic devices, thermocouples, and the rest from the 1830s? Might this not leave Page as an important, perhaps outstanding exception to the de Tocqueville critique of science in Jacksonian America? The question embodies deliberate hyperbole, quite so, but perhaps it also merits a moment's consideration.

36

Chapter Two

Washington

> In February, 1841, a summons came for me to leave in a few
> days for *Washington*. Had I been called to enter Alladin's
> palace by the light of the wonderful lamp, I could not have
> been more overcome with pleasure and excitement. . . .
> *Priscilla Sewall Webster Page, 1886*

Someday, when somebody edits and publishes *The Scientific Writings of Charles G. Page,* one of its striking aspects will be the amplitude of engravings of three-dimensional objects, many bearing a plaque reading:

> DANL. DAVIS JR.
> MAKER No. 11
> Cornhill. Boston

Davis was the first American manufacturer to specialize in electrical apparatus. His initial catalogue, which came out in November 1838, described nearly two-dozen instruments designed by Page, and surviving examples bear witness to his ingenuity no less than to Davis's skill. Page's involvement in this sort of activity has apparently proved misleading to historians, however. Because those who have treated the development of such apparatus have usually done so within the context of technology, it is here that Page is found—when, indeed, he is found at all—in the specialized literature.

Yet, to reiterate the thesis of the opening chapter, if technology is defined as that branch of knowledge relating to engineering and applied science, then it needs be asked of this paraphernalia: applied to *what?* And the answer must be: nothing of any immediate utility, nothing beyond the expansion of human consciousness regarding the properties of electricity and magnetism.

It is true that there are definitions of technology which *do* seem appropriate to Page's pursuits—"a question of process, always expressing in terms of 'things'," or "activities of man that result in artifacts."[1] Even so, I think there is a crucial distinction to be drawn between things conceived to advance science and the artifacts of applied science. Admittedly, the distinction can be most subtle, for a device such as an induction coil may be either, depending on the circumstances. As our understanding of the relationship between science and technology in the 19th century improves, it seems certain that "Instead of a simple picture of theory yielding practice (or the reverse), we will encounter complex, ambiguous social and intellectual situations."[2] Page's early career appears to epitomize such a situation, for here was a very capable experimental physicist whom historians ever so readily mistake for a prosaic "ingenious mechanic" (or, perhaps, a *non*-ingenious mechanic, since so little of what he designed "worked").

It is simply a truism that a rudimentary historiography renders oversimplifications inevitable: to take another facet of the same period, before historians understood the substantial distinctions between, say, William Lloyd Garrison and James G. Birney, their approach to Abolitionism inevitably distorted a "complex, ambiguous social and intellectual situation. . . ." I suggest that it involves a similar distortion to pigeonhole Page with Thomas Davenport, as he so often has been. Now, Davenport was a very clever man, who may well deserve veneration as "the Watt of the electric motor,"[3] and who perhaps ought to have a spot in the Pantheon of America's hero-inventors. But intellectually he was about as different from Page as, yes, what he was, a back-country blacksmith. The foremost Henry scholar, Nathan Reingold, thinks it injudicious to presume too much of a semblance between Page and Henry either, suggesting instead that he resembles no other American so much as he does the Englishman, Charles Wheatstone. Fair enough. Certain characteristics shared with another Englishman, William Sturgeon, have previously been noted. In any event, if Davenport, or Samuel F. B. Morse—men eager to harness electromagnetism to one or another pet application yet relatively indifferent to comprehending the full range of its attributes—typify some peculiarly "American" attitude, Page was exceptional, at least as exceptional as Henry, in regarding this sort of research with anything but indifference.

Unfortunately for Page, though, there were very few others who felt likewise. Patronage for the sort of "career of science" he set out to pursue in 1836 was scarce anywhere in the world; in

America it was simply not to be had. The consequences were predictable: more and more he felt compelled to draw attention to potential workaday applications for his innovations. At one point, "several gentlemen in Boston" interested in the development of a useful motor provided him with financial backing, but after investing something over $500 they gave it up.[4] By contrast, Davenport, who focused almost exclusively on trying to render motors practical, succeeded in attracting substantial sums of entrepreneurial capital. Page was envious. Late in April 1838, while he was evidently trying to decide whether or not to remain in New England, he approached Davenport with an offer of partnership: "I am now under obligation to no one here," he wrote,

> and before I get up another interest I should like to know your views. I believe it would be for your advantage and mine, and contribute much to the success of the experiment [i.e., with electric motors], if our interests should be united. If you will make me a reasonable offer, I will take hold with you heart and hand, and there is no question but that in a short time we could make an excellent business of it, as we could cover the whole ground.[5]

Despite Page's claim that he could "make any machine of yours in five minutes time half as strong again," Davenport was probably not much impressed by this "scientific gentleman." Indeed, he may have felt that Page was simply trying to avail himself of some good practical expertise he himself did not possess, and he curtly replied that he was "not in a situation to make or receive propositions relative to a union of interests."[6]

Such a union with Mr. Davenport was certainly not Page's last possible option on his home ground. But sometimes he could be as easily discouraged as he could be stubborn at others. He could also be petulant, and probably brooded over Davenport's indifference to his offer of "heart and hand." Next, one finds that he has suddenly wound up his affairs and moved on.

By no means would this be the last manifestation of a peculiar impulsiveness in Page's character. Yet he liked to finish what he began, and, even though he cut out further experimentation altogether, he still had on hand quite a backlog of research notes. In 1839—a year he did nothing in science—he published more papers than any other time in his life. Sometimes he mentioned projects he expected to undertake in the future, particularly with energy-conversion apparatus. Davis marketed Page's little rocking-beam motor for $12, and his magnetos cost $35 to $75. That was not really cheap, yet even the largest magneto was decidedly feeble. Page wanted to try building a large rotating motor, one with a hundred-pound armature, and a magneto with a multiplicity of armatures. But either would be an expensive venture, and investors were not optimistic about his chances of devising anything very powerful.

On that score, his image as a "scientific gentleman" did not help at all. Davenport's cast of mind was such that he could observe Henry's great electromagnet at the Penfield Iron Works in Crown Point, immediately be overwhelmed by the certainty that "ere long this mysterious and invisible power will super[s]ede steam,"[7] and throw himself unstintingly into that task. Page would always know far more about why electricity behaved the way it did, of course, but for practical purposes this could actually be a handicap, because he might continually get distracted by methodological niceties, lured into curious byways, detoured from any utilitarian goal.

Besides, it seems rather unlikely that Page could have attracted private backing after mid-1838 even if he had been armed with a substantial record of practical achievement. First, his residence was as far from the places where skilled mechanics maintained shops as it was from the wellsprings of entrepreneurial capital. Second, this was not exactly a propitious moment in American history, even for someone with a technological novelty of great promise—Professor Morse, say. Davis no doubt paid Page royalties, but, with the nation mired in its worst depression, the market for philosophical instruments must have been rather slack. That the federal government might somehow be persuaded to underwrite private research and development was a possibility in the minds of certain individuals, notably Henry L. Ellsworth, the Commissioner of Patents. For the time being, though, this was obviously out of the question, considering the makeup of the 25th Congress and a President steadfastly dedicated to the tenets of *laissez faire*.

Page's primary choice for his life's work had been experimental science. By 1838 he would have settled for a career of applied science, of the sort in which the federal government later offered many opportunities. But the hard fact of the matter was that there was precious little to which his scientific specialization could yet *be* applied directly, and he now found himself in the distressing position of lacking a sufficient source of income.

40

Backing up a bit, the question recurs: why *did* Page choose to depart his Salem-Cambridge-Boston milieu? Whatever his opportunities there, would they not have been broader than in the Old Dominion? He surely must have had his regrets at leaving behind a large circle of friends who shared one or another of his own enthusiasms—Daniel Davis in Boston, Benjamin Peirce in Cambridge, Henry Oliver in Salem. He was also leaving behind ready access to such civilized appurtenances as libraries. When he replied from Pageville to Henry's first letter, he promised to check his sources "as soon as opportunity offers," but implied there might be a delay since he was residing "some distance from the city [Washington] and have therefore no means of immediate reference to journals."[8] Had Page still been in Salem he could have found what he needed to know in a few minutes.

It is true that in some respects Salem was not the place it once had been. The nation's seventh largest city at the time of the third census in 1810, its population remained virtually static for decades thereafter. As an entrepôt, it was struck devasting blows by Jefferson's Embargo and the outbreak of war with England the year Page was born, blows from which it never fully recovered. Although the seaport "died hard,"[9] its decline was inexorable, and the late 1830s were especially doleful. While some South American and African trade persisted until after the Civil War, the last entry from Europe was recorded in 1837, the year Jere Page made up his mind to leave.

Yet, Salem's allurements for someone like Captain Page's son, Charles, would scarcely have been affected; two of his most illustrious successors in electrical science, Moses Gerrish Farmer and Alexander Graham Bell, both found it a congenial environment. For Page himself there would have been diverse opportunities nearby to find employment as a teacher. On the other hand, there were only two institutions of higher learning anywhere near Pageville. One, Georgetown College, employed only Jesuits. The other, Columbian College, was a school whose very survival seemed chronically imperiled until it entered its third decade in the 1840s. Pageville, moreover, was rather remote for daily commuting. In retrospect, it seems inevitable that soon enough Page would have settled in the capital itself. What remains not entirely clear is why he would have left Massachusetts for Virginia *or* Washington, although the less timorous among us sometimes do things like that just to be doing them. It is also a valid presumption that he was acting under some of the same motivations which pulled other scientists such as Henry School-

41

craft off into the West, or which induced James D. Dana to embark on a four-year cruise in 1838 with Charles Wilkes.

Indeed, with an eye to the Wilkes Expedition, a man as imaginative as Page might well have glimpsed the important potential for institutional science in the capital. To be sure, this would not be science as it was done, say, in the capital of France. The goals, at least as served up for public consumption, were couched in the rhetoric of utilitarianism—charting the wilderness, plotting the seas, fostering inventive genius. The authenticity of this rhetoric varied, but in no case were the pursuits involved not of considerable benefit both to science and to its practitioners. This was becoming so even in the 1830s. As Hunter Dupree has written, these scientific activities

> . . . must not be discounted simply because they all sprang from definite needs and because the subject of the ultimate nature of scientific institutions in the government was usually avoided. All advocates of scientific enterprise learned to side-step constitutional issues and discussions on the ultimate responsibility of the government to aid science. The really striking thing is that, given these limitations, so many activities sprang up and so much was accomplished.[10]

Thus, even when Page left Salem, there were opportunities in Washington for a scientific career that were not available elsewhere. There was nothing tailored to fit him precisely—one can scarcely envision the Chief of the United States Coast Survey, Ferdinand Hassler, performing bureaucratic legerdemain to make room for an experimental physicist. There was another sort of job, however, one whose prime requisite was general scientific expertise. Not many emphasized the physical sciences, but even in 1838 there were at least two—the $1,500 per year positions as patent examiners. Then, both incumbents seemed comfortably ensconced. Yet the Patent Office appeared to have an expansive future indeed. Who could fail to be impressed by its new building under construction on F Street, a replica of the Parthenon, designed to be one of the most beautiful and impressive structures in America? It would be overshadowed only by the Capitol itself and the Treasury, also still under construction. Did this not suggest that aside from the essential chores of legislation and finance, the encouragement of progress in the inventive arts was regarded as the most important federal function? Did this not betoken a Patent Office humming with activity, a staff comprised of *many* professional scientists? Invention was a pursuit that surely had much in common with science; indeed, several of Page's scientific heroes were also patentees—Davy, for example, and Professor Hare.

As for the city itself, despite its sprawling, roughhewn aspect—there were not even any public streetlights until 1842— Washington had already begun to acquire something of the same aura which more recently has proved so attractive to the young and adventurous. The reaction of one girl who came in 1841 to live with her sister's family is quoted at the beginning of this chapter.[11] True, that girl had spent most of her 18 years in the northern marches, Maine, whereas her future husband had grown up amid the most richly textured civilization in America. But Charles Page was an exceptionally free-spirited individual. He settled down relatively late—only falling into a steady job at 30, not marrying till 32—and at 40 or again when nearly 50 he could fundamentally change course with few qualms. A mariner's heritage had not failed to affect him: he sought variety and loved adventure—the adventure of scientific discovery, of course, and perhaps too the adventure entailed in picking up and starting anew in a completely strange setting.

Even Joseph Henry, a rather stodgy character personally, seems to have been pleased by the notion that Washington was a place "where everyone does as he chooses."[12] Yet, when Henry arrived he bore a commission to become "the great founder of a great Institution," no less.[13] Page came with no definite prospects at all and his rationale for departing Massachusetts for Virginia remains something of an enigma. His next step, however, seems the logical product of a simple process of elimination. As of 1839, no appropriate government positions were open, nor any of even modest status for a teacher. But Page was, after all, trained as a physician. No doubt he had considered his time in medical school primarily as a period of post-graduate work in science, a not unusual attitude. Henry Wheatland, for example, never had any intention of practicing medicine "unless forced by circumstances to earn a living in that way."[14] Wheatland managed to get along as a professional naturalist for a decade after taking his M.D. Then, in 1848, a unique opportunity opened up for him, and he commenced a long and rewarding career as secretary of the Essex Institute in Salem. In some ways the Essex Institute grew to resemble a locally oriented Smithsonian, with Wheatland its Joseph Henry. But, for his classmate, Page, no comparable

43

challenge presented itself. Although he regarded his medical education in much the same light as Wheatland—"as a way to get your living ... [only] if you have to"[15]—in 1839 he found it necessary to exercise that option.

For three years he became a practicing physician, a country doctor in northern Virginia. Fairfax County was in no sense the wilds; the fifth census reported nearly half as many residents there as in Washington City itself. But Page's new career was scarcely remunerative. In 1840 he was forced to put one of his prized possessions up for sale, running the following notice in *Silliman's*:

> Dr. C. G. Page wishes to dispose of his entomological cabinet, comprising about two thousand species and nearly a thousand duplicates. Two thirds are natives, and with the exception of about one hundred, were obtained from the vicinity of Boston, Massachusetts. The remainder is a choice selection from Maranham, Java, Japan, and China. The cabinet is in excellent order, and the characteristic distinctions of the Lepidoptera particularly are uncommonly well preserved, as most of them were raised from the eggs, in a cocoonery, purposely for the cabinet. (The specimens are mostly classified and named.) This collection is offered for four hundred dollars.[16]

Page may never have pursued his medical career with even the vigor he once devoted to botany. He visited Washington often, and lived there periodically before his permanent move in 1842. Several years later, a friend of Henry's could still describe the capital as a "desert,"[17] yet even at the beginning of the 1840s its community of amateur and professional scientists had begun to show signs of lasting vitality. One event of more than symbolic significance was the founding of an organization called the National Institute for the Promotion of Science.

With respect to its grand aims—which included gaining control over James Smithson's bequest—the National Institute ultimately proved a dismal flop. This was partly because it was, in Henry's words, "unfit ... to decide questions of a strictly scientific character."[18] Yet the very existence of such an organization was a boon for Page. First of all, unlike its predecessor, the Columbian Institute, it was not overladen with dabblers. Its meetings provided the opportunity of getting acquainted with genuine professional scientists, engineers, explorers, and inventors (as well as government officials and politicians), many of whom would become his friends, colleagues, and allies. For example, nearly all the most prominent members of the Corps of Topographical Engineers belonged, including John C. Frémont, who in 1841 married Jessie Benton, daughter of Senator Thomas Hart Benton of Missouri. It was no doubt through Frémont that Page got to know Benton, who later managed a $20,000 Congressional appropriation for him to investigate the feasibility of applying "electromagnetic power as a mechanical agent for the purposes of navigation and locomotion." Although historians characteristically assess institutional success primarily on the basis of how closely attainment measures up to aspiration, institutions which were apparent failures may well have had considerable impact in facilitating social interaction that otherwise would not have taken place.

Resident members of the National Institute included government scientists such as Ferdinand Hassler, J. M. Gilliss, J. H. C. Coffin, and Matthew Fontaine Maury; political friends of science such as John Quincy Adams, Joel Poinsett, and Francis P. Blair; entrepreneurs such as W. W. Corcoran, George W. Riggs, Joseph Gales, and W. W. Seaton; and miscellaneous luminaries such as Francis Scott Key and Daniel Webster's son, Fletcher. Page never knew *all* of these men well, but some he did—Maury for one, and Corcoran and Fletcher Webster. And he did form many close friendships with other members of the Institute, in particular Dr. Harvey Lindsly, who would become his brother-in-law, and Professor Walter R. Johnson, subsequently a staunch proponent of Page's costly experiments with large electric motors. He made enemies, too, such as Francis Markoe, Jr., that mysterious figure who hankered to take over the Patent Office before becoming Henry's one serious competitor for the post of Smithsonian Secretary. He met future colleagues such as J. M. Thomas, Thomas Miller, J. F. May, William P. Johnston, and Joshua Riley, all physicians and fellow faculty members when Page taught at the National Medical College later on.

Finally, and ultimately most important, the Institute's membership included: Henry L. Ellsworth, Thomas P. Jones, William P. Elliot, Charles M. Keller, Thomas W. Donovan, Henry Stone, W. P. N. Fitzgerald, John J. Greenough, Charles L. Fleischmann, C. B. Moss, and Samuel Cooper. While in some ways quite diverse, these men shared one distinction: all were, had been, or would be associated in some way with the Patent Office. Ellsworth was the commissioner, Keller and Donovan the examiners, Fitzgerald and Stone the assistant examiners. Elliot was the designer of the building itself. He and Jones, a man of many parts, including a stint as superintendent of the office in the 1820s and another as examiner in the 1830s, were the first Americans to make a profession out of counseling aspiring patentees. Greenough, who, along with Fleischmann, had been employed to re-do patent drawings lost in the fire of 1836, was an important inventor in his own right and also a pioneer patent agent. Keller resigned a few years later to form a partnership with Greenough. In the 1850s Fitzgerald also established himself as a patent attorney. Cooper and Moss both worked as examiners; Cooper later became proprietor of the largest patent agency in Boston. Page got to know them all, for in 1842 he moved permanently into Washington and took a job whose prime formal requisite was general scientific expertise, the job of examiner of patents.

One of my primary aims in detailing Page's subsequent career is to elaborate upon the significance of the antebellum Patent Office. It was important to the history of American technology, of course, but also to administrative history and the history of *science*. Page found his new job much more congenial than practicing medicine, because it offered "unusual opportunities for pursuing scientific studies and experiments." [19] The great variety of his avocational pursuits during his first decade in the Patent Office, 1842–1852, indeed tends to confirm the general point that an examinership was to some extent a sinecure—"a way in which men of scientific interests were given an income" without being required to devote full-time to their official duties. [20]

As far as Page was concerned, the Patent Office became the single most important institution to him personally for the rest of his life. This relationship assumed several forms; in the 1850s he left the office and became a patentee himself, an agent for prospective patentees, and a journalistic advocate of procedural reform. Partly as a result of pressure he helped generate, during the interlude separating his two terms as examiner the system's administrative philosophy underwent a fundamental transformation. While this had no basis in formal statute, it was of a magnitude sufficient to render an examiner's role qualitatively different when Page returned in the 1860s from what it had been in the 1840s.

Besides examiner, agent, patentee, and reformer, Page's role with regard to the Patent Office assumed yet another dimension. Though never quite such an embattled pawn of patronage as

46

some other federal agencies, within a decade after 1836 it had clearly become sensitive to the vagaries of partisan politics. The occupant of the White House often made a great deal of difference. So did the composition of Congress, since by no means did the commissioner invariably have final say on policy matters. Occasionally Congress simply rode roughshod over his vested authority. Most often this amounted to passing legislation extending the life of a patent even though the commissioner had refused to do so, but occasionally it entailed exceptional grants of special privilege. Privilege-seekers were always around, and Page was not averse to joining their ranks when conventional procedures failed to meet his desires. Indeed, the two most publicized episodes of his entire career each stemmed from a special act of Congress, one waiving the statutory proscription on employees of the Patent Office obtaining patents, the other legitimizing an exception to the assumption that the federal government's proper mode of fostering private research and development was constitutionally restricted to the maintenance of the patent system. Naturally, both these episodes raised a storm of controversy, and by having given the appearance of courting political favor in too heavy-handed a manner Page seriously marred his public image as a selfless "labourer in the cause of American Science." Still, in no objective sense could anything he did in the 1850s or 1860s alter the reality of his earlier motives and achievements.

I suggested at the beginning of this chapter that Page's activities in the 1830s epitomize an intellectual situation for which "conventional rubrics" prove confusing or useless. It is even more difficult to pin a label on him in the decade after 1842. The question has been asked of Alexander Bache, "How does one deal with a man simultaneously concerned with organizing a solar eclipse expedition and harbor improvements?"[21] It might be asked of Page, how does one deal with a man whose pursuits ranged from experimental physics to practical pharmacy and the application of electromagnetic power to useful purposes, and who all the while held down a regular job with the State Department's Office of Patents? That was Page in the middle and late 1840s. In what pigeonhole does he belong? Again, my closing question is deliberately rhetorical, because Page can no more be confined in this sense than Bache can. Even his role as a patent examiner is deceptive, for he was expected to be a public servant and a scientific expert at the same time. Though not immediately apparent, this entailed a contradiction whose repercussions would affect Page deeply.

Chapter Three

America's Parthenon

... a visit to our new and beautiful Patent Office will convince the close observer that the inventive genius of America never was more active than at the present moment.

Robert Walker, 1844

The great mass of inventions are of a character to make us alike proud of the genius of our countrymen, and the Government which fosters and protects it. Man's wants increase with his progress in knowledge; and hence the paradoxical truth, that the growing number of inventions, instead of filling the measure, increases its capacity.

Charles Grafton Page, 1844

On April 28, 1836, while Page was just about to submit his first paper on induction to Benjamin Silliman, in Congress a committee of three New England senators issued a report on "the state and condition of the Patent Office, and the laws relating to the issuing of patents for new and useful inventions and discoveries."[1] Along with its report, the committee also introduced a bill to revamp both the legal underpinning and organizational superstructure of the American patent system.

Since 1793 American patents had been registered in much the same way they were handled in England. The law required compliance with certain procedural formalities, but made no provision for a disinterested investigation of originality, novelty, or utility. Administration fell within the domain of the Secretary of State, and in 1802 James Madison established a separate Office of Patents. He awarded the superintendency to William Thornton, architect of the Capitol building and a close personal friend. Dr. Thornton remained as superintendent for more than a quarter-century and came to feel a "sense of personal ownership in the Patent Office."[2] His actual power was deliberately circumscribed, however. He managed to wangle an assistant in 1810, but Congress studiously ignored each of his subsequent pleas for additional clerical help. Moreover, when he recommended the withholding of letters patent "in cases notoriously without merit,"[3] the Secretary of State rarely backed him up, for even a

48

"judicious exercise of a discretionary power,"[4] amounted to subverting the Patent Act of 1793.

Thornton died in 1828. He was succeeded briefly by Dr. Thomas P. Jones, editor of the *Journal of the Franklin Institute*, who was in turn succeeded by John D. Craig. Craig was dreadfully tactless, and his superintendency during the early 1830s was a stormy period indeed. Individual personalities aside, however, by the time Secretary of State John Forsyth replaced Craig in 1835 it seemed clear that the ground-rules of the patent system were in need of major revision. This had been proposed as early as 1816 by President Madison, but not until Craig's time, when legislative investigations became endemic, did Congress authorize even piecemeal reforms. Nevertheless, a tide of opposition had begun to push against the whole system.

One individual it especially displeased was a young employee of the Patent Office named Charles M. Keller, who had inherited from his father in 1829 the job of maintaining the collection of patent models. So many applications seemed totally devoid of any originality that Keller had begun unofficially "advising applicants as to the novelty or want of novelty in their inventions."[5] By 1835, he had worked out a reform plan, and had also aroused the interest of the new superintendent, Henry L. Ellsworth of Connecticut, and the support of Senator John Ruggles of Maine. In December, Ruggles proposed an inquiry, which he and his two colleagues completed in the spring of 1836. The Ruggles committee reported that

> the Department of State has been going on, for more than forty years, issuing patents on every application, without any examination into the merits or novelty of the invention. And the evils which necessarily result from the law as it now exists, must continue to increase and multiply daily until Congress shall put a stop to them.[6]

After the addition of several amendments, including one prohibiting Patent Office employees from holding patents, the bill Ruggles drafted "to prevent these evils in the future" was signed into law by President Andrew Jackson on the 60th anniversary of the Declaration of Independence, July 4, 1836.[7]

The law provided for elevating the Patent Office to the level of a bureau within the State Department. The President was to appoint a commissioner at a salary of $3,000, the same as that of the Commissioner of Indian Affairs. (Ellsworth, who was carried

49

over as the first commissioner, had once held the latter post too.) The commissioner in turn would name several functionaries including an "examining clerk," all nominations being subject to ratification by the Secretary of State. Another law passed simultaneously provided for constructing a special building for the Patent Office on F Street between Seventh and Ninth. This was the site Pierre L'Enfant had picked in his 1791 Plan of the Federal City for a great National Church, and in popular mythology the Patent Office assumed an aura not inappropriate to that concept. The first of its four wings was under construction when Page arrived from Salem in 1838, the last was completed just before he died 30 years later—an appropriately symbolic note, considering his long and intimate association with the Patent Office.

The classic south facade of the Patent Office soon acquired a distinct symbolic significance of its own. Pictorial representations, every bit as ubiquitous as the Capitol or the White House, served as a constant reminder of the inventor's key role in building America's national might. Yet, even before the second wing was begun in 1849 the government began allocating office space to other bureaus, and this had the effect of turning the building itself into an object of a dispute which flared periodically throughout the 19th century.

But no provision in the legislation of 1836 ultimately led to such heated controversy as the creation of the post of examining clerk. It was the examiner's duty to scrutinize each application and the accompanying model for novelty, originality, and utility. In case he found it wanting on one or more count, he was to reject it and explain why to the applicant. The latter might then modify his application and re-submit it. Occasionally this jousting continued for several rounds, until the applicant either abandoned his application or satisfied the examiner regarding the phraseology of the claims.

For the examiner's reference, Congress appropriated an initial sum of $1,500 to establish a *Scientific Library*. Superficially, this suggested that decisions would be grounded in the straightforward logic revealed by an objective—"scientific"— examination of all relevant facts. Soon enough, however, inventors realized that an examiner's views were highly subjective, especially with regard to questions of novelty. Then, as now, patent examining was "not a mechanical process but almost an art."[8] Examiners could differ greatly in the thoroughness with which they searched for precedents, in the degree of originality they thought sufficient, and, especially, in their propensity to take into account parallel physical principles between one sort of device and another. None of these matters was delineated in any formal sense. Nominally, the commissioner had the final say on all such questions, since the examiner's function was ostensibly only advisory. But Ellsworth showed little inclination, and his immediate successors even less, to countermand examiners' decisions. Inevitably this generated concern about vesting the latter with what was essentially a judicial authority.

Not that the qualifications for nomination as an examiner were not rigorous, ideally at least. In the words of Senator Ruggles:

> An efficient and just discharge of the duties, it is obvious, requires extensive scientific attainments, and a general knowledge of the arts, manufactures, and the mechanism used in every branch of business in which improvements are sought to be patented, and of the principles embraced in the ten thousand inventions patented in the United States, and of the thirty thousand patented in Europe. He must moreover possess a familiar knowledge of the statute and common law on the subject, and the judicial decisions both in England and our own country, in patent cases.[9]

Individuals meeting these criteria, Ruggles mentioned rather superfluously, "are rare." By 1861, when the number of examinerships had been increased to twelve, thirty-two men had held the post. Not every one possessed all the qualities Ruggles enumerated, yet on the whole they were remarkable. As it turned out, examiners of "extensive scientific attainments" often proved most resourceful at ferreting out evidence on which to base rejections for want of novelty. For a time around mid-century such men thoroughly dominated office policy. Even at the beginning of the Civil War first-rate chemists like Thomas Antisell and Benjamin S. Hedrick were employed by the office, yet by then the dominance of "scientific men" had been broken. This was largely the result of agitation by the patent lobby which began to find its voice around 1850 and demand relaxed standards of examination, even if this meant the removal of "illiberal" examiners.

The first appointee to the post of examining clerk was Charles Keller. In a sense this was appropriate, even though Keller lacked "scientific attainments," since it was he who had been unofficially examining prior to the reconstitution of the office. At the outset he denied three-fourths of all applications, but that was as much attributable to technical errors in their preparation as to any marked "illiberal" streak in Keller. Indeed, by the time those who bandied this term about began to acquire political influence, he had moved to the other side of the desk and set himself up as an agent whom inventors could entrust with the job of steering applications successfully through to approval with their original claims as much intact as possible. Virtually all patent agents, it goes without saying, were stout proponents of a "liberal" policy, Keller being no exception.

Initially, most inventors submitted their applications without enlisting the assistance of a professional agent, although members of Congress sometimes acted in lieu: by 1839, for example, one finds Senator Franklin Pierce, Senator James Buchanan, Congressman Millard Fillmore, and Speaker of the House James K. Polk performing that service for constituents.[10] This practice died out, however, as an increasing number of agents established themselves in Washington and the major Eastern cities. The first of these was Thomas P. Jones, who worked the field until March 1837, when Congress authorized the employment of a second examiner and Ellsworth named him to this position. He remained through 1838, after which he resigned and revived his agency. This sort of crossing from one side to the other was not uncommon, and it fostered many touchy conflicts of interest; indeed, it appears that in a few instances Jones *examined* applications he had previously *drawn up.*[11] Later, it became commonplace for former or even incumbent commissioners to endorse one or another agent as, say, "a gentleman worthy of confidence,"[12] and agents who had recently resigned examinerships naturally found themselves confronting their former colleagues, often close friends, in what ostensibly was an adversary relationship.

The second to establish himself as a patent agent was William P. Elliot. Like Keller, Elliot's father had worked for the office under the old regime. Elliot, *fils,* drafted the original design of the Patent Office building, although the ultimate design was the work of several architects and draftsmen and it therefore reflects "the confused rivalry that so characterized the American architectural profession in the early 19th century, especially in the capital city."[13] By the time the building opened in 1840, Elliot and Jones had a good jump on the patent soliciting field: Elliot negotiated 50 letters patent in 1839 and 34 in 1840, Jones handled

29 and 50. Though no other agent had nearly as large a clientele, a few of subsequent importance were already in business by 1840, among them Richard Eddy and Ezra Lincoln in Boston, William Serrell and J. P. Pirsson in New York, and, in Washington, John J. Greenough.

For several years the amount of business transacted by the Patent Office remained static. Patents totaled about 500 annually, with a low of 425 in 1839 and a high of 531 in 1843. These figures represented about 60 percent of the applications received. After 1843, however, two telling changes began to occur. First, the number of applications started rising sharply, from 819 in 1843 to more than 1,000 in 1844, 1,500 in 1847, and 2,200 in 1851. Superficially this seems to fit Professor Rostow's designation of 1844 as the "take-off point" in American economic history. Yet the number of patents was actually *less* in 1845 than in 1844, only *one* more in 1847 than in 1843, and—relative to the number of applications—only *half* as many in 1853 as in 1842. As Ellsworth's successor noted in one of his annual reports,

> The rigid examinations now made in the Patent Office, with regard to originality and patentability of new discoveries and improvements, result in the rejection of a much larger proportion of the applications than formerly, when a less scrutinizing system of examination was pursued.[14]

Before the Civil War, however, this tendency towards greater stringency in the examination procedure had been decisively reversed. In 1858 and 1859, when the number of applications topped five and six thousand respectively, nearly seven were approved for every ten received, as against a ratio of one to three during the early 1850s. I shall treat some of the factors that precipitated this turnabout, and its relevance to the history of American science and technology, in subsequent chapters. But it might bear mentioning here that this must be considered against the background of conventional political history. The rhetoric of those who pushed for "liberalizing" Patent Office policy in the 1850s was often indistinguishable from that of Jacksonian egalitarianism in the 1830s. Occasionally, they yearned openly for a return to the old registry system, when anybody could have his patent simply by paying his fee and filing the proper papers. That became impossible, of course, after the passage of Senator Ruggles's reform bill in 1836, the last year of Jackson's presidency.

What happened at the Patent Office during the Pierce and especially the Buchanan administration may be regarded as a recrudesence of Jacksonianism, a rebellion against policies that seemed weighted against the man whose attributes were those of common sense rather than erudition.

Blame for the "illiberal" tack taken by the office was laid squarely at the feet of certain old-timers on the examining corps whose forte allegedly was books and laboratories, not practical matters at all. Inventors and their journalistic and political lobby became increasingly incensed about the dominance of these "scientific men." The repercussions of this controversy affected Page in several ways, but primarily in his capacity as examiner. Even though the new system had been in effect for nearly six years prior to his appointment, only three others had previously held the position, and none of them had enjoyed anything approaching Page's scientific reputation.

After Jones resigned, Ellsworth named Thomas W. Donovan to serve with Keller, and together these two—each with the help of an assistant—divided the examinations between them for three years. Applications were routinely assigned to one of 20 broad categories, and within Donovan's purview fell the classification "chemical processes, manufactures, and compounds." On December 11, 1841, the office received an application from Dr. Jones on behalf of a New Yorker named John H. Smith for a patent on a "mode of manufacturing elaine and stearine from lard." In the normal course of events it ended up on Donovan's desk. There was nothing very recondite about Smith's process; he simply boiled the lard with a small amount of alcohol, allowed it to cool and granulate, then placed it in cloth bags and pressed out the elaine. Smith conceded that "in analytical chemistry" elaine and stearine were separated by dissolving lard in heated alcohol, but pointed out that this was too costly for commercial purposes. What he claimed as original was the employment of alcohol as a catalyst which, although it was "driven off at an early stage of the ebullition," left the two substances "with a disposition to separate from each other." [15]

Strange to say, Smith's application seems to have been one of the most perplexing involving a chemical process that the Patent Office had yet been compelled to pass upon. Donovan noted that the process of boiling lard in alcohol was described in William Henry's *Elements of Experimental Chemistry*, but he was unable to assess the originality of its use as a catalyst, and sought

54

Commissioner Ellsworth's opinion. Ellsworth in turn sought Keller's. Keller begged off, disavowing "any knowledge of chemistry." [16] The office tabled Smith's application.

Then, on March 16, 1842, Page went on the payroll, and two days later Donovan went off. It is not clear whether he was dismissed or resigned, probably the latter, but in any event the Smith application must have made Ellsworth realize the necessity of having a chief examiner with formal training in the physical sciences. Ellsworth and Page had been acquainted for some time, and it seems likely they had discussed the possibility of his filling the first vacancy. Aside from Jones, who had once held a professorship of natural philosophy at the Franklin Institute and had edited a work on chemistry, Page was the first examiner who truly met Senator Ruggles's criterion of "extensive scientific attainments." Though many others later met it well, he met it best of all.

So, at the age of 30, Page had finally found his life's work. He would spend every one of his remaining 26 years in the Patent Office, either as an examiner or as the examiner's adversary, an agent. This was perhaps not the ideal "career of science" of which he might have dreamed a decade earlier as a college senior, but it must, nevertheless, have appeared quite attractive. Among the classes of inventions assigned him besides chemical processes were mathematical, philosophical, optical, surgical, and medical instruments, calorific, hydraulic, pneumatic, and lever devices, and "arts—polite, fine, and ornamental." The pay was certainly on a par with a good professorship. And, whereas Alexander Bache had recently lamented the scarcity of "positions now attained by scientific men in the United States where there is sufficient leisure for research," [17] Page's was an exception, for the hours were but six or seven daily, depending on the season. He would have time to resume the pursuit of his personal research, while simultaneously getting paid for the exercise of his expertise. Page was now a true professional scientist.

As it turned out, opportunities for virtuoso displays of his erudition were rare. The great majority of applications that came across his desk belonged to the more mundane classes assigned him and provided scarcely any challenge. Though he later became much more stringent, at first he did not look too far for analogies, and rejected outright only about a third of the applications he examined. Smith's catalytic process he regarded as obviously patentable, and he passed it at once. Initially he had to complete about two examinations per day to keep his in-box clear. Among the applications he reviewed during his first months on the job were many for heaters, lamps, and cookstoves, brick-presses and stone-dressing machines, bee-hives, umbrellas, and water-wheels. He approved "Sam Brady's Pennsylvania Labor-Saving Corn Planter and Cultivator," an "Improvement in the Apparatus for the Resuscitating of Persons from Suspended Animation," an "Improved Mode of Disconnecting Horses from Carriages," "Seger's Axilla or Armpit Measure," and "a new and useful preparation for . . . preserving and beautifying the human hair" compounded from oil of bergamot, rum, and carrot juice.[18]

Page had a lively sense of humor, and he probably responded to contraptions and concoctions of the sort one historian calls "Patent Nonsense"[19] much as we would today. But he took his duties as seriously as warranted. Inside a few weeks he had dealt with the leading agents, such as Jones, Elliot, and Greenough, and knew what to expect from each of them as businessmen as well as informally. Finding the work pace leisurely, he had ample time to resume the pursuits he had dropped when he left New England. In 1842 he sent Jones two papers for publication in the *Journal of the Franklin Institute;* in 1843 he picked up his experiments with electric motors, and the next year he plunged into a great diversity of part-time pursuits.

In 1844 Ellsworth started having each examiner write a personal review of his activities, for publication in the commissioner's annual report. Looking back over his first two years, Page recounted having examined 824 applications, passing "in whole or in part" 527. After noting what he thought were the more important inventions he had seen, Page took leave to offer "some reflections of a general character." A visitor to the model room at the Patent Office, he wrote, would find "no idle schemes . . . nothing of the philosopher's stone—but everywhere the utilitarian efforts of inventive genius, so to arrange in other forms existing materials, as to subserve the interest and enhance the comfort of mankind."[20] Such an observation perhaps hints at the potential for a profound shift in Page's personal philosophy, yet the invidious comparison implied in his juxtaposition of "the philosopher's stone" to "the utilitarian efforts of inventive genius" was more apparent than real. He probably saw no reason to draw any definite line of demarcation between science and invention; fundamental to each was the accretion of knowledge and an expanding range of inquiry. "The greater the circle of

56

light," he quoted Humphry Davy as saying, "the greater the boundary of darkness which surrounds it." [21] He still regarded piercing that darkness as mankind's most compelling challenge.

The observations quoted at the head of this chapter are also from Page's first report to the commissioner. He continued by declaring that "the offspring of each distinct and notable invention may be hundreds, or even thousands; and each of these may claim its host of descendants. In an incalculable ratio will inventions increase, till space will hardly be found to preserve their representations." [22] Nothing much needs be made of the prescience of this, although it surely stands in marked contrast to Commissioner Ellsworth's feeling that invention was due to begin tapering off. In 1842, the year Page took his job, 517 inventions were patented; when he left the office 26 years later, that annual total had multiplied 26-fold. As he suspected, within a short time there was simply no more space "to preserve their representations," and the stipulation requiring the submission of models along with applications had to be dropped. Yet, Page's years were in truth almost bucolic compared to those that followed. The last patents bearing his signature of approval were numbered in the 70,000s—that many inventions had been patented since the examination system was put into effect 32 years earlier. The same number of years *later,* at the turn of the century, the number had passed 700,000. In the last year of the 19th century more than 26,000 inventions were patented—and even that figure would subsequently double.

During Page's third year on the job, by contrast, the number of applications topped 1,000 for the first time ever. In 1845 the total rose yet another 200, though the number approved was actually less. More applications, but fewer patents—this meant, among other things, that the examiners were working harder, for a rejected or drastically amended application almost inevitably entailed a larger amount of research and correspondence. While the range of outside activities for which Page found time would scarcely suggest he was overworked, in 1844 Commissioner Ellsworth presented the first of a series of pleas to Congress to enlarge the examining corps and give them "more adequate compensation for their services":

... Deep study and knowledge of different languages, a minute acquaintance with the arts and sciences, and much experience, are all required to fit an individual for the office of

57

examiner; and yet his pay is only $1,500—less than is paid for clerical duties in many of the bureaus. The present compensation will be inadequate to induce those in the office to remain. . . .[23]

As a matter of fact, Keller did tender his resignation in 1844, and Ellsworth induced him to stay only with the hope that Congress might authorize a raise. "I beg to ask," he wrote, "if while the income of the office is fully sufficient to meet all necessary expense, whether it would not be a matter of deepest regret to part with experienced help for new and untried hands. What blunders, what errors, what litigation would ensue."[24] But Congress would not authorize a raise, and Keller left early in 1845 to form a partnership with John J. Greenough. Next to the one run by Thomas P. Jones, Keller and Greenough's firm became the most successful of its time. Their clients included some of the most illustrious American inventors, including S.F.B. Morse, who, while he did not invariably pay his fees promptly, lent great prestige to their business.

Page, too, had become closely associated with Morse, as a technical consultant. He was also responsible for examining Morse's patent applications (as well as any from his competitors, of course), a conflict of interest that later caused a bit of a stir. Nobody expressed any concern then, however, and with Keller's resignation Page became senior examiner. To fill the vacancy, the commissioner promoted one of the assistants, William P.N. Fitzgerald. Fitzgerald had an interesting past. Nineteen years before, he had stood second on the list of most distinguished cadets at West Point, and first in mathematics and natural philosophy. Then, following a Christmas celebration at which he allegedly conducted himself in a riotous manner, he had been summarily drummed out of the service. The best he could do while that scandal remained fresh was take a lowly instructor's position at the Mount Pleasant Classical Institution in Amherst where he roomed for a time with one of his students, Henry Ward Beecher. But later he read and practiced law, then came to Washington and the Patent Office in 1840.

Although Page was generally decorous in his behavior, he and Fitzgerald were amiable friends and compatible colleagues. And, with these two, the Patent Office for the first time had well qualified scientists occupying both principal examiner's positions. But that was only the beginning. About a year later, Leonard Gale became Page's assistant. In 1848, Gale was promoted, and Henry B. Renwick, Jonathan Homer Lane, Titian R. Peale, and Thomas Everett were hired. The next year, President Zachary Taylor named the redoubtable Thomas Ewbank commissioner. In short order, Lane was promoted, and George C. Schaeffer, Edward Foreman, and William B. Taylor came on board. I shall have more to tell about these people later; suffice it for now to say that all of them moved in the same circles as Professor Henry, all were regarded as worthy "scientific men." And there were still others of commensurate stature—in sum a most impressive cast of experts—but one never universally applauded, indeed, one which soon enough began to draw far more catcalls than cheers.

Chapter Four

Statesmen, Promoters, Professors, And Scientific Gentlemen

> Mr. Calhoun once remarked to us . . . that "the subjugation of electricity to the mechanical necessities of man would mark the last era in human civilization."
>
> *Charles Grafton Page, 1853*

> Please let me know when you will be at license to consult.
>
> *To Samuel F. B. Morse, June 14, 1844*

> I would be glad if you would think of establishing an Electrical Association, Society or Academy . . . I should be ever ready to cooperate in any such movement.
>
> *To Robert Hare, Feb. 17, 1848*

> Dr. Page requests the pleasure of Prof. Henry's company on Tuesday evening May 30th to meet a few scientific gentlemen.
>
> *To Joseph Henry, May 5, 1848*

Page felt most fortunate in having Henry Ellsworth as his superior. First, he was a good friend and kindred soul. His imagination could be set soaring by "what is now accomplished by the electric fluid, when confined and tamed, as it were, to the purposes of life,"[1] and he was pleased when Page had time to pursue his own research on government time. Second, Page found his administrative policies admirable. Some years later, he wrote that when he started to work Ellsworth presented him with a set of instructions which evidenced

> a proper appreciation of his own position, the true relation of his subordinates to himself and to the public, a just estimate of the character of rights of the class of citizens he was to deal with, and of the high responsibility imposed upon him by the statute in the execution of a law replete with intricacies.[2]

Finally, Ellsworth was always eager to praise the expertise and industry of his examiners. Even though he failed to win them a raise, he set a precedent for his successor who reiterated the same plea so persistently that eventually Congress yielded.

Despite the urgency with which Ellsworth endowed his

appeals for a larger staff and increased pay, in 1845 there was good reason to doubt whether sufficient justification existed for either. True, it proved impossible to keep Charles Keller. But Keller had no rival in his knowledge of the American patent system, and, if his successor perhaps exaggerated in calling him "one of the master minds in the arts," [3] it certainly was not unrealistic for him to anticipate a lucrative career as a patent agent. One of Ellsworth's ploys was to pose comparisons between an examiner's salary and those of "other officers of like capacities"—among whom he included assayers, melters, coiners, and engravers at the Mint ($2,000), top-rank naval engineers ($2,500-$3,000), assistants to the chief of the Coast Survey ($2,000-$3,500), and the chief himself ($6,000). Ellsworth felt that "the discharge of the duties of several of the above stations does not demand the talents or acquirements necessary for an examiner of patents." [4] He surely knew that this was not so of the $6,000 man, Alexander Bache, whose talents were prodigious. Still, maybe it *was* incongruous that Page made only one-quarter as much.

On the other hand, very few college professors did as well as Page, and only one scientist in academia earned substantially more, Robert Hare at the University of Pennsylvania. Hare was extraordinarily prolific—no American physical scientist came close to matching his publication record—for his was the closest thing to a research professorship in the country. Page's income was a far cut below Hare's $5,000 plus, but his job too allowed him a certain amount of free time. He handled 644 applications in 1844. Less "liberal" than previously, he passed only 48 percent. With more applications and more rejections, his work-load was naturally heavier. By no means was it overbearing, however: for better than half the year he was required to be in his office only from 9:00 a.m. to 3:00 p.m. He did not let his spare hours go to waste.

Shortly after beginning his new job, Page published two brief papers, his first since 1839. One stemmed from his previous investigation of "closed secondary currents," which he had ascertained must be developed not only in the winding of a magnet but also in the core. Although Henry had inferred the same thing, as had at least one Continental physicist, Page devised a means of actually demonstrating the existence of this phenomenon which later came to be associated with the term hysteresis. [5] The other paper described what he called a "quantity helix," a stack of annular copper plates designed to get "the

61

greatest number of circumvolutions of conducting metal within a given space, and to bring those conducting circuits as near as possible to a direction at right angles to the axis of a magnetic bar."[6]

This foretold a crucial experimental reorientation: here, Page was seeking not to induce high voltages in the secondary winding of a coil, but to intensify the magnetic influence on the core. The operational prototype was his 1838 device "for exhibiting the magnetic forces in the centre of a helix"—fundamentally, an electromagnet with a sliding core, a solenoid. What he had in mind was reducing this principle to practice in the form of a motor. Theretofore, his and all other rotary motors were woefully deficient in power. Perhaps developing a dynamic power comparable to the enormous static power of an electromagnet was merely a matter of constructing *reciprocating* electric motors, or, as Page preferred, "axial engines."

Commencing work on these during 1843, he came up with a promising design early the next year. In May 1844, when the Association of American Geologists and Naturalists met in Washington, Page exhibited his "new electro-magnetic instruments to produce a reciprocal motion."[7] This was important "as a token of the broadening interests of the Association,"[8] soon to be transformed into the American Association for the Advancement of Science. And for Page himself it was indeed a key event, because the reaction gave him heart to set out on a long quest that ultimately succeeded in one sense, failed in another, and left him quite literally exhausted.

Meanwhile, he had also spent time improving his magnetos, and by the end of 1844 had developed one capable of energizing Morse's Washington-Baltimore telegraph line just as satisfactorily as a chemical battery. Likewise in 1844 he assumed the professorship of chemistry and pharmacy at a fledgling institution called the National Medical College. These pursuits I shall detail in due course, but it would distort the picture of what meant most to Page personally to omit yet another event of 1844, one more important than medical college, motors, or magnetos— namely, romance and matrimony.

One of the first Washingtonians with whom Page made friends was Dr. Harvey Lindsly, a fellow member of the National Institute, practicing physician, and Professor of Obstetrics at Columbian College. An old-timer in the capital, Lindsly had married Emelyn Webster, formerly of Maine, in 1828. Emelyn was the elder sister of Priscilla Webster, who had come to live with the Lindslys in 1841. Page had occasionally seen Priscilla at their Pennsylvania Avenue home, especially in 1843 during a visit by the daughters of a Salem surgeon who was related both to the Pages and the Websters. But he had actually met Priscilla Webster socially only once.

In her *Personal Reminiscences*, written in the 1880s, Priscilla recalled the evening nearly 40 years before when "A card was brought to my room . . . upon which I read the name of 'Dr. Charles G. Page'." Since she hardly knew Dr. Page, she assumed there was some mistake and told the servant, "This is for Dr. Lindsly." He assured her, however, that it was *Miss Webster* that Dr. Page had asked for, so she went down to the parlor. "I did not fall in love with him at once," she wrote, "but I admired him greatly, and found him far more interesting and fine-looking than any of the gentlemen who were then attentive to me." Before their conversation ended, she added, "the thought flashed through my mind, 'He will ask me to be his wife, and I *think* I like him'."[9]

In truth, Dr. Page swept Priscilla quite off her feet. Though she had several suitors, none had made much of an impression. Her feeling as soon as Charles left, on the other hand, was "as if I were in a dream; that my fate was sealed, without any effort or even choice of my own." A day or two later he brought her some engravings to look at, then spring blossoms from the country. Flowers were a mutual fancy; they soon discovered many others— long walks, quiet talk, romantic fiction. At 32, Page was indeed a fine figure of a man: small—smaller than Priscilla—though physically very powerful. He spoke carefully but had a quick mind and a vast repertoire of talents. When Emelyn asked him to a little social gathering, he charmed everybody "with his delightful music, singing, and playing the flute exquisitely."[10]

In April Charles and Priscilla became engaged. His parents took to her at once, and there were many gay times that summer at Pageville. In September they were married. They honeymooned in New England, boarded during the winter, and in the spring of 1845 "went to housekeeping, in a pleasant little house on C Street, embowered in roses and honeysuckle."[11] In June, a daughter was born, Emelyn, and two years later a son, Charles Grafton Page, Jr.

Though not even 20 when she and Page met, Priscilla Webster was quite a sophisticate. While thoroughly imbued with the characteristic New England equation of Democrats with disaster, she was nevertheless proud to have made the acquaintance of Millard Fillmore and Henry Clay. An uncle who resided in Washington was married to a sister of Senator Rufus Choate, and she had passed many an hour in the home of that estimable gentleman and leading light of Whiggery. But the family she came to know most intimately, next to the Lindslys, was that of another Massachusetts Whig—Choate's idol and Priscilla's cousin, Daniel Webster.

A towering personality who had a far greater impact on 19th-century America than many Presidents, Webster became Secretary of State a few days after Priscilla's arrival in Washington (she called him "Premier"). 1841 and 1842 were a busy time, and he was absent from his home on President's Square (as Lafayette Park was then called) for long periods. Priscilla often stayed with Webster's wife, Caroline, to keep her company, and when Daniel was there she was occasionally treated to a unique inside-view of the social side of statecraft. Even though she had attended White House receptions with thousands of guests, the Webster home was truly special. Mrs. Webster made it "the center of brilliant society, drawing around them the finest spirits of the century." [12] Recalling her times there, Priscilla wrote,

> . . . the charm of society as it then existed in Washington can, I am sure, never be repeated. Elegant dinners were given to Lord Ashburton [the British Minister, with whom Webster negotiated a major treaty in 1842], to the President and Cabinet, and foreign Ministers, to which I was sometimes invited; and as I would not infrequently be the only lady present except Mrs. Webster, the seat of honor would be given me by Mr. Webster's side. [13]

As time passed, Daniel Webster grew extremely fond of Priscilla. Not only was she invited to grand dinners, but also to cozy little affairs for special friends only. Sometimes just the two of them would be alone, and often Priscilla read poetry to him. His favorite was *The Winged Worshipers* of Charles Sprague, which she came to know almost by heart. In August 1844, a month before her announced marriage, he wrote his "Dearly Beloved Priscy" from Boston to express his sadness that "hereafter you must belong, principally, not to former friends and connections, but to another." Still, he felt that her choice for a mate was "exceedingly good." "I have not much personal acquaintance, my dear cousin, with Dr. Page," he continued, "but have ever

64

received an excellent character of him. He is a friend, I believe, of Fletcher's [Webster's son], and I know much of him, also, through Mr. Ellsworth and others. You cannot doubt that I think him a most fortunate man. . . ."[14] Webster concluded by asking Priscilla to relay his respects and felicitations to Dr. Page, and his anticipation of getting better acquainted.

The newlyweds spent part of their honeymoon in Massachusetts at Marshfield with Caroline Webster. Although family illness forced them to cut short their visit and they did not see Webster then, he and Page subsequently got to know each other well. Webster had charge of the Patent Office, of course, during his first tenure as Secretary of State, 1841 to 1843. He had strong opinions on the patent system, opinions that later had a decided influence on Page's own thinking. Once, in the midst of a conversation Page never forgot, Webster turned and exclaimed, "You examiners have too much power! Too much power!" If that power could not be reined in, he insisted, it "would be better to go back to the old system, and give every man his patent."[15] Page perceived that "such a system might please the lawyers" (Webster, whose private clients included Charles Goodyear, was involved in litigating several major patent cases), but could not agree, not then at least. Eventually, however, he understood what Webster meant: even this Whig of Whigs could stand unequivocally for "liberalization."

Although Page was a steadfast Whig too, he was not usually partisan in choosing his companions, and his acquaintances included many important Southern and Western Democrats. When he needed a letter of personal recommendation, he might turn to Choate (whom he had first met in Salem), but he could also speak with warm regard of John C. Calhoun's "beautiful, extraordinary and *bold* conceptions,"[16] and rely on Thomas Hart Benton to plead a cause for him in Congress.

Among all the great politicians of the era, though, it was Webster that both he and Priscilla knew best. One of Priscilla's most profound memories was her last visit with the old gentleman in August 1852, two months before his death. Her sister Emelyn had brought him out to "Grafton Cottage," in the country four or five miles north of the city where she and Charles had resided since the late 1840s. Emelyn remarked, "Priscy and I think and talk of you a great deal." Webster replied, "When you think of *me*, you think of the *past*; when you talk of me, your conversation is historical." Priscilla lifted each of her children—

by then there were three—for a farewell kiss, then, she recalled, "Our last good-bye was spoken, and we met no more." [17]

Much to his regret, Page simply had too much to do that day, and found it impossible to be present. While he was in no sense addicted to work—he often spent Saturdays tending his garden or botanizing; he always had time to play with the children; and he frequently hosted social gatherings—Page did drive himself very hard for an entire decade, 1844-1854. Those years no doubt constituted his prime, a period which has been defined in another context as "the time when energy and experience are in the equilibrium that yields peak efficiency and output." [18]

During this period, his circle of friends and associates grew to encompass not only political luminaries, but also men of science and inventors whose repute was comparable to Webster's in politics. The inventors included Alfred Vail and Samuel F. B. Morse, who were attempting to commercialize the most truly practical application of electromagnetism so far devised in America, the telegraph. On March 3, 1843, at the strong urging of Commissioner Ellsworth, Congress had authorized an unprecedented appropriation, $30,000 to finance a telegraph line connecting Washington and Baltimore. As superintendent of construction, Vail's was the key role in the ultimate success of the project. He made a serious tactical error, however, by first attempting to place the wires underground inside lead conduits. Short-circuits made this unworkable, and Page advised him to string a bare wire overhead, returning current via the earth itself, as was the German practice.

Usually, either Ezra Cornell or Professor Henry is credited with having pointed this out, but Page evidently did it first. He inferred from Ohm's Law and also from an experiment which entailed wiring instruments to the roof of the Patent Office— 22,000 square feet of copper—"that the poorest conductor, or what has usually been considered a non-conductor, would become a conductor if the area of its cross section were indefinitely increased and its length remained nearly nothing." [19] In fact, the "cross firing" problem could have been solved simply by insulating the wires more carefully, and in retrospect Page's theoretical explanation seems a bit strained. Still, by now he could handle a deductive methodology with considerable skill, proceeding from hypothesis to experimental test to the inference of a general principle—as when he set out to corroborate "the law of Ampere as to the modifying influence of distance upon induction," and

66

established that "The inductive action of a helix upon inclosed bars of soft iron of uniform lengths and transverse diameters, is directly in proportion to the weight of those bars."[20] And Morse, for his part, was astute enough to see that here, in Page, was a valuable fount of expertise, be it theoretical or practical.

Not long after the Washington-Baltimore line was completed, Morse inquired when Page would be free to discuss a certain matter, and thenceforth the two frequently consulted about technical problems. Page's youngest son, Harvey Lindsly Page, later tried to establish his father along with Morse and Henry as "The Three Inventors of the Telegraph." He was scarcely convincing, yet the fact remains that Page did devise significant improvements in telegraph technology, one being the arrangement of adjustable stops for the armature to vibrate between, another, a miniaturized form of receiving magnet.[21] Most interesting, though, was his experiment with an alternative to galvanic batteries as a source of power.

Page probably *does* merit designation as one of "the three inventors of the magneto," with Hippolyte Pixii and Joseph Saxton. He designed the first one made in America (Saxton built his while residing in London). He pioneered in the utilization of an electrically excited field magnet, and also in deriving direct current by means of a commutator (or "unitress," in his personal terminology).[22] Moreover, it was Page who first devised a magneto wherein the armature rotated between *two* sets of magnets in order to intensify the field. In 1844, at the urging of Morse, he resumed experimenting along these lines, and a month after the wire to Baltimore was put in operation Morse paid him $99.50 for "one magnetic electric machine." Subsequently he invested an additional sum for a large quantity of copper plate.[23]

For assistance Page relied chiefly on Vail, who kept track of their progress in his diary. Often he phrased these entries in a manner such as this: "Studied Farraday [*sic*], and after dinner spent 2 hours experimenting with Dr. Page with his Magneto Electrical machines. . . ."[24] We know that "Faraday's experiments and his observations on them actually contained a number of clues to effective generator design."[25] Clearly, Page and Vail were striving to unravel these clues. Though reluctant to describe the experiments in any detail, partly because he was seeking to obtain foreign patents, Page did acknowledge that his ultimate aim was to develop a machine with the property possessed by a battery "which chemists call quantity, or that power upon which depends its ability to magnetize."[26] At this he did succeed, eventually building a magneto capable of sustaining 1,000 pounds.

The most noteworthy accomplishment, however, occurred on Christmas day 1844. Vail described it:

> This morning a beautiful experiment was tried at Washington on Morse's magnetic Telegraph—Prof. Charles G. Page, examiner in the Patent Office well known for his many ingenious inventions in electro magnetism, has been engaged for some time in improving his original magneto electrical machine, which has now attained such a degree of perfection as to answer all the purposes of the Galvanic battery in the Telegraph. The first experiment tried this morning in presence of Prof. Morse & Mr. Vail his assistant, fully tested the practicability and importance of the invention. The Telegraphic instruments were operated to Baltimore and back to Washington, a distance through 80 miles of wire, by means of this new improvement—thus establishing the fact that the Galvanic Battery, an expensive and disagreeable apparatus may be dispensed with. The instrument was made by Dr. Page for Prof. Morse and we are happy in announcing the complete success of the experiment, adding another instance of a new discovery bearing upon the Telegraph and economizing its operation so far as to remove all objections on the score of expense to its extensive introduction.[27]

Page felt that he had come up with a significant piece of apparatus, not only for practical uses such as telegraphy and for "blasting at a distance," but also for experimentation, since it enabled "the man of science . . . to have always at hand a constant power" without any wasteful consumption of chemicals. Certain elements of its construction, especially the nature of one "very important discovery" pertaining to the derivation of large quantities of low intensity electricity, Page did not want to make public "until his rights [were] in some way secured." Nevertheless, in 1845 he let Vail publish a partial description along with illustrations (Fig. 7) in his book on the telegraph. (Page was the sixth person to whom Vail gave a copy of this work; the first five were Leonard Gale, two of Vail's relatives, Amos Kendall, and F. O. J. Smith; Morse and Henry were both far down the list.)[28]

More than a year after Page performed his "beautiful experiment," *Scientific American* still anticipated that the use of

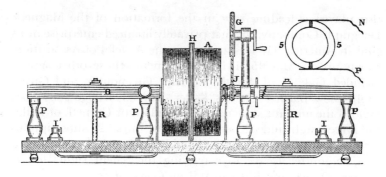

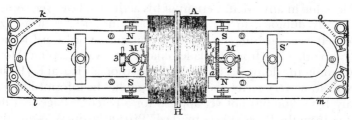

Fig. 7. Magneto developed by Page for Morse, 1844. (From Alfred Vail, THE AMERICAN ELECTRO MAGNETIC TELEGRAPH [1845], p. 147.)

batteries in telegraphy "may probably be superseded by Dr. Page's improved magneto-electrical machine." [29] He pursued this work no further, however, and no other American took up where he had left off until the Civil War. Page later mentioned that his magneto embodied a plate helix nearly two feet in diameter which "required the full strength of a man to turn." [30] This, of course, helps explain why it never "superseded" batteries in telegraphy. Had it been possible to harness water-power, the utilization of Page's machine would have made sense; otherwise, it was nothing more than a museum piece. In 1852 Page donated it to the Smithsonian—probably the Institution's first accession of a technological artifact. Henry had some repairs made, and promised that it would "be carefully preserved." [31] Alas, it was destroyed in the fire of 1865, along with a number of other objects Page had donated and all the apparatus given by Robert Hare.

The idea of generating elecricity without consuming chemicals was an intriguing one. It simply turned out that, for Morse's purpose, Hare's sort of electrochemical apparatus was not so "disagreeable" after all. But Page stayed on as his consultant, and

69

also played a leading role in the formation of the Magnetic Telegraph Company, the first privately financed enterprise of its kind in America. He was a party to the Articles of Association, drawn up on May 15, 1845, a document whose other signers included Gale, Vail, Smith, Cornell, Greenough, and Greenough's new partner Charles Keller. The $500 Page subscribed equaled the amount subscribed by Kendall, or Cornell, or Keller and Greenough; indeed, only five of the initial 27 subscriptions were larger. Along with Kendall and B. B. French, he was named to a committee to see to conveying the patent rights to the trustees, French and William Wilson Corcoran.[32]

While there is some question whether Page ever paid his subscription, his services to the new company were of considerable value in any event. Certain of his activities, however, seemed ethically dubious, to say the least. For instance, even as Ezra Cornell was pushing his construction crew northward toward New York City from Philadelphia, Page was keeping Morse posted on the doings of potential competitors: "[Royal E.] House seems to be very secret about his telegraph," he informed him in July 1845; "he has not yet applied for a patent." Page sent this letter from the Patent Office marked "Private business"—and that it was, for whether or not anyone had applied for anything was simply not a matter to be treated as public information. Nevertheless, here was Page assuring Morse a few days later that "you may rely upon my warmest advocacy whenever occasion may require."[33]

Page was then receiving money regularly from Morse—most often, no doubt, for services and advice rather than "warmest advocacy." He was not especially impressed with Morse's ingenuity, and his advice was sometimes blunt and unembellished: "I do not like your mode of mounting the lever," "The feature of bevelling the poles I object to entirely," "let well enough alone." Certain problems he discussed with considerable circumspection, however, and in such detail that he could easily have published his letters as articles—one of 500 words, for example, dealing with a plan for laying lines beneath "large bodies of water."[34] Page also designed an improved form of receiving magnet for Morse, and saw to making several of these, for which he was paid cash sums ranging from $20 to $50. Later a dispute over the receiving magnet would instantly destroy what had remained a close friendship for nearly two decades, but that blowup was still a long way off in the 1840s when Page obliged Morse in a great variety of

70

ways. Certainly not the least important was his role in the first of the major telegraph lawsuits, Morse *vs* O'Reilly (1848), in which Page starred as a key witness.

Morse's attorney, Amos Kendall, took great pains to make sure everyone understood exactly what Page's position was, by repeatedly having him identify himself for the record as "Chief Examiner in the Patent Office." In one interrogatory he asked Page,

> Have you not made Electricity and Electro Magnetism to a great extent your study, and have you not read all or most of the publications describing the progress of that science, and its applications to telegraphic purposes at home and abroad? If so, do you know any fact which could impair Professor Morse's right to all he claims in his patents if this were now for the first time submitted for your examination?

Next, he inquired whether Page was

> not familiar with the origin and progress of most of the plans for Electric and Magnetic Telegraphs which had been invented and patented in Europe, particularly with Wheatstone's, Davy's, and Steinheil's? . . . To your knowledge, is any telegraph now in service in Europe which writes or imprints telegraphic characters by means of Electro Magnetism, like Prof. Morse's?

To these questions Page responded,

> I have made the subject of Electricity and Magnetism a special study for more than twelve years and knew of nothing before the issue of Letters Patent to said Morse which could have interfered with his claims nor has any fact come to my knowledge since the grant of said Letters Patent which would in my judgement in any way impair his rights as secured to him under said patent.

> I am familiar with the origin and progress of the Electric and Electro Magnetic telegraph and have never known of one that marked signs by indentation after the manner of said Morse's invention, and to the best of my belief and knowledge the telegraphs of Steinheil . . . Wheatstone . . . and Davy . . . have been found impracticable and are not now in use.

Last, not only did Page affirm that Morse himself had invented every component of his telegraph system including the receiving magnet, he also stated, "I have not now, nor ever had, any interest in any of the Patents granted to said Morse." Although this was the truth, it was not an answer to the question Kendall had asked him, which was, "Were you ever or are you now interested in Professor Morse's Telegraphs?"[35]

The story of Page's role in refining the receiving magnet had already been accorded some publicity, and eventually the blatant conflict of interest in which he had allowed himself to become entangled began to attract considerable attention. Henceforth, he realized, discretion must prevail. In mid-1849, when Elias Loomis of Yale queried Page on the subject of Morse's patents, he replied in a very curt manner, insisting that "the pressure of business upon us will hardly permit [even] these few lines." Late in the year, one of Morse's attorneys reported he had called repeatedly at the Patent Office to see Page, but had "never as yet found him." Simultaneously, Gale informed Morse that Page had determined to keep his peace, "as the opinions and affidavits already out had created much disturbance." Page thought it important both for Morse's sake and for the reputation of the Patent Office "that the Examiner's names should not be too often brought before the public."[36] Finally, he had decided to cease relaying information to Morse on the activities of his competitors. (Gale stepped in to fill that breach, however, disclosing in some detail the current dealings of Alexander Bain vis-à-vis the Patent Office.)

Even though Page at last mended his ways, his relationship with Morse between 1844 and 1849 left his sense of ethics appearing somewhat tarnished, even by contemporary standards. But another of his pursuits during those same five years does much to restore its sheen. In 1844, with the backing of Harvey Lindsly, Page obtained a teaching position in the Medical Department of Columbian College. Thanks to the labors of President Stephen Chapin, this school had been put on a sound financial footing and was entering a period of "gradual but consistent progress."[37] After having been moribund for several years, the Medical Department was revived in 1839, and its condition had remained stable. The faculty comprised Dr. Thomas Sewall, Professor of Pathology and the Practice of Medicine, who had been present at the creation in 1825 and delivered the introductory lecture; Lindsly, who ranked second in point of seniority; Thomas Miller, anatomy and physiology; John M. Thomas, materia medica and therapeutics; and William Johnston, surgery. Page's appointment was as Professor of Chemistry and Pharmacy. He already

72

knew each of his colleagues, for all were fellow members of the National Institute, but he joined them at an especially opportune moment.

In 1842, Congress had appropriated $10,000 to convert the old jail on Judiciary Square into an insane asylum. After the alterations had been completed, however, this location was deemed unsuitable for such an institution. At that point, the Columbian faculty petitioned Congress for permission to take over the building, and received approval to utilize it "for the purpose of an infirmary, for medical instruction, and for scientific purposes."[38] Shortly afterwards, the six of them jointly leased the building and put up a bond to return it in good repair whenever Congress should request. Sewall, Lindsly, Miller, Thomas, Johnston, and Page, wrote Joseph Toner, the historian of the D.C. medical profession, "deserve the lasting gratitude of this community and the highest respect and admiration of their professional brethren for the tact, energy and enterprise displayed in establishing the Washington Infirmary."[39]

Congress initially refused to provide any funds for the institution, thus rendering rather incongruous its denomination as the "National Medical College." The faculty bore the cost of procuring furnishings, and in July 1844 opened the first general hospital in the capital. Patients were admitted upon payment of a token fee for board, and cared for gratis. (Beginning in 1845, Congress began appropriating a small amount annually for the care of non-resident paupers.) Meanwhile, Page and his colleagues had made ready to commence instruction. After recruiting another M.D. as a demonstrator in anatomy, they advertised a four-month course of lectures for $70, plus $10 for dissecting tickets.

During Page's five years at the college, the number of graduates ranged between five and eleven—so, obviously, he did not realize much in the way of financial gain. A few months after he resigned in 1849, he wrote Henry about a replacement for Gale, who had also served on the faculty for a time. Page wanted Henry to find out whether his friend Edward Foreman would be interested in the job. So that Foreman might know what to expect financially, Page informed Henry that "the receipts for tickets last winter were $412." He quickly added, however, that "with an effort to make up a class among the citizens it might easily have been $500."[40] Foreman decided against taking the position, though later he did give up his job as general assistant at the

Smithsonian for one as a patent examiner. He lost that job in a sweeping purge at the outset of the Lincoln Administration. Shortly before, the government had commandeered the hospital; shortly after, it burned to the ground.

Page's letter to Henry regarding Foreman is one of several dealing with personal matters still extant in the Smithsonian Archives. By 1849 he could address himself to Henry in terms of easy familiarity; indeed, he now included among his intimates not only inventor-entrepreneurs like Morse and politicians such as Webster, but also the kingpins of professional science in America. Page was genuinely thrilled by the prospect of Henry coming to Washington to take the reins of the Smithsonian. The day after the regents elected him secretary, he sent him the following letter:

Patent Office
Dec 4 1846

Sir

Among all the true lovers and followers of Science in this place, there appears to be a deep felt pleasure and satisfaction at the Election of yourself by the Board of Regents of the Smithn. Instn. No one has more cause for hearty congratulation than myself. The whole interests of this Institution have long been threatened by the *influential* labors of Mr. [Francis] Markoe, a clerk in the State Dept., to place himself at its head, an issue which I labored hard to prevent. As our best wishes for yourself, the Institution and the Cause of Science, are thus far fulfilled, I most sincerely trust that the inducements will be sufficient to rupture the strong ties that bind you to Princeton and that there will be no impediment in the way of your acceptance. I had a long conversation with Mr. Choate last evening, and though I should not anticipate any of the movements of the Regents, yet I could not fail to be delighted at his liberal views from which I infer that there is a disposition to offer high compensation, that you will have pretty much a Carte Blanche and that the actual labors will be light and agreeable. Please accept the congratulation and best wishes of

Yrs truly with
Respect & Esteem

Chas. G. Page[41]

Here at last was a fellow townsman with whom Page could converse on the same plane about electrical science. One typical exchange took place in July 1847, just before Henry once and for all left Princeton for Washington. "My dear Sir," Page wrote him,

> I have just rec'd yrs of 30 inst. and am much delighted to hear of your decision to adhere to the Smith. Inst. I was over yesterday to look at the work, which appears to be going on well and rapidly. The appearance of the stone is fine and will I am satisfied prove a most popular and valuable selection. . . .
>
> I have looked at subject of Rotations a little further and find experimentally that the magnet must revolve under the conditions I stated to you. That the revolving force is greatest when contact is made at (a) and that it diminishes on either side of (a); xx is of course constant and when xa and ab are in opposition to each other xx is still left. So far as I can find, the operation of the terminated current xx has not been considered in this connexion. Placed any where between the two poles the terminated current (c) revolves in one direction by the conjoint action of the two poles. Roget makes out in paragraph (274) of his treatise the rotation of a magnet on its own axis; but I think it is all wrong, and incompatible with Ampere's theory. Of this however I will explain more when I see you. . . .[42]

Page followed up the next day with a letter in which he told Henry about two other experiments "in connexion with a subject upon which we conversed lately."[43] Then on the 8th, he received a reply to his letter of the 6th. Henry wrote that he had

> given a hasty glance at article 274 of Roget's Treatise but I do not find the error you mention. The radiating current through the mercury is a true cause of motion though not the only one. The radiation through the magnet from this axis is another and also the current from the top of the bar down to its middle, if it happens to be excentric [sic], is a third.
>
> The current from the top to the middle must in all cases be excentric for according to the law of galvanic conduction the current must pervade the whole bar and consequently but a very small portion of it will pass a long the axis. . . .

Henry concluded by allowing that "There may however be some points which I do not see but which would be presented in a conversation with you. I shall therefore be pleased to converse with you on the subject when we next meet." [44]

Henry evidently had questioned some point in a paper Page published in the March 1847 issue of *Silliman's*. [45] Exactly what that point was is not really important; what *is* significant is that this reads like correspondence between two men whose natural inclination is to treat each other as intellectual equals, and whose personal relationship is more than just a formal one. In that regard, Page even took to sending off a few lines simply when he had a spare moment. In one such note he mentioned having recently looked over the Smithsonian building, and his pleasure at the rapid progress, "i.e. rapid for Washington and considering the season." Turning to politics, he expressed satisfaction at the defeat of Congressman Robert Dale Owen. "The issue was made upon his writings," Page observed, "and I think it a signal triumph of *good principles*." Then he moved on to the Patent Office, apologizing for the "brevity and incompleteness" of his most recent report. At the beginning of the year, he explained, the commissioner had assured the examiners that they would not be required to write any report at all, so they "were very much surprised at a demand made upon us at the eleventh hour." "The materials for my report were collated and the whole of it finished in three days," Page explained, "when it should have occupied as many weeks." He concluded by telling Henry not to consider "this epistle as entitled to a reply or acknowledgement, for your time is precious and duties onerous." [46] He did remind him, though, that he and Priscilla would ever be happy to have the Henrys come visiting at Grafton Cottage, their new home on Missouri Avenue.

Page's correspondence with Henry during the late 1840s ranges from experiments with a polariscope, to the study of whirlwinds, to his ongoing work with motors—from what today we would call pure science, to applied science, to technology. He presented public demonstrations often, and always sent an invitation to Henry. For example, on April 25, 1848, he invited him to witness an exhibition of polarized light in his laboratory at the Infirmary, "if the Sun should shine." [47] And he also invited Henry to social functions, as he did a few days later, requesting "the pleasure of Professor Henry's company . . . to meet a few scientific gentlemen." [48]

Not long after Henry arrived in Washington, Page turned 35. Though no longer a young man, he could rest confident that he

76

was considered erudite, imaginative, and versatile. He kept up with foreign journals, repeating and building upon the experiments of men such as Arago, De la Rive, and Grove. He had published some of his best and most original work during the past year. The one person in America who most closely shared his scientific enthusiasms had just moved to Washington too. He had a lovely wife, a growing family, a good job. But it was not a consistently interesting job. He could point to no single accomplishment of transcendent significance, in the sense that Henry or Morse could. His future appeared comfortable but not very exciting. Like many another person finding himself in a similar pass, Page began to toy with the idea of a radical personal reorientation.

Since beginning to lecture at the Medical College, he had rediscovered how much he enjoyed teaching, a pursuit at which he clearly excelled. Now, then, where might a man of his training and capabilities obtain a good teaching job? One possibility immediately suggested itself. Exactly a week after writing Henry to congratulate him on his election by the Smithsonian Board of Regents and to express confidence that the inducements to accept would "be sufficient to rupture the strong ties that bind you to Princeton," he addressed a second letter to him:

> Patent Office
> Dec. 11, 1846

Dear Sir

Permit me to trespass upon your time to answer the following inquiries. What is the salary or compensation for the Professorship you have vacated? When is the next meeting of the Trustees? Did you hear recitations in any other Branch than Natural Phil? And lastly do you intend to continue your services in the College any longer? By responding to this with return mail, if convenient, or as early as possible you will confer a great favor upon

> Yrs truly

> Chas. G. Page[49]

Henry responded on December 29 that his duties entailed teaching analytic mechanics, experimental philosophy, and theoretical geology, that his connection would terminate at the end of the current college year, that the regents would meet in June, and that the salary for a new professor was $1,300.[50]

77

Page apparently pursued the matter no further. Probably what discouraged him most was the salary—nearly 15 percent less than the government was currently paying him. Moreover, it was rumored that Congress at long last might approve a raise for the examiners—perhaps to $2,500, nearly twice the starting pay at Princeton. In fact, few American professorships paid nearly so much as $2,500. But it just so happened that the one which paid a great deal more became vacant too just a few months later, the chair of chemistry in the Medical Department of the University of Pennsylvania—a post which has been called "the most desirable scientific position in America."[51]

Henry was the first to whom the vacancy was offered, although Page perhaps was aware of it earlier. At least, he himself seems to have thought so, for on May 25, 1847, he wrote Henry:

> Prof Hare was here a few days since and informed me that he had resigned. His succession rests with the Trustees, all of whom are unknown to me. Can you do anything with them in my behalf? If so, please use your own discretion entirely as to the mode of proceeding. From some intimations I am stimulated to present myself as a candidate although I have it from the highest authority that there are two persons in Philadelphia in high favor, one of whom will undoubtedly receive the appointment should he consent to serve. I am in honor bound not to mention their names. Hare stated that he had thought of me, but that I was in the predicament with himself, having paid more attention to the physics of Chemistry than other branches. He stated that they would require a medical man, which qualification I can present, as I was four years in the Boston School, and three years in practice. I do not intend to fortify myself with recommendations, but trust to such friendly efforts as may be made in my behalf to bring me before the Trustees in the event of their failure to secure either of the above named candidates.[52]

Henry never seriously considered taking the job, but Page— despite his studiously casual attitude—was definitely interested. For someone who claimed that he did "not intend to fortify [himself] with recommendations," he seems to have been responsible for generating a considerable amount of correspondence. Three days later, Lindsly repeated Page's request to Henry for a letter of recommendation:

My dear Sir,

I have had some correspondence with gentlemen in Phila. in relation to Dr. Page's becoming a candidate for the chair of chemistry in the University of Pa. and altho the chances perhaps are decidedly against him, yet this is sufficient encouragement to induce his friends here to make a decided effort in his behalf. Now it has occurred to me, that your recommendation as a *scientific* man, in respect to his *scientific* qualifications (if you can consistently give him a strong one) might be of great avail. *We* think here very highly of Dr. P's capacity as a Teacher of Chemistry and indeed I have never known one whose manner was better fitted to excite the interest & command the attention of his class. He is clear, animated, enthusiastic, even eloquent & has always been a great favourite with the students. His turn for mechanics too peculiarly qualifies him for success in his experiments & hence he very seldom fails. I have not the slightest doubt of his being able to sustain himself nobly in Philadelphia shd. he receive the appt. He is, & always has been enthusiastically devoted to the pursuit of chemical science and I shd. be glad to have him secure a situation where his whole energies could be applied to its cultivation.

Some very strong recommendations will be forwarded to the Faculty & Trustees—and I shd. be much gratified if yours could be added to the number.

> Please present my regards to Mrs. H.
> & believe me
>
> Most truly Yrs.
> H. Lindsly [53]

The next day Lindsly wrote to Pennsylvania himself. Page had been, he related, "ardently and enthusiastically devoted to the pursuit of chemical science from his earliest youth—& has established a very high character as a man of science & a lecturer both here and elsewhere." Lindsly emphasized that he held degrees both from the Classical and Medical Departments at Harvard, was "of a highly moral and religious character," had "few superiors in his power of interesting young men as an experimenter very expert and skillful," and as a writer was "practiced, ready and eloquent." If Page were given the position, Lindsly felt certain that "he would sustain himself nobly and confer honor on an institution already very distinguished." [54]

He enclosed a copy of a recommendation signed by the entire medical faculty at Columbian College. These gentlemen indicated that they would "sincerely regret the loss which their own school will suffer, should his application be successful," but thought it "their duty to bear their hearty and united testimony to the satisfactory and able manner in which he has discharged his duties here." Like Lindsly, they pointed out that Page had "from his earliest youth, been an ardent, industrious & successful votary of natural science and particularly of chemistry." They went on to say that he had "instituted and carried out many important & original investigations," that as a lecturer he was "peculiarly excellent and forcible: clear, animated and self-possessed," that his "natural talent for mechanics preeminently fits him for skillful manipulation & experiments, on which success of a Lecturer on Chemistry so much depends," that he was a "ready, elegant, interesting, and forcible" writer, and that his demeanor was invariably "gentlemanly, courteous & conciliatory."[55]

Page also enlisted the assistance of some of his political friends: Rufus Choate, for example, attested to his "love of science, & high talent for its successful pursuit."[56] Knowing that his chance for succeeding to Hare's position was rather slim, however, he also applied for yet another teaching job, in the new Lawrence Scientific School at Harvard. This he did evidently at the suggestion of Henry: "In regard to the [Professorship] in Harvard I think it would suit me and on the whole be pleasant," he wrote Henry on July 6, 1847, "and [I] shall be greatly obliged if you will be on the lookout to serve me there."[57] While it is not inconceivable that Page might have got a job there, neither was it very likely, and he apparently pursued the matter no further.

In fact, one senses that he was not enthusiastic about any prospect that involved leaving Washington. Although interested in "Prof. Horsford's school,"[58] he must have had serious doubts about returning to New England. First, to do so would be to deprive himself of the opportunity to sit down and consider with Henry whether or not certain ideas were "incompatible with Ampere's theory." Second, he surely did not lack for prestige in his present position. Even to such a towering figure as Hare himself, who had written to sound Page out on the possibility of "establishing an Electrical Association," he could respond, "I must prepare a hasty reply to your kind letter of the 13., as public duties now press upon me. . . ."[59] Beyond that, chances for Congressional approval of a pay boost looked increasingly good.

80

By the end of 1847, Page had decided to stay put. Whether or not he might actually have obtained any of the professorships in which he had expressed an interest remains a moot point. But it is certain that among the duties that "pressed hard" upon Page, all were not connected with the Patent Office, or with his teaching, or otherwise "official." Ever since unveiling his new form of motor in 1844, he had been striving steadily to improve it. Indeed, for all the diversity of his pursuits during the late 1840s, his "electro axial engine" provided the main focus of his personal attention. This was something he talked about as heralding "an entirely new era in the science of electromotion,"[60] and which he exhibited to enthusiastic audiences on numerous occasions.

Its fundamental components were two, a helix (or solenoid) and an iron axial bar (or armature). The helix, when energized, induced the bar up into its orifice; a circuit breaker then cut off the power and the bar dropped out. This reciprocating action was converted to rotary by means of a clevis, crank, and flywheel. Augmenting that basic concept in the years after 1844, Page went to horizontal motors with adjacent helices and a U-shaped axial bar, then he incorporated tandem rows of helices successively cut in and out, and finally he utilized two opposing sets of them which pulled dual axial bars first one way then the other. But the underlying principle, essentially the same as today's linear induction motor, remained unchanged (Fig. 8).

Page first demonstrated the utility of his motors by coupling them to implements such as planes and circular saws. He envi-

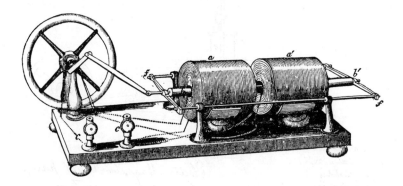

Fig. 8. The Axial Engine that Page unveiled at the 1844 meeting of the Association of American Geologists and Naturalists. (From AJS 49 [1845]: 133.

81

sioned numerous other uses—pumping, for example (Fig. 9). But a singularly dramatic means of employing electricity more and more captured his fancy. In February 1849, while in the course of presenting a series of exhibitions under the auspices of the Smithsonian, he sent a petition to the Senate requesting "an investigation of a mode discovered by him of applying electro-magnetic power to purposes of navigation and locomotion." He invited a committee to assess the capabilities of his motors and decide upon "the propriety of further action for the development of this important invention," which he termed "a general substi-tute for the dangerous agency of steam." [61] Page wanted, in modern parlance, a research and development grant.

Thus began one of the most interesting episodes of his entire career—simultaneously the most famous and the greatest failure. The reason it was doomed was because Page evidently allowed his personal enthusiasm to get the better of his scientific acumen. He knew that it might be *possible* to employ battery powered motors to do many kinds of work. But even by 1849 their *practicality* was generally regarded as extremely dubious—unless money were no object. Yet Page was by no means ready to concede this, even though it had been more than five years since James P. Joule had read his paper on the mechanical equivalent of heat to the British Association, and nearly two since Joule and Hermann von

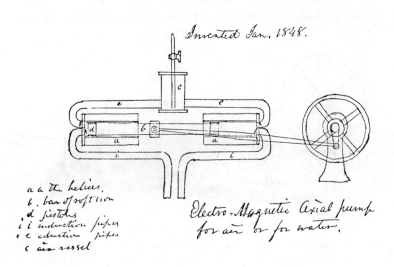

Fig. 9.   Sketch from a Page notebook, 1848. (Courtesy Joseph W. Hazell.)

82

Helmholtz had both given a clear exposition of conservation of energy. To be sure, some of their ideas remained controversial, but most good scientists were now certain that the battery powered motor was a hopelessly impractical device.

Not so Page. In September 1848 he wrote to Henry: "The more I experiment and reflect, the more am I convinced of the fallacy of making the heating power of the current the exponent of its mechanical power."[62] Moreover, Page had little difficulty attracting allies who shared his vision of a "new era." Many were not scientists. But that was beside the point, for some—one in particular—had power, political power. While this politician had probably never heard of James P. Joule, he knew all about S.F.B. Morse, and he knew that it was only because of assistance from the federal government that Morse had been able to introduce his important innovation. Now, he was going to try and see that the government did the same thing for Page as it had done for Morse.

Chapter Five

To Harness the Forces of Nature

> This invention of Mr. Page's is undoubtedly a great invention, and we see no reason why it should not in time supersede the use of steam, at least as a propelling power.
>
> American Railroad Journal, *1851*

> The Americans are still ever striving to harness the forces of nature and to let them work for mankind. . . . and perhaps the Americans will be the first to travel over the sterile areas between the Mississippi Valley and California, where neither wood nor water is found, not by steam but by electromagnetic force instead.
>
> *Charles L. Fleischmann, 1852*

> The successful application of electricity for practical purposes, as a motive power, would truly form a brilliant "page" in the annals of science and art.
>
> American Telegraph Magazine, *1853*

> With all proper respect for the opinions of Mr. Joule, and other writers, upon the subject of the cost of this power as compared with steam, we must say that we . . . . have no desire to be met on the very threshold of experiment, with a discouraging limitation of mathematical reasoning.
>
> *Charles Grafton Page, 1854*

> . . . the mathematical mind . . . . could not discover dynamic electricity, nor electro-magnetism, nor magneto electricity, or even suggest them; though when once discovered by the experimentalist it can take them up with extreme facility.
>
> *Michael Faraday, 1857*

The man who took up Page's cause in the Senate was Thomas Hart Benton of Missouri, that body's senior member and chairman of its Committee on Military Affairs. Benton told his colleagues that he had known for three years about Page's experiments "in the application of this great power to the useful purposes of manufacturing" and was "seriously inclined to consider them of importance." While he conceded that he himself did not understand the principles involved, for he did not "have science," he hastened to add that men who did understand were also impressed.[1]

But Samuel Phelps, a Vermont Whig, voiced reservations. Asserting that Thomas Davenport, one of his constituents, had built axial motors antedating Page's, Phelps cautioned that "we had better not have any action upon the subject until we [have] found out who was the original discoverer of the power." To this Benton replied, "I expect that it is the same with this invention as with all others—new claimants to its discovery will arise and affirm that they are the original inventors." While Page, he insisted, had given Davenport full credit for his attainments, he himself was "far in advance in his experiments of any others of a similar character that have been attempted." [2] Without a doubt, Page's motors could outdo Davenport's in sheer horsepower. After all, he had been experimenting for nearly five years, whereas Davenport had been inactive since the early 1840s for want of funds. He had once tried to get a Congressional subsidy and met with rebuff. Page of course felt completely at home not only in academic and scientific circles but also amid leading politicians.

Named to Benton's committee was Phelps—who could hardly have been kept off—along with Senators James Wescott, John Berrien, John Dix, Joseph Underwood, and William King. Together they attended Page's exhibition the very next evening, February 21, 1849. Page prefaced his customary routine with a discourse entitled "Electricity vs. Steam." It was a rather whimsical admixture of fact and fancy, sober analysis and hyperbole. He made no claim that electricity could yet compete with steam on a comparative-cost basis. While he deplored that "the saving of human life is a very trifling item in our calculations upon the cost of any enterprise," he admitted that electricity must be proven economical before it could be introduced as a substitute for steam. As for the fear that galvanic power entailed any dangers itself, he refuted this possibility convincingly, at least until he added an aside that "if perchance a man should get knocked down by a shock, you have only to give him another [to] raise him up again." [3]

He commenced the next portion of his talk on a less facetious note. While it was "not [his] wish to excite any undue enthusiasm," he did suggest that there was as much hope of successfully utilizing electricity for motive power as there had been for steam at a commensurately early stage of its development. Surely it was "not safe even for the most learned and skilful, in these times, to prejudge inventions." That was obviously a sound observation, but once more he shifted from the sensible to the silly by proceeding to recite in full some unnamed bard's epic entitled "The Song of Lightning," which concluded with this stanza:

> At last the hour of light is here,
>   and kings no more shall blind,
> Nor the bigots crush with craven fear,
>   The forward march of mind;
> The words of truth and freedom's rays
>   Are from my pinions hurled,
> As soon as the sun of better days,
>   Shall rise upon the world.[4]

This was a bit mawkish, perhaps, yet even the overwrought imagery of his own concluding paragraph could not becloud the authenticity of Page's faith in both the inevitability and beneficence of technological progress. His hopes for electric power, he said,

> seem to spring from a kind of intuition, an almost unavoidable conviction, that this mighty agent, which rends the stately trees, and hurls the mountain top from its throne will one day serve some other purpose than to excite our fears and admiration. . . . Shall the power that holds to our admiring gaze, the ponderous mass of iron, suspended between heaven and earth be ever our master, and never our servant? Shall this last of nature's Titans lie buried forever under an immovable mountain? No! The mind of man will not rest, till by faith and works, it has torn down this mountain, and tried the monster's strength.[5]

Page followed up by running through a series of his most imposing demonstrations. When he spoke of a "ponderous mass of iron, suspended between heaven and earth," he was referring to the capacity of his helices to sustain a 50-pound weight in mid-air. These theatrics clearly impressed the seven senators present. A week later they issued their report. Because Page had shown that his motors could perform useful work, the committee members saw no reason why he could not build one on a scale capable of propelling a vehicle. All that was needed now, they felt, were experiments to determine whether power "can be produced at a rate to justify its common use as a mechanical agent."

Page claimed to have discovered how to cut costs substantially already, and the committee was "satisfied that his past success, with his limited means, justifies the expectation of further success from large means." It therefore deemed a full test program "an object of national interest" and recommended that financing be provided out of the naval appropriations bill.[6] On March 2, Benton offered the following resolution: "For testing the capacity and usefulness of the electromagnetic power as a mechanical agent for the purposes of navigation and locomotion, and the probable cost of using the same according to the investigation of Professor Page, the sum of $20,000, to be expended under the supervision of the Secretary of the Navy in making a practical experiment of said invention, according to the plan to be proposed and conducted by Professor Page."[7]

The appropriation was passed, so far as can be ascertained from the published record, without dissent. While it is true that precedents existed—especially Morse's $30,000 grant in 1843—the absence of opposition is curious, particularly with the South growing increasingly rigid in its opposition to federal sponsorship of almost any project. Even the six members of Benton's committee—one northern Democrat, one northern Whig, and two of each from the South—should not have been expected to approve the appropriation unanimously. Still, it did include two of the most outspoken partisans of the inventive arts, James Wescott of Florida, who had lately led a move to double the salary of patent examiners, and William King of New York, always effusive in his praise of their talents. As for Benton himself, while his power was on the wane, he still loomed larger than life amongst his colleagues.

Benton apparently had two reasons for championing Page, one rather narrowly political, the other conceived more grandly, or, if you will, romantically. First of all, he believed that if Page's experiment were successful it would redound to the benefit of a body of his constituents in Missouri. He unquestioningly accepted the notion that an electric motor was simply a prime mover which consumed the metal in a voltaic cell for fuel, just as a steam engine burned wood. The metal most commonly used for battery plates was zinc, an element not theretofore considered especially useful by itself. It was often regarded as virtually a waste product of lead, with which it was usually found. The nation's greatest lead deposits were located in the upper Mississippi Valley, to a large extent in northeastern Missouri. Benton, who had always sought to help the mining interests, envisioned a burgeoning demand for zinc opening "a market for an article now thrown away."[8]

Yet, Benton's motivations were not wholly mundane. His sponsorship of Page was also part and parcel of his almost mystical concept of the role of the West in American history and of the part federal internal improvements were to play in fulfilling its destiny. In early 1849 Benton advanced a western internal improvements scheme which, although the theme was familiar, dwarfed all previous proposals of its kind. On February 7, just two weeks before he presented Page's petition to the Senate, he had introduced a bill to utilize proceeds from the sale of public lands to finance a "Central National Road" stretching from St. Louis to San Francisco Bay, with a branch to the Columbia River. For such a project, he perceived, "no private means would be equal . . . or fit to be trusted with it."

Specifically, Benton suggested that a one-mile swath be reserved, wide enough "for all varieties of roads that are now in use, or which may come into use in the unnumbered generations which the road is to benefit." There would be a steam railway, of course. There would also be a plank road, a macadamized road, and "a plain old English road." And there would be room for yet another kind of road—"a track by magnetic power—according to the idea started, I believe, by Professor Henry, and, to me, plausibly pursued by Professor Page, of the Patent Office, if that idea ripens into practicality."[9]

Benton was not the only person to perceive that battery power would make most sense in regions where wood and water were scarce.[10] But he did have a grand imagination and he did flaunt considerable erudition, summoning forth analogies with classical Rome, Renaissance Italy, ancient Phoenecia, and the mysterious Orient. The concept of a "passage to India" had become virtually an obsession with Benton.[11] He concluded by declaring that "the state of the world calls for a new road to India, and it is our destiny to give it—the last and greatest. Let us act up to the greatness of the occasion, and show ourselves worthy of the extraordinary circumstances in which we are placed, by securing while we can an American road to India—central and national— for ourselves and our posterity—now and hereafter, for thousands of years to come."[12]

However fanciful some of this may seem, it does show that, their imaginations unfettered, Page and Benton were cut from much the same cloth. Page had an "almost unavoidable conviction" that galvanic power could be made practical, while Benton himself would not "undertake to say that any idea will not become practicable in the present age." And the idea of a "track by magnetic power" could easily have seemed plausible to Benton. For one thing, numerous copies of his speech were run off by a Washington printer "on a single Napier press, bed 24 by 41 inches, driven by Professor Page's Electro-Magnetic Engine, at the rate of 1200 impressions per hour."[13] If electric printing presses, why not locomotives?

Page began preliminary work in the early summer of 1849. Because the Secretary of the Navy had no real comprehension of what Page was attempting, he evidently approved all expenditures simply as matters of routine. Not until seven months after the appropriation was voted did he ask for some accounting. Page prepared a brief summary, barely one printed page long. He reported that he had just recently found a manufacturer in Connecticut who could provide him with the large quantity of square-drawn copper wire he would need, and he had also contracted for the assistance of a New York mechanic. This was Ari Davis, brother of the Boston instrument maker with whom he had worked in the 1830s. Aside from devising some testing paraphernalia, Page had accomplished little more. He excused this by saying, "The great result I am seeking, will not justify haste in the proceeding, and it is due to the government conferring upon me so great a privilege, that I should proceed with deliberation and realize the full advantage of the appropriation."[14]

This remark was directed, not so much at the secretary or at Congress (which in fact ignored Page), as at certain skeptics who had begun to accuse him of deliberately dawdling. During 1850 adverse criticism started to appear in *Scientific American,* and by July that journal was calling for a full disclosure of Page's expenditures: "Uncle Sam's funds belong in trust to his children, and it is right they should know something about 'how the money goes;' $30,000 [*sic*] is a sum not to be sneezed at."[15]

In the fall, Thomas Davenport decided to have his say. He published a lengthy statement in his home-town newspaper declaring that since he had built motors many years previously identical in design to the most advanced model displayed by the "scientific gentleman" (Page), he "could have saved him the needless expenditure of several thousand dollars, by giving him the results of some of my experiments of 1838-9-40."[16] *Scientific*

American excerpted a portion of Davenport's letter, then commented disingenuously, "It seems that Mr. Davenport is not aware of the fact that $20,000 was appropriated to Prof. Page for his experiments . . . and after all here is a poor man who obtained as great results ten years ago. . . . 'Honor to whom honor is due,' and the laborer is worthy of his reward." [17]

Page had borne a substantial amount of abuse silently, but this indictment finally drew a public reply. Honor was due, he declared, to a number of men—to Henry, Sturgeon, and others. Honor was even due to Thomas Davenport, for his invention reflected "great credit upon his genius and perserverance." Nevertheless, he added, "so far as I can learn from any publication, record or evidence of any sort, the peculiar principle of my present engines was first adopted by myself, and some time after by Mr. Davenport." [18]

A soft answer turneth away wrath. *Scientific American* appended a conciliatory rejoinder to Page's letter, and printed nothing more about him, good or bad, for some time. Page could certainly do without its reproach; in the summer of 1850 he had a host of other reverses. One was tragically personal: on August 4, his third child, a son, died at less than a year. Then, while he and Priscilla were in New England regaining their composure, the Senate paused briefly after finally hammering out one of the most controversial provisions in what became known as the Compromise of 1850. Benton availed himself of the opportunity to deliver a written report on Page's experiments, the first official mention of him in that chamber since his appropriation was voted 17 months earlier. He began by reviewing the bright side of the picture. Page had informed him that "with the same size battery, and much less cost, I am enabled now to exert a force of six hundred pounds where, little more than a year ago, I obtained a force of only fifty pounds. With a consumption of two and a half pounds of zinc, I now produce one horsepower for twenty-four hours. This is nearly as cheap as the cheapest steam engine in the world, and much cheaper than steam under some conditions."

Benton commented that if this assertion were correct "the hitherto insuperable objection to [the use of electromagnetism] as a propelling power is entirely obviated, and the cost actually converted into a consideration in its favor." Then he took a new tack, one which hinted at what he was leading up to. A distinctive advantage of electricity was that it enabled "instantaneous communication of full power, so important in changing course and avoiding collision—capacity to run a blockade, making no noise, and showing no light."

Obviously, the senator was talking about something other than a locomotive, but before getting to the point he indulged in some boasting. "I took the risk of moving [for an appropriation] in the matter at the last session," he stated, "the risk of ridicule which attends great projects ending in failure. . . . I have taken the risk of this ridicule, and mean to take it still deeper." Then, with all the grandiloquence that only a man 30 years in the U.S. Senate could muster, he declared:

> I mean to move another appropriation for Dr. Page—one that will enable him to make an experiment on a scale commensurate to the grandeur of the enterprise, the stake which the human race has in its success, and the wealth and power of the United States, to whom its first advantages and entire glory is to redound, if successful. I shall move an appropriation to work a ship of war or a merchant vessel by this new power, and deem the decision of the question worth all the money to be expended, and all the risk of the ridicule to be incurred. If successful, it will be an advance upon the use of steam power equal to the advance of that power over sails, oars, and wheels.[19]

Page rather expected Benton's move for a second appropriation to succeed. He informed his assistant, Lane, that, should it pass, "I shall resign forthwith, and you must take my place. (Say nothing about it) but make up your mind for such an event."[20] Yet, while Benton was blithely proposing something far more costly, down at Page's shop in the Navy Yard there were not even the rudiments of a vehicle to ply the Central National Road, or any other road. Not for the first time in his career he had gone too far. Many of his colleagues immediately wanted to know just what had happened to the *original* idea—and the original appropriation. The Secretary of the Navy was directed to find out precisely what was going on, and on September 3 he forwarded to the Senate a report from Page. Since this was the first document that described his expenditures and accomplishments in any detail, it was immediately published and reprinted both here and abroad.[21]

Page had constructed four different motors, each of which he had tested with a dynamometer and a special galvanometer (Fig. 10). He had performed an exhaustive series of trials, check-

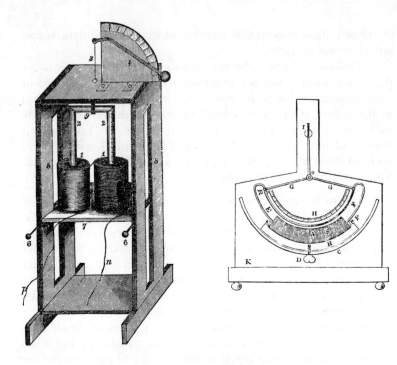

Fig. 10. *Page's first Axial Galvanometer (1845), and an improved version that obviated the necessity to incorporate a spring balance. (From AJS 49 [1845]: 137, and AJS, 2d ser. 1 [1846]: 243.)*

ing the efficiency of axial bars and helices of various dimensions, diverse sorts of cutoffs and reversing apparatus, optimum working velocities, and sundry mechanical arrangements. All this was of considerable interest to Page's fellow scientists. At the 1850 meeting of the AAAS in New Haven, Alexander Bache had relinquished an hour allotted him so that Page might describe his experiments. His audience was large and enthusiastic. Walter Johnson and Benjamin Silliman, Sr., seemed convinced that he had vanquished certain hitherto critical problems. Benjamin Peirce commented that he "felt astonishment and great delight at the results obtained by Dr. Page." And Joseph Henry was quoted as saying that "he had witnessed with great interest Dr. Page's experiments before the Smithsonian Institution," and that Page "had produced by far the most powerful electro-magnetic engine ever made, within his knowledge." [22]

As for the matter of economy, however, there were no more claims about electricity being "nearly as cheap" as steam. For one thing, after trying out a variety of battery components, Page had concluded that the most effective combination was the one devised by the British electrochemist William R. Grove. Grove's batteries had two metallic electrodes. One was zinc, and Page's expenditure for supplies of that metal seemed nominal, $70.68. His outlay for the other element, platinum, was more than 36 times greater. Electric power, he had to admit, still entailed "fifty times the cost of the dearest steam engine." In addition to this formidable drawback, "much remain[ed] to be done with the galvanic battery to render its action regular and durable, and in other ways to establish a certainty of action, so that the engines may be managed by persons not thoroughly skilled in the subjects of electricity and magnetism."[23]

This was hardly encouraging; nor were some of Page's other findings. He even confessed to having second thoughts about the design of his motors. For propelling a ship at least, he thought that a rotary axial engine—a unique contrivance he had toyed with for several years—might possibly be more suitable (Fig. 11). Finally, even though he had not even begun constructing a conveyance of any kind, land or water, nearly two-thirds of the appropriation was gone. He subjoined to his report a breakdown of expenditures. His figures certainly did not suggest any dissimulation, but neither did they bespeak a keen sense of thrift. More than $3,500 had been spent on wages for a retinue of helpers, and nearly $1,000 more had gone for such things as shop fixtures, a horse and wagon, and postage and printing. As might have been expected, Benton's move for an additional $40,000 appropriation, plus personal compensation for Page, aroused no little dissension. Benton recited the complimentary remarks of other scientists and reminded the senators of the farsighted wisdom they had shown by backing Morse. He even invoked the hallowed name of Newton and earnestly attempted to link it with that of Page. But no ploy could stem the tide of opposition. Page might have become friendly with many a Washington politico, but hardly with *all* of them.

First to rise to the challenge was Lewis Cass of Michigan, the Democratic presidential candidate in 1848. Cass wanted to know how much the government had expended in "abortive experiments." It would amount, he suspected, "to a fearful sum." Though willing to concede the possibility of merit in Page's work, Cass felt that the government "should be the last agent to interfere in these matters. . . . If we are to meddle in this case, why

93

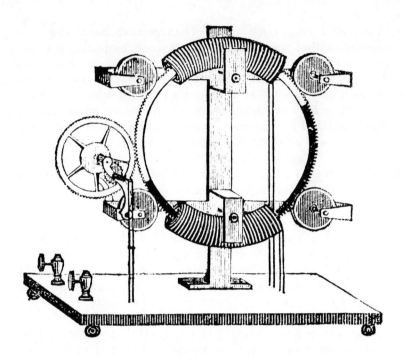

Fig. 11. Axial Revolving Circle, for converting axial motion into direct rotation. Half the toothed ring is iron, half brass. (From [Davis's] MANUAL OF MAGNETISM [1848], p. 179.)

not in every other by which science and the arts are to be promoted?" As Senator Daniel Dickenson of New York pointed out, other inventors seeking appropriations were already beginning to cite Page's grant as a precedent.

The principal opposition was voiced by the two senators from Mississippi, Henry Foote and Jefferson Davis. Both were fearful of any measure that might tend, even in the most roundabout way, to strengthen the federal government. Internal improvements schemes, unless directly beneficial to the South, were anathema. Foote confessed that in a moment of indiscretion he had voted for Page's original grant. As a consequence, he had suffered pangs of conscience for what now seemed "the most wasteful expenditure of public money in a small way that this government has ever practiced within my recollection." To be sure, Foote and Benton were caustic personal foes. Even so, Foote's attitude toward Page rather typified that of the opposition. He could not see that Page was "much better in-

94

formed . . . now than he was a year or two ago," or that his exertions had benefited the country in the slightest, or that there was any reason to assume they ever would do so, or that the best rule of thumb for all Congressional policy making was not the "great principle of frugality."

Like the other dissidents, Jefferson Davis also touched on these matters. But to him the problem at hand was not primarily a practical one. It was a legal one. As he saw it, at the very heart of the whole affair lay the question of constitutional legitimacy. The other objections—that "perhaps $80,000 will be asked" at the next session, that Congress was not qualified to pass on the hypothetical merits of inventions, that Page's grant gave him an unfair advantage over such a "poor and friendless" inventor as Davenport, that there was sure to be an "uprising" of inventors demanding appropriations, and that Benton was attempting to make the government not merely the guarantor of patent rights, but also "the patron of arts and inventions"—all these were subordinate to one paramount issue: "the power to make this appropriation . . . is surely not in the Constitution."

Benton's rejoinder was uncharacteristically lame. He confined himself largely to emphasizing how candid Page had been about the results of his experiments and to denying the likelihood of there being repeated requests for appropriations in the future. He never once tried to parry the charge of unconstitutionality. Nor did the only other senator to go on record in favor of the appropriation, William Gwin of California. Gwin remarked that Morse's telegraph "would not have been put in operation for years had the Government not assisted him." To this, Foote replied without artifice that there was no reason to suppose Page's idea and Morse's were equally sound scientifically.[24] Page's appropriation never even came to a vote. Any chance for reconsideration died a month later when Benton finally fell victim to his own pro-free-soil pronouncements and lost the Senate seat he had held for three decades. Not a man to call attention to his failures, he omitted Page entirely when he published his memoirs a few years later.

In March 1851 the scene shifted to the House. During the waning days of the session, Tennessee Congressman Frederick Stanton, chairman of the Committee on Naval Affairs, tried to rush through an appropriation for Page. Stanton's measure called for giving him, not $40,000, but only enough to enable him to finish his partially completed locomotive (a cost overrun, in modern jargon). The sum was a mere $4,000. But such appropriations, whatever their size, naturally had their dedicated foes in the lower house too. One of them was another Tennesseean, Andrew Johnson. Thus, the phalanx of Page's vocal adversaries now included a President-to-be, as well as an unsuccessful candidate and the future President of the Confederacy.

Johnson so feared the "extravagance, folly, aristocracy, and corruption of Washington" that he had once voted to reject James Smithson's bequest and send it back to England.[25] His rhetoric often made him seem like a reincarnation of Andrew Jackson, and never more expressly than when he opposed Page's relatively modest grant. Page, he thought, already was the recipient of too much special privilege; indeed, there was no telling "from how many sources he draws revenue." If he really had something, Johnson declared, he should resign his job, "come forward with his improvement, and if it is worth anything, why the country can pay him for it."[26]

Johnson carried the day; Page got no more government money. Nevertheless, he decided to try and complete his locomotive anyway. By this time, doubts about the worth of what he was doing had become widespread. A report was circulating, for example, which claimed that his motors "lost speed in a wonderful manner when set in motion to do something useful."[27] Such an allegation smacked of calumny, and Page was not the sort to let it pass lightly. After his government funds ran out, he used up his own personal savings, then borrowed heavily from friends. In order to keep costs down, he designed most of the running gear and superstructure himself—although he had little experience with the sort of engineering problems this entailed.

The finished product had a wheel arrangement of 4-2-0, with five-foot drivers and 30-inch wheels on the truck. The weight was 21,000 pounds. The length over end-sills was 21 feet; the beam, six feet. The rods were connected outside and had a stroke of 24 inches. The arch-roofed cab was 15 feet long, sufficient to accommodate several passengers in addition to the crew. Indeed, the superstructure looked like an ordinary railway coach (Fig. 12). The engine, mounted inside on the floor, superficially resembled a slide-valve duplex steam pump. The reciprocating members consisted of two iron rods four feet long and five inches in diameter, which were attracted alternately back and forth by a series of short helices successively thrown in and out of the circuit by sliding contacts. Suspended between the drivers was an oblong

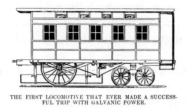

THE FIRST LOCOMOTIVE THAT EVER MADE A SUCCESS-
FUL TRIP WITH GALVANIC POWER.

*Fig. 12. Page's locomotive. (From AMERICAN POLYTECHNIC JOURNAL 4
[1854]: 257.)*

trough divided into 100 cells, each occupied by a pair of plates, one immersed in sulfuric acid, the other in nitric.

While the chances of putting on a passable demonstration would have been slim in any event, the first preliminary road test revealed a serious design flaw. The vibration of the motor made the locomotive ride very roughly, and Page's battery was a very fragile thing indeed. The least jolt could easily fracture one of the diaphragms. Ari Davis did get a local potter to mold some new cells, but neither he nor Page was able to figure out an adequate way to cushion the battery from the "jostling and oscillations." This was only one of the imperfections that remained. But, as Page's friend Greenough wrote, "prudence and necessity demanded a cessation of all further expenditures."[28] Page was already $6,000 in debt. This was the moment of truth, his only chance to attract additional backing. With a great deal of luck, he might have been able to conceal the technical deficiencies. Ill fortune plagued him, however, throughout his final month of preparation. On April 2, the 11:00 o'clock train from Baltimore "got on the wrong track and drove into the house occupied by [his] locomotive." "Fences, doors, and timbers flew in all directions," but the locomotive itself sustained only minor damage.[29] In the long run, it might have been better had it been demolished.

The public demonstration took place on Tuesday, April 29, 1851, with a substantial crowd of spectators on hand. Save for a single bright moment, it was a disaster from start to finish. Page rated his locomotive at 24 horsepower. This was an exaggeration to start with, but, no matter how much power was initially available, it was not available for long, because almost immedi-

97

ately the insulation surrounding some of the helices broke down under the strain. These short-circuited and had to be disconnected. Worse, the new battery cells turned out to be even more delicate; the clay from which they had been molded was impregnated with particles of iron which the acid naturally attacked. Six cells cracked open before the locomotive even turned a wheel, two collapsed on an upgrade outside the yard, and seven more a little further on.

The speed dropped literally to a walk. Page had to ask the passengers to get out in order to reduce the load, but since that did not help they soon climbed aboard again. All the while, he and Davis were working feverishly to isolate the broken cells and get the wiring jury-rigged. As to what took place when they finally did so, one of the riders, Greenough, had this to relate:

> Now came the cheering realization of travelling by lightning. . . . On reaching the level we carefully timed the revolutions of the driving wheels, and found that at our highest speed we had attained the unlooked for rate of nineteen miles per hour. . . . We were greeted by waving of handkerchiefs from windows, and . . . even the negroes on the plantations stare[d] in utter astonishment to see what had the appearance of a passenger car posting along at a very respectable railroad speed . . . propelled by some invisible giant, which by his silence was as impressive as his noisy predecessor, although less terrific.[30]

One can either take this account or leave it, especially the proclaimed speed. Still, Greenough's commentary generally embodied a matter-of-fact air, and he made it quite clear that after the one exhilarating romp practically all else was dreary anticlimax.

Page's announced destination had been Baltimore. Upon reaching Bladensburg, not even a mile beyond the D.C. boundary and nearly 35 short of Baltimore, he deemed it prudent to turn around. And prudent it was, for as soon as he headed back more battery cells began rupturing. At one point, there occurred what Greenough called "a general *stampede* of cells," which drove him, Page, Davis, Lane, and the other riders from the car, choking on acid fumes. When Page got the circuits cross-wired again, less than half the cells remained fully operative. While the outbound trip had taken only 39 minutes, a fair pace, it took

98

nearly two hours to limp back downtown. The number of unanticipated stoppages was reported at up to 15.

Both Page and Greenough claimed that most of the difficulties could be traced directly to the "makeshifts and expedients" necessitated by the shortage of funds. This contention was not without plausibility. Although the battery cells would have been deficient in durability even if cast from the best clay available, they surely could have been molded from some material more rugged than that from which potters made "common brown pans." The suspension and running gear could no doubt have been revamped advantageously. As for the damage to the helices, that was evidently intrinsic to the design of the motors, for a highly destructive spark was set off each time the current was switched between opposite sets. While Page had devoted much ingenuity to circumventing the sparking problem, he never fully succeeded.[31]

A few private entrepreneurs did show some interest in further experimentation, but they were unwilling to provide any money. This was understandable. Although the *National Intelligencer* called the trial run a "great triumph," and optimism continued to prevail even in certain technical periodicals,[32] it appeared as if the entire locomotive, inside and out, needed fundamental alterations. But, more important, it seemed increasingly clear to almost anyone who understood current physical theory that any mechanical improvements, whatever their extent, would simply be an exercise in futility. How in the world, knowledgeable observers were asking, could there be the slightest chance of acid and metal—platinum, zinc, or whatever—displacing water and wood with any acceptable degree of economy? For example, while P. H. Vander Weyde, a long-time consultant to Peter Cooper, thought Page's system was noteworthy for its large scale, he advised Cooper to keep his money to himself.[33]

During 1853 and 1854 Page published a running series titled "Electro-Mechanics," in which he steadfastly affirmed his preference for "experimental to hypothetical deductions." Despite his reverses, he was able to close out this phase of his career on a note of optimism:

> Long as we have been engaged in the pursuit of this subject, our faith has kept steadily up to the opinion that the electromagnetic power would be at some time used as a motive power for many and various purposes, and as so

many collateral arts and discoveries continue to throw light upon the intricacies of this subject, we believe the time is near at hand. Enterprise seems to be all that is needed.[34]

Indeed, enterprise *was* all that was needed. But that enterprise had to entail a thoroughgoing reexamination of theory, not merely additional refinements to existing paraphernalia. Although Page may have suspected this, he and his apologists insisted to the end that the only substantial impediments to the success of his locomotive were mechanical. Nevertheless, the limits of empiricism had been reached. Moreover, because Page thought in terms of developing an analogous "substitute for steam," he devoted his inventive energies to a form of power that was self-sufficient, as if electricity were another kind of prime mover. That was a fatal error.

Page now found himself in desperate straits, financially and emotionally. To pay off his debts he began presenting lecture-hall exhibitions again, and at one point a young assistant examiner from the Patent Office reported finding him in a New York hotel "in a critical state, alone, unattended. . . ."[35] Yet, he was resilient in the face of adversity, and was naturally encouraged when Henry Varnum Poor's *American Railroad Journal* reported on his exhibitions with nearly unqualified enthusiasm, and they even won accolades from *Scientific American*.[36] Nevertheless, success in this respect did not alter the now-prevalent supposition that his locomotive was an outright failure. Greenough assumed the role of his chief defender, upholding the merit of his electrical apparatus while continuing to blame the botched demonstration on the design of the vehicle itself, which made it, he said, "a matter of wonder and surprise that this rude structure would move at all."[37] The engineering was not all that primitive—Ari Davis was a successful inventor of machine tools, among other things. It did provide a convenient excuse. But it was also a classic red herring. For Greenough's apologetics decidedly underplayed the fundamental stumbling block, the inherent limitations of the primary-cell battery.

Here the problem of breakage was really incidental, for galvanic power made an extremely poor showing costwise even under the best of circumstances. Joule, Scoresby, Petrie, Rankine, Hunt, and others of comparable stature, a formidable consensus, insisted that the expense was prohibitive. Page was aware of their arguments, but showed an unfortunate tendency, said to be

100

common among inventors, "to apply such tests to his ideas as are likely to exhibit their best features, and genuinely to forget to apply those tests which will exhibit their worst features."[38]

He had, of course, made cost analyses, but often he airily dismissed "mathematical reasoning" or equivocated by insisting that definitive statistics on the matter were a chimera—as well he might have, when at one time he decided galvanic power was no more expensive than steam, while at another he found it 50 times as costly. Usually he fell back on the contention that any short-coming in economy was justified by greater safety. That senti-ment, as far as railroad transportation was concerned, was largely specious. After the tryout of his locomotive, Page did concede that galvanic power had drawbacks, yet never did he admit the possibility of it being utterly impractical for the purpose to which he was trying to apply it. As late as 1854, in criticizing Joule's formula for comparing the cost of steam and electricity, he wrote that he objected "to any formula at all." The question of economy, he thought, "involves more elements of practice than has or can at the present time enter into any formula which may be set up as a standard."[39]

An eminent historian of technology has suggested that grandly conceived but stillborn innovations may indicate "the perception of an incomplete pattern in respect of a strategic invention. They are inventions in the strict sense of the word, but they raise more problems than they solve, so they have no separate significance of their own."[40] While this historian specifically had in mind the incandescent lamps devised by Joseph Swan and Moses Farmer 20 years before Edison's, Page's locomotive might also serve as an example. First, it undeniably *was* an invention— in the sense of a group of elements "combined to produce results which are more than the details from which they are formed"— but whatever advantages it may have possessed *vis-à-vis* steam were outweighed by its shortcomings. Perhaps, however, Page's failure might more precisely be attributed not to his "perception of an incomplete pattern" but to his reliance upon what was from an economic standpoint an unsuitable combination of compo-nents.

Galvanism was a scientific discovery of great moment, a discovery that underlay a vast new field of research with whose exploration Page felt a keen sense of personal involvement. Moreover, it was a phenomenon that by the early 1840s had yielded promising new commercial technologies—electroplating, for one, and especially telegraphy. Telegraphy also derived from electromagnetism, whose period of great experimental discovery was the 1830s; indeed, among those who helped expand the frontiers of knowledge in this realm, Page's role was far from inconsequential. By 1840, a remarkably compact battery could energize an electromagnet capable of lifting literally tons of iron, or telegraph an audible impulse dozens of miles. Electromagnetism had also been shown to possess numerous other properties, and there was no telling how many might be harnessed to useful purposes.

Able to look back through time, "wise after the event," we can see that whereas galvanism plus electromagnetism was an appropriate combination for separating ore or sending messages through wires it was inappropriate for propelling vehicles. During the 1840s, British and Continental scientists began calculating and comparing the cost of the work available from various chemical, electrical, and mechanical processes. Out of this emerged the principle of conservation of energy. One of the two or three foremost figures in explicating this great generalization was James P. Joule, formerly rather an optimist about the potential utility of battery powered motors. Indeed, it is noteworthy that those who once shared Page's hopes were extraordinarily dissimilar both in their erudition and their technical skill. Nowhere is this heterogeneity more striking than in the contrast between Moritz de Jacobi, a member of the Imperial Russian Academy of Sciences, and Davenport, the paragon of Yankee ingenuity, yet almost totally ignorant of electrical science *per se*. Jacobi and Davenport, Page, Sturgeon, Joule, Moses Farmer, and Robert Davidson of Aberdeen [41]—first-rate theoreticians and talented experimentalists, or mere backyard tinkerers—all accepted for a time the same paradigm regarding electromagnetic motive power. All knew that galvanism plus electromagnetism combined effectively for some purposes, and assumed there might be others as well. The key question to be asked about any of these men is when he *stopped* accepting the paradigm.

Page knew all about Robert Davidson's electric locomotive of 1842, the *Galvani,* and he knew exactly what European scientists had decided about the economics of battery power. Yet he spent years and used up at least $30,000 on his own experiments. The most obvious problem with the *Galvani* had been its impotent motors—it could never be coaxed faster than four miles an hour. So Page devoted the bulk of his resources to designing and

102

building motors which 20 years later still ranked as the most colossal ever made. He should have known this would not be sufficient to transcend the strategic problem. Perhaps he did know it. Perhaps he was more interested in what was possible than what was practical. Perhaps he pursued this project simply because it was technically exciting, an act of creativity not unlike an artist working a novel medium. It *did* make him famous: when the great Ampère's son visited this country, for instance, he indicated that "à part un intérêt de famille assez naturel, j'étais très curieux de voir l'appareil inventé par M. Page pour remplacer la vapeur par l'électro-magnétisme." [42]

Or perhaps he pursued it because he could not understand those who argued that it was an *ignis fatuus,* because as a scientist he was the product of another era—an era when experiment, not "mathematical reasoning," constituted the most fruitful methodology in electrical science. Indeed, Page's bibliography for the decade after 1845 does suggest a picture of a scientist getting trapped beyond "the edge of incomprehensibility." Much of what he published up through 1847 and again just after mid-century derived from his experiments with motors, although several papers reflect a revival of his interest in chemistry, and two represent the apex of his sophistication as an electrical theorist. An 1851 paper, however, entitled "On the Time Required to raise the Galvanic Current to its maximum in Coiled Conductors, and its Importance in Electro-Mechanics," [43] finds him attempting an experimental solution to a problem which can only be satisfactorily approached through mathematics.

The words from the greatest of all experimental physicists quoted at the beginning of this chapter [44] convey a poignant hint as to how any scientist in that tradition must have been affected by the realization that his day was over. Page never conceded any such thing openly. But all of his post-1851 publications treating either physics or chemistry were based on experiments conducted considerably earlier. Like Henry, Page became interested in such relatively unsophisticated sciences as meteorology and acoustics—although even here he remained only a dilettante compared to Henry—and his most original research concerned floriculture, a field still wide open to fruitful investigation by a diligent amateur.

By 1854, when he published his last significant paper on electromagnetism, Page had become an anachronism—an old-fashioned natural philosopher in a day when the science of

103

electricity was becoming the province of mathematicians. Essentially the same thing happened to Henry, of course; in fact, he published virtually nothing more on electricity after coming to Washington. At that point, though, Henry had only just embarked on the career which marked the true measure of his greatness, his illustrious role in fostering the institutionalization and professionalization of American science. There seems to have been a popular misconception, deriving no doubt from the close relationship between Page and Henry during the late 1840s, that Page's motor experiments bore an official sanction from the Smithsonian. Scattered throughout the historical literature are many references to "Prof. Page of the Smithsonian Institution," or even to him as "Henry's successor."[45] Aside from the work he performed for the building committee in 1847, however, Page never had any formal connection with the Smithsonian. Moreover, while Henry expressed enthusiasm for Page's motors as late as 1850, by the time he actually took his locomotive out on the road Henry had apparently decided to eschew further comment.

Shortly before the public demonstration, Page sent Henry a note requesting "an investigation by the best authorities as to the actual cost of power in my Electro-Magnetic engine." With this in view, he continued,

> I should be pleased if you would consent to give me your assistance in this important inquiry in conjunction with several other gentlemen I may name. Three would be a sufficient number and I would like to have Prof. Bache and Prof. W. R. Johnson added if such an arrangement should prove mutually agreeable. I will afford every facility in my power and it can be so arranged that the result can be determined in a few hours. Please let me hear from you as soon as convenient.[46]

It is not certain that either Henry or Bache obliged Page's request; probably they did (and Johnson surely, since he was one of Page's most faithful allies), but both must have known in advance the outcome of any such investigation. Henry no longer kept pace with the leaders of physical research either, but he would have had no trouble grasping Joule's analysis of the relationship between electrical, chemical, and mechanical effects. He must have been disappointed in his friend, Page, for there seemed to be only two viable explanations of his motivation: either his optimistic posture simply amounted to whistling in the

104

dark, or else he really meant such assertions as the one concerning Joule and the "discouraging limitation of mathematical reasoning."[47]

In either event, Henry could scarcely have regarded Page any longer as an ally in his efforts to upgrade the image of scientific professionalism, though he does seem to have given the benefit of the doubt to his honesty of purpose. This was not necessarily conceding a great deal, however. In March 1853 he declared in a public address that

> From a want of a knowledge of the state of science, many ingenious minds have wasted their energies in fruitless labor, waged with fortune an unequal war. . . . The true man of genius never lives before his time; he never undertakes impossibilities, and always embarks in his enterprise at the suitable place and period.[48]

Henry pointed to no special individual who had "waged with fortune an unequal war," but many who heard or read his talk would have suspected that he had in mind Page's "fruitless labor" to harness electromagnetism as a motive power. Henry's words evidence not only the basis for an incipient personal estrangement, but also a broader polarizing tendency that had become increasingly evident since mid-century.

Fundamentally, this polarization derived from the anomalous status of scientific and technological enterprise in a democratic society; on the level of ordinary disputation, it was concerned with conflicting notions about the hierarchical relationship between the two. Page's experiments failed to win plaudits from inventors or their press (as witness the attitude of Davenport and of *Scientific American*) largely because they still regarded him as a "scientific man," pursuing another one of those fanciful projects for which scientific men had such a notorious weakness. This image tended to remain in clear focus so long as scientists the stature of Silliman, Peirce, and Henry continued to treat Page as one of their own, and an organization such as the AAAS could treat an address by Page as interchangeable with one by Bache.

Though sometimes conceding that what he was doing was interesting, Page's opponents could scarcely see any more practical value in it than in the experiments of his intimate, Jonathan Homer Lane, who had become interested in determining the velocity of solar heat. Henry and his kind clearly approved of *that*

105

sort of investigation; indeed, Henry had assured Lane that he would procure some of the apparatus he would need "at the expense of the Smithsonian Institution."[49]

Now, it is not unlikely that certain of the most outspoken partisans of the "ingenious mechanic" could have become excited even about Lane's esoteric experiments, *if* they had perceived that much of what concerned either scientists *or* inventors was significant only from what we might today term an existential perspective—only, that is to say, as an act of individual self-expression whose objective significance is literally irrelevant. Scientists had tried hard to fabricate utilitarian rationales for what were in truth quests of pure intellectual curiosity; but they were coming under increasing fire for indulging in "useless" pursuits while diminishing the just desserts due "practical" men of invention. And they were firing back. Henry and like-minded scientists thought that *they* were the ones bearing the burden of injustice—that the inventor was attempting to steal the scientist's fair due. They were increasingly insistent that without the "theorist" the "ingenious mechanic" was nothing. As a rule, this was just not so—technology owed very little to science. Yet, neither had the majority of inventors ever contributed significantly to the betterment of mankind. Many attempted to harness the forces of nature, but relatively few succeeded.

Still, there was private satisfaction—the simple satisfaction, say, of receiving letters patent for the product of one's own ingenuity and handiwork. This was closely akin to the satisfaction a scientist received from seeing a paper he had written in print. There, however, was the rub. Those who decided what was published in *The American Journal of Science* were individuals whose judgement was rarely mistrusted (as yet) by men of science. All of them were personally immersed in scientific enterprise. On the other hand, the men charged with deciding who was to be awarded patents were not primarily thought of as inventors at all (not even Page), but as *scientists too* who, as such, lacked sympathy for the peculiar subtleties of technological innovation and consequently dismissed the validity of far too many patent applications.

At the outset, then, animus between inventor and scientist tended to find a primary arena in the Patent Office. A lobby coalesced whose main aim was to see that patent examiners stopped applying "illiberal" notions of novelty. Even though most patents, like most scientific papers, were rarely worth

106

anything save private gratification, this lobby began deliberately constructing a rationale for the social value of invention. It also began to evolve a calculated defense of the inventor's methodology, and much of the contretemps came to focus on the question of what sort of endeavors were "really scientific." Page's persistent defense of empiricism would eventually help cleanse his reputation in inventors' circles—at the expense of his reputation among scientists. This conflict over fundamentals was intimately tied to the rise of a periodical which assumed leadership of the patent lobby while treating the Smithsonian and the AAAS in terms ranging from lukewarm to openly hostile. Editorially, it disputed the right of any self-selected elite to appropriate the designation "scientific," for it had its own very definite ideas about the meaning of that word. On its banner this periodical carried the name *Scientific American*.

Chapter Six

What Then Is This Scientific American?

> In urging an increase in the salaries of the examiners the undersigned is happy to find himself sustained by the great body of the enlightened inventors of this country, who desire earnestly that the men who are to pass upon their valuable rights shall be not only men of integrity, but of the highest order of talents and scientific qualifications.
>
> Edmund Burke, Commissioner of Patents, 1846

> Scientific men, without practical experience in mechanics, are generally governed in their opinions by what they have read in books.
>
> Edmund Maher, in Scientific American, 1849

> Dr. Page, formerly, had a bad name for want of liberality and sympathy, but a change has evidently been wrought in him. . . . We welcome him into our ranks,—he, like Paul, has been a great sinner,—but, like Paul, we hope he will become distinguished for his conversion to right.
>
> "Daclede," in Scientific American, 1850

Despite consuming a substantial proportion of his energy, Page's consulting, his popular and academic lecturing, his R & D, were all essentially spare-time pursuits, for he had never relinquished his job as a regular employee of the federal government. Within a few years after Charles Keller's resignation advanced him to the position of senior examiner in 1845, the Patent Office became the focus of a rekindled controversy over procedural reform, with a concerted effort being mounted to "liberalize" the criteria for patentability. It also became vulnerable to the vicissitudes of partisan politics.

Commissioner Ellsworth had managed to survive Presidential turnovers from Jackson to Van Buren to Tippecanoe and Tyler too. But the election of James K. Polk in 1844 presaged the departure of this remarkable man who, so said John Quincy Adams, had "turned the Patent Office from a mere gimcrack-shop into a highly useful public establishment."[1] Polk was a ruthless spoilsman, and Adams assumed that Ellsworth's exit resulted from pressure by Southern Democrats. While there is reason to doubt this, it is true that by aiding and abetting the allocation of a large sum of public money to finance Morse's initial telegraph line he sinned unforgivably in the eyes of strict-constructionists (and Ellsworth was the son of a leading participant in the Constitutional Convention at that!).

It is also clear that after 1845 the Commissionership remained forever ensnared in the spoils system. No appointee during Page's time would enjoy a tenure even approaching Ellsworth's full decade. More typical was that of his successor, Edmund Burke of New Hampshire, which terminated almost exactly four years later following the party turnover of 1849. Burke had been a lawyer, editor, and three-term Congressman, but, unlike Ellsworth, was not reputed as a special enthusiast for science and invention. He grew into his office, however, compiling an index to American patents, cataloguing the Scientific Library, and even publishing an able report on steam boiler explosions a few months before the end of his term. Moreover, he respected his examiners highly, and from the very outset yielded nothing to Ellsworth when it came to extolling them to the public and Congress.

In his first annual report Burke declared that the "interesting reviews of the progressive march of the arts" submitted by Page and Fitzgerald constituted "very favorable proof of the talents and industry of these two officers." He lamented losing a man of Keller's caliber for purely mundane reasons. Surely, he insisted, an occupation that entailed "the most attentive and incessant mental labor" and required one to be "a living encyclopedia of science" merited a salary greater than $1,500.[2] Executives in positions such as Burke's characteristically emerged as champions of their staff, while economy remained ever the watchword in Congress. The result, as Leonard D. White has shown, "was a continuous struggle between the executive and legislative branches."[3] Congress held firm for several years, yielding only when it became obvious that Burke's proposals had picked up a substantial body of adherents outside the government.

Yet, even in 1845 the office was beginning to fall behind in transacting its routine affairs. Four or five months often elapsed between receipt of an application and its examination, and soon it had "become a common question among petitioners for letters patent . . . why there should be so much delay in deciding cases."[4] Burke answered that business had "increased beyond the physical ability of the present examiners and assistants to keep up with it, although constantly and industriously engaged in the performance of their onerous and fatiguing duties." He also reiterated his view that there were very few government posts requiring "more ability for sound and nice discrimination, more extensive and varied acquirements . . . than the office of examiner of patents."[5] In private, however, he had to warn the examiners, Page especially, that "The government is entitled to *all* the time of its officers," and that they had no right "to claim any part of it to engage in other pursuits not connected with their official duties."[6] Whether or not Page complied is a moot point. But one thing is certain—both he and Fitzgerald were finding a mounting proportion of applications unacceptable. During Page's first year in the office, 1842, the ratio between patents issued and petitions received was nearly seven in ten, but this had dropped to five in ten by 1846 and to less than four in ten during the next two years. Page thought this might partly explain the backlog, as it frequently happened that an application was rejected not just once but two or three times, and each re-examination required "new investigations and elaborate reasoning to meet the new claims and views of the applicant, and to sustain the decision of the office."[7]

Understandably, most applicants found it difficult to savor the "elaborate reasoning" and "nice discrimination" embodied in Patent Office rejections. When the examination system was barely a decade old, an organization calling itself the "National Association of Inventors" proposed returning to "a simple registry," but such abolitionists attracted little support, then or later. Nor did the majority of inventors immediately rally to the point that patent examiners must be men of "liberal spirit." The first principle on which they all agreed was that applications should always be processed expeditiously.

Soon they acquired a forum, *Scientific American*. Orson D. Munn and Alfred E. Beach, *Scientific American's* proprietors, were two ambitious young men barely into their 20s who had purchased a floundering weekly for a few hundred dollars in July 1846, and during the next half-century were to make it an enormously significant influence on the history of American technology—an influence "unapproached in kind and effect by any other periodical."[8] Their initial crusade concerned the lengthening delay between the submission of applications and the issuance of letters patent. It would be easy, Munn and Beach knew, to speed up the machinery of the Patent Office. Because the two examiners apparently could complete no more than three examinations a day between them, Congress simply had to authorize more examiners. That was that—but how to overcome its chronic sloth whenever this reform came up? Previewing the sort of élan that would make their enterprise an instant success (circulation had reached 10,000 by 1848 when they took in a third partner, Salem Howe Wales, and five years later neared 25,000), they suggested the following means of stimulating the Solons: "Some torpedo inventor" ought to send "some strange locomotive thundering through the Capitol with its broad banner waving boldly amid the din of dismay, the wreck of overturned inkstands, singed wigs and broken winded speeches, and on which shall be inscribed 'immediate patent rights to prevent further damages'." [9]

Munn and Beach did not so much as hint at one obvious way of minimizing delays—merely conduct less exhaustive examinations. In no year since 1843 had patents amounted to even half the number of applications received. When Page passed only seven of the 27 applications for patents on lever and screw devices in 1846, they acknowledged that this naturally left a score of applicants "dissatisfied with the management of the Patent Office." [10] Yet, they traced the root of the problem not to unreasonably stringent standards of examination but to the difficulty inventors had in "informing themselves concerning the construction of various articles already patented" [11]—keeping up with "the state of the art." Again, the most easily identified villain was Congress, which habitually quibbled over the appropriation for publishing the commissioner's annual report. Burke's for 1847 did not appear in print until June of the following year, an absolutely inexcusable delay, Scientific American felt, since it embodied "more truly useful information than all the [other] Reports presented to Congress during this term put together." [12]

When it finally did come out, it included a familiar pair of entreaties: better pay for the examiners, and more examiners. The number of applications had doubled since the staff had last been augmented, and examinations were now seven to eight months in arrears. At the beginning of his personal report, Page apologized for a brevity necessitated by the great accumulation of business, and he and Fitzgerald both echoed the commissioner's plea for a larger staff.

Part of the difficulty stemmed directly from a clutter of applications whose novelty was marginal at best, and in 1848 Scientific American began calling on "the Smithson gentlemen" to publish a comprehensive illustrated history of American

111

inventions, a work that would become "the Urim and Thummin to all our inventors."[13] This suggestion was reiterated periodically for some time thereafter. Gradually, though, its utter futility became obvious to Messrs. Munn and Beach and to their rapidly growing constituency. Such a disposition of any part of the Smithsonian bequest was just about the furthest thing from the desires of Joseph Henry, a fact he was at no pains to conceal. Partly because of this, American inventors were starting to feel vaguely apprehensive about being victimized not only by tight-fisted politicians, but also by their erstwhile bedfellows within the scientific community. The former, instead of attending to vital legislation on Patent Office affairs, apparently regarded "Party spirit, bitter personal feelings, war, blood and bones [as] finer subjects for the orator to declaim upon"[14]—an allusion to the Mexican War—and scientists also seemed unduly engrossed in their own sort of "blood and bones" affairs.

In particular, Professor Henry was steering the Smithsonian—by far the best endowed organization of its kind in America—on a course that was deliberately unpopular. *Scientific American* could perceive nothing worthwhile resulting from "Expeditions to the Dead Sea, & c," or from "analogical research to prove the absurdity of the lost *ten tribes* of Israel having been dwellers either in Chilicothe or Canajoharie," or even from the Smithsonian's initial publication, the study of American Indian archaeology by E. G. Squier and E. H. Davis titled *Ancient Monuments of the Mississippi Valley.* "We hope that such a work may do some good," Munn and Co. editorialized, "but so far as true science, and the majority of our people or any other nation will be benefitted by it, we are more than doubtful."[15]

At issue was nothing less fundamental than a disagreement over the nature and definition of "true science." Here was a periodical calling itself *Scientific American* expressing grave doubts whether the "antiquarian zeal" of Squier and Davis would be of any benefit at all, while urging Henry to publish a history of inventions and thereby "open up to the world a vast laboratory of American science."[16] That such a proposal could be advanced in all seriousness is rather persuasive evidence for the observation that Henry's conception of the Smithsonian "was probably incomprehensible to many of his contemporaries."[17] Having long since resolved in his own mind a key issue that had continually befuddled the debates over the disposition of Smithson's bequest, "Henry clearly separated the increase of knowledge

112

from its diffusion."[18] He felt that the Smithsonian should be devoted to the former, while the appropriate vehicle for the diffusion of knowledge was the press. Indeed, he may well have wondered why Munn and Beach themselves did not undertake the task they were asking of him.

Henry's ideology of original scientific research was *not* something readily understandable to most Americans, not even to the unusual group that comprised the readership of *Scientific American*. Yet, the exact point of contention was badly blurred by the fact that a periodical which could speak disdainfully of Squier and Davis's book as "the popingjay of curious cabinets" went by the name it did. Many impartial witnesses must have wondered who in fact *did* have the most valid claim to the appellation "scientific," and there were certainly those to whom *Scientific American*'s seemed the more compelling. The impression that it stood for what was "scientific," the Smithsonian for what was "antiquarian," would scarcely have been weakened when the Patent Office later succeeded in unloading on the Smithsonian the rather disheveled collection of specimens it had inherited largely from the Wilkes Expedition and known as the "National Cabinet of Curiosities."

Henry was no great enthusiast for museums, of course, and it also needs be said that he himself remained relatively immune to criticism, even when he joined the fray personally by disparaging "mere empiricism" before a group who, by and large, knew no other method.[19] This was perhaps because the heuristic virtues of his own scientific discoveries were beyond dispute. The enemy had to be sought elsewhere, in the person of such as Squier and Davis, or, later, among a clique that apparently had managed to wheel a Trojan Horse right into the Patent Office. Page fell under heavy fire for going his own merry way with his motors, while simultaneously being altogether too stringent in performing his official duties. The issues, however, still remained too unclear for anyone to be concerned about the presence of possible subversives in 1848, when agitation for accelerating the machinery of the Patent Office finally began to receive serious attention on Capitol Hill.

Congress, which held sole responsibility for determining the number of federal employees and fixing their pay, considered itself the final bulwark against the spendthrift propensities of the executive agencies. Nevertheless, in 1847 a bill got through the Senate providing for the employment of two additional patent

113

examiners and two more assistants, and also for revising the salary schedule. It died in the House, but on February 1, 1848, the same Senate bill once again came over. It immediately encountered stiff opposition, especially the provision boosting the examiners' pay 60 percent, to $2,500. As it was, this amounted to less than originally asked by the Senate sponsor, James Wescott of Florida, who had wanted to double the salary. Congressman Andrew Johnson moved to cut the figure back to $2,000 and Robert Toombs of Georgia deemed any increase at all an "unnecessary and profligate expenditure."[20]

Upon reconsideration Johnson agreed. Debate focused primarily on the question of how much expertise an examinership actually necessitated. One proponent of the bill, William King of New York, stated that "There was not in any department of the Government an Officer of whom so much was required nor who was so poorly paid." Others spoke of protecting "the property of the intellect and genius . . . which shed lustre upon the American name in distant climes," and of the necessity for paying a salary that would attract men competent to judge inventors' claims "with as little delay and upon as enlightened and correct principles as possible."

But Toombs and Johnson could not be dissuaded from striking out the $2,500 salary, an amount "as much as the judges and the most honorable state officers received." Indeed, Johnson not only wanted to cut that, but for good measure he also proposed reducing the commissioner's salary from $3,000 to $2,500. This left him vulnerable to charges of being "opposed to the arts and sciences" in general, and neither of his amendments regarding salaries carried. The next day, though, Robert McClelland of Michigan did secure affirmation of a provision setting the examiners' pay at $2,000.

The Senate would not accept the bill as returned—its original sponsor insisting that examinerships "cannot be filled by mere politicians or mere clerks," but only by gentlemen "qualified for one of the learned professorships in our institutions of learning"—and sent it back to the House with the $2,500 sum restored. An impasse ensued which dragged on well into the spring. By late April *Scientific American* had grown tired of waiting, and proceeded to inform the House in no uncertain terms that "the country demands a speedy action and a liberal one upon this bill." Those opposing the bill, it continued,

114

are not aware of the qualifications required for an Examiner nor the labor he has to perform. The duties . . . are more arduous than an Ambassador's or a Cabinet Minister's, and their pay is not disbursed by a tax upon the nation, but paid by inventors. These are the very people that desire the increase. . . . Congress must not adjourn without passing the bill. . . . Why do [Congressmen] seek to cut down the $2,500 . . . ? They surely do not know that there are but few men in the country capable of filling the [examiner's] offices. . . .[21]

Within three weeks the House capitulated, though not without a parting shot from McClelland of Michigan. McClelland thought it perfectly logical "that science commanded more when it was free and independent than when it was employed by the government," and quite obvious that "whenever an officer found he could make more out[side] of an office than in he could go out." Finally, in a closing remark whose snide overtones were scarcely mistakable, he said that

the heads of bureaus, the engineers of the military service, topographical and artillery officers and officers in the military and navy service, where science and extensive information and much talent were required, received no more than the Senate proposed to give these examiners of patents.[22]

McClelland was obviously not convinced that "these examiners of patents" had or needed much "science." Proponents of the bill contended that they did—indeed, that they had to be qualified for a "learned professorship." The lobby led by *Scientific American* agreed. Its warning that the House must step lively lest it "be remembered with ill will" apparently had some effect, an intimation of the influence it would soon achieve. Of more immediate significance, however, was its assumption that the interest and outlook of its constituency, inventors, coincided with that of Patent Office professionals. It even suggested that the $3,000 salary initially proposed by Senator Wescott was fully warranted and that passage of a bill which embodied this sum "would have met the wishes of all our inventors."[23] A year or two later, *Scientific American* made a crucial turnabout, concluding that examiners who were *too* "scientific" were not even fit for their positions. And a year or two after *that,* Page began saying the same thing.

Obviously, this was not something he could say as an employee of the Patent Office; first, he had to give up his job which, since May 27, 1848, had paid him nearly $50 a week.

That was a handsome salary by practically any standard, and there were dozens of applicants for the newly created positions. An assistant examiner who expected a promotion but got by-passed proceeded to stir up quite a fuss by filing 21 charges against Burke, including "giving improper information to Amos Kendall about pending applications and caveats; thus violating the confidential character of the Patent Office." [24] After a thorough investigation, the House Committee on Patents exonerated Burke in August 1848. Nevertheless, his day of reckoning was fast approaching, as the victory of Zachary Taylor in November foretold his ouster. Although there is no evidence he ever played the partisan in the performance of his official duties, Burke made no secret of his Democratic sympathies, and soon after inauguration day Old Rough and Ready rotated him back to private citizenship.

Burke's successor was Thomas Ewbank, an English-born polymath eager to arouse popular enthusiasm for the industrial applications of science, a patentee as early as 1823, and an author whose works included a treatise on hydraulics that had become a classic in its own time. Since retiring from business as a manufacturer of tubing in 1836, he had "devoted his entire attention to travel, to science, literature, the history of invention, and speculations respecting its future development." [25] His reputation was of exceptional erudition and "great scientific attainments," a philosopher—indeed, a philosopher of science and technology. [26]

The two new examiner's positions likewise went to individuals regarded first and foremost as "scientific men." One was Henry B. Renwick, whose family name practically every American associated with signal achievements. His father, James, came from the same mold as Ewbank and had published an enormous amount. His younger brother, James, Jr., had already made his reputation as the designer of Grace Church in New York and the new Smithsonian Institution; another brother, Edward, was becoming established as one of Washington's most highly re-garded patent experts. As for Henry himself, he was something of a prodigy. He had graduated from Columbia at the age of 16, then spent two years studying engineering and several more as a civil engineer for the government. After the Civil War he was to become one of the most respected technical consultants in Wash-

116

ington, but even in 1848 his formal expertise was such that he bore scant intellectual resemblance to the typical patent applicant.[27]

The other new examiner was Professor Leonard Gale, Page's assistant since 1846, and a scientist with whom he of course had much in common. But the colleague whose enthusiasms most closely coincided with his own was one of the new assistants, Jonathan Homer Lane. While an undergraduate at Yale in 1846, Lane had published a paper noteworthy in the history of American science as the first to deal with electrical phenomena mathematically. It was basically nothing more than an explication of Ohm's Law (which Lane mistakenly called "the law of Lenz," confusing Ohm with one of his European interpreters), yet Page immediately perceived its significance, as did Michael Faraday himself: according to Page, Lane's paper had elicited Faraday's "unqualified encomiums."[28]

In 1847, Lane had taken a job with the Coast Survey, but soon began seeking a teaching position, fortified with recommendations from Page and Henry, among others. When the Patent Office job became available, however, he decided to apply— mainly, it seems, because of Page's presence on the staff: "Consider myself fortunate not only in securing a place in the patent office but also in being associated with Dr. Page in it," he wrote in his journal shortly after starting his new job.

> He is a really fine man [Lane continued]. I have been acquainted with him for more than a year and familiar since taking up my residence here last December. He is a scientific man of high order, of a quick discriminating judgement and very great mechanical ingenuity. He is most particularly distinguished for his numerous inventions of electromagnetic machines &c as well as his discoveries and experiments in electrical science.[29]

After 1850, when Page's personal contacts with Henry, Bache, and the leading lights of the Washington scientific establishment became increasingly rare, he still remained close to Lane. Although Lane himself never sat in the seats of the mighty, he held the esteem of both Bache and Henry as long as each lived; he did become a charter member of the redoubtable Philosophical Society of Washington; and he was admitted to the National Academy. After the Civil War, it was Lane who reminded his fellows of something that many seemed to have forgotten, namely, that Page had been "a scientific man of high order," who in days past "contributed greatly to extend a knowledge of, and excite an interest in, electrical science." [30]

When he wrote this after Page's death in 1868, it could scarcely have escaped Lane's memory that the Patent Office as it was when he first joined the staff two decades previously had been truly remarkable for its concentration of scientific expertise. The commissioner and four principal examiners—Ewbank, Page, Fitzgerald, Gale, and Renwick—were all men who commanded substantial respect as scientific experts. For that matter, so did the assistants, the other three of whom were Thomas Everett, a professor of mathematics and meteorology, Samuel Cooper, a former military engineer, and Titian R. Peale, a famous naturalist and pioneer photographer. Peale and Everett moved in the same circles as Henry and Lane, about whom Page could write: "His attainments in mathematics & physics are such as would do honor to the best Professorship in the Country." [31]

One might presume that a periodical calling itself *Scientific American* would have been most pleased at the makeup of the professional staff of the Patent Office, perhaps the best assembly of physics and mechanical engineering brainpower under one roof anywhere in the country. Moreover, these men regarded examining patents as serious business; Lane was not atypical in being "laborious and thorough, cautious and critical, conscientious in the extreme." Inevitably, however, such an examiner "could not be popular with the exterior world of inventors," [32] and quite soon *Scientific American* was to begin seriously reconsidering whether these were truly the ideal sort to have passing upon patent applications.

Before that, though, its attention was diverted by the first appearance of a perennial bureaucratic problem. In 1849 Congress transferred jurisdiction over the Patent Office to the Home Department, or Department of the Interior. No longer a relatively small and incongruous appendage of the State Department, it now comprised a major component of a brand-new cabinet-level arm of the executive. The bill creating the department, which passed despite alarming forecasts that it would soon embrace "everything upon the face of God's earth," [33] assigned it jurisdiction over three other agencies—Pensions and the Indian Bureau, formerly part of the War Department, and Lands from the Treasury Department. But there was no place available to quarter these except the Patent Office; the Home Department, which

118

"might well have been designated the Department of the Great Miscellany,"[34] had no home. Much to the distress of inventors and their allies, the department began progressively appropriating space in "their" building for the use of these agencies.

Rarely after 1849 were controversies involving the Patent Office long absent from the news. If "encroachments" upon its domicile were not at issue, it might be proposals and counter-proposals for organizational or procedural reform. Aside from occasional legislation affecting the size of the staff, Congress did little about these. Nevertheless, through its advise and consent prerogative, it had much to do with determining who sat in the commissioner's office. And, if that individual put a broad interpretation upon his mandate, he could get away with a very cavalier treatment of formal regulations. While the patent lobby was rarely able to prevail against any unsympathetic Secretary of the Interior (one of whom was Robert McClelland, who as a Congressman in 1848 had displayed such antipathy, and as Secretary was accused of "a deep hostility to the Patent Office"),[35] it did manage to apply sufficient pressure to vitiate the policy of subjecting applications to examinations it regarded as hyper-critical.

Between the beginning and the end of the 1850s the ratio of patents to patent applications rose fully 100 percent—the result of concerted demands for "liberalization" which first began to command serious attention just before mid-century. While several major newspapers supported the cause, including Horace Greeley's New York *Tribune,* the strategic headquarters was unquestionably the editorial offices of *Scientific American.* The initial sally in the spring of 1849 was almost diffident, tucked away in an item ostensibly devoted to commending the examining corps for how well it was "making the business fly." The number of patents being issued had risen dramatically since 1848, the backlog was dwindling—indeed, the present situation was "almost perfect." But one matter still merited attention: there needed to be "a widening of the field for decision respecting what is new." While the office was accommodating about re-examining rejected applications, *Scientific American* felt that "great care and kindliness should be exercised on the first examination." As it was, the examiners' initial decisions were "frequently too contracted in spirit, as if ingenuity was exercised to invent objections."[36]

Now, this was scarcely a devastating assault, yet it was a definite omen. Less than a year previously, a one-time associate of

119

Joseph Henry's in Albany named R. Varick DeWitt told of selling the Patent Office a copy of Agostino Ramelli's 16th-century treatise, *Le diverse et artificiose machine,* the only one in America so far as he knew. And *Scientific American* had commended the office for its "large and valuable library of works on all branches of the arts and sciences." Since this enabled it to decide questions of novelty with strict authority, inventors had no call for surprise at "the great number of rejections." [37] *Scientific American* did not reorient its thoughts about this matter all at once, though some of its contributors were utterly appalled by the idea that examiners would actually search out precedents in a work as ancient and obscure as Ramelli. Here, indeed, was precisely why their decisions tended to be "contracted in spirit."

In late April 1849, *Scientific American* began to serialize an essay by a Washington inventor named Edmund Maher, whose ideas presaged a crucial change in Patent Office policy. First, he indicted Congress on two counts: for failing to enact legislation "defining in terms, clear to the understanding of all, what shall constitute a patentable subject," and for failing to pay sufficient heed to "the selection of offficers [*sic*], to interpret and carry out the Laws." The Ruggles law of 1836 left "the discriminating power of judgement, *ostensibly,* with the Commissioner of Patents . . . but *in fact,* with the Board of Examiners. . . ." [38] Were it not for the "extreme discretionary power" allowed the examiners, Maher felt that "many useful inventions that have been rejected, and consequently lost to the world, would have been patented." He also felt that "Many of the greatest inventions ever produced [had] met upon their first introduction with . . . lukewarm receptions from scientific men," and their acceptance long delayed because of "erroneous opinions formed in the public mind, through the agency of adverse opinions of persons professing to be versed in the mechanic arts and sciences. . . ." [39]

Now, Maher began to get to the crux of the matter: "Scientific men" should no longer be permitted to dominate the examining corps of the Patent Office. In order to guarantee inventors "a fair and candid examination and decision," he declared, the majority of examiners should be "thorough bred mechanics" who had served a minimum three-year apprenticeship. "A proper numerical representation of intelligent mechanics" was requisite not only "by reason of their peculiar fitness for the trusts and duties reposed in the Examiners," but also for a secondary reason—"as a return for the shameful neglect of the government

120

towards this industrial [*sic*] class of citizens in the bestowal of its patronage. . . ." Pursuing this strangely mundane embellishment of what was essentially a philosophical point (the point, quoted at the beginning of this chapter, that scientists relied too heavily on what they "read in books"), Maher declared that since "Mechanics [were] virtually excluded from all other departments of the government, the assignment of them to the offices of this mechanical department [the Patent Office], which had its origin and present elevation from their exertions, [was] no more than a just and merited return for their labors." [40]

Or was it a strange embellishment? Maher's style of expression had an unmistakable Jacksonian flavor, and perhaps he regarded the proposition that a share in the spoils of office was "no more than a just and merited return" for the mechanic's labors as virtually self-evident. In any event, this was far from the last time that advocates of Patent Office "liberalization" were to be heard saying things which sounded so much like old-fashioned Jacksonian egalitarianism that one would have thought it was the 1830s, not the 1850s. Historians have been able to discern hardy elements of Progressivism persisting throughout the 1920s; likewise, the debate over Patent Office policy during the 1850s suggests that the Age of Jackson still retained a certain vitality beyond 1841, or 1845, or even 1849.

Little of Maher's scheme for removing "the obstacles in the way of inventors to a just and fair reward of their genius and toil" was ever written into law. Nevertheless, it is noteworthy as the first detailed plea for "liberalization," with its corollary proposition that too "scientific" a cast of mind was an undesirable trait in a patent examiner. During the 1850s, proponents of this view would attain considerable influence, with direct and personal results for some of Page's cohorts such as Gale and Lane.

Following the publication of Maher's essay, *Scientific American* became an open forum for any who would second his ideas, restate them, or embellish them. There was, for example, "Junius Redivivus." Junius agreed wholeheartedly with Maher's notions concerning the shortcomings of scientists ("professional wise men"). An adherent of the Biblical stricture that "great men are not always wise," he thought it especially unwise not to resolve all borderline questions of novelty in favor of an applicant. Yet this had become extremely rare. The cause lay in "the great fault with some analytic minds," namely, their tendency to "pulverize the spirit of the law as unscientifically as a miller does his wheat,

121

by setting his upper stone too close."[41] "We are afraid that in adjudicating upon applications for new improvement," Junius wrote with his knack for homely analogy,

> some of the Examiners look upon the law in the light which Pollock's rural peasant looked upon the moon, as a light 'no bigger than his grandsire's shield.' In such a case, (and there have been many such cases) the *guillotine* falls and the victim expires *legally,* a great consolation no doubt to the faithful executioner.[42]

By the time he got to the fifth in his initial series of epistles, Junius was addressing himself almost exclusively to the problem of "narrow mindedness." "A right spirit," a "generous spirit," a "candid spirit"—were all qualities sorely lacking at the Patent Office. He had to concede that there was another problem involved, however, poor transmission of information about inventions, and he sought to revivify *Scientific American*'s proposal that the Smithsonian publish a comprehensive work on the subject. As it was, it seemed virtually impossible for an inventor to anticipate possible objections to his claims, inasmuch as the Patent Office had been known to reject applications "on the ground that they [had] been described in *Rabelais,* a work in a foreign language and more than two centuries old, and of which, there is not perhaps more than two copies in the United States." Junius of course meant Ramelli, and (if he was not being deliberately cute) his very unfamiliarity with that name tended to confirm his contention that the average inventor was laboring under an enormous handicap in attempting to pit mere ingenuity against the book-learning of the patent examiners. He concluded with a call to action: already "treated as a set of beggars," it was now absolutely imperative that American inventors "unite to sustain their rights or matters will get from bad to worse."[43]

While *Scientific American* concurred in much of what Junius said, the editors were still not able to resolve an ambivalence concerning his fundamental point—that the Patent Office defined novelty too rigorously. Previous remarks about decisions being "too contracted in spirit" indicated that they were leaning toward this view also, yet they now responded by upholding the duty of the office to deny patents for any of the "many things invented every year, which to our knowledge are old."[44] As far as they were concerned, the worst villainy was perpetrated by politicians. Congressmen, for example, were ever ready to appropriate funds

122

for publishing "huge documents on agriculture," while the commissioner's reports on mechanics "presented a miserable appearance in comparison with their buttermilk neighbors, for whom the inventors did all the churning, and made the churn too." Why should Patent Office publications deal with anything other than what was "relevant to patents and improvements in the arts"? And finally, why should the office have the slightest involvement with partisan politics? Here, Ewbank's appointment seemed encouraging, for he was "not a hot partisan, but a good quiet citizen." *Scientific American* thought this "a good recommendation to inventors," asking with no apparent artifice, "What do they care about party?"[45]

To wish the Patent Office altogether dissociated from politics was chimerical, even insofar as the routine appointment and promotion of examiners was concerned. When Burke submitted nominations for the new positions Congress authorized in 1848, Secretary of State James Buchanan asked to discuss these with him personally. This aroused the curiosity of one of the nominees, Lane, and after dinner one evening he stopped by Page's laboratory in the Washington Infirmary to seek an explanation. Page told him that "Mr. Buchanan's object in sending for Mr. Burke was to inquire after the *politics* of the gentlemen nominated." Buchanan was under the impression that Burke was "appointing nearly all Whigs," and indicated there had been "some complaint about it."[46] Burke replied that he failed to see how the politics of his appointees was relevant. Buchanan initially refused to confirm one of them, but soon backed down, perhaps embarrassed by the realization that Burke's appointment of Whigs certainly could not have been motivated by his own political predisposition.

Several years later, after getting bypassed for promotion despite continued efforts on his behalf by Henry and Bache, Titian Peale finally confessed to a friend in Philadelphia that "Nothing but strong political backing can secure my rights." Though he felt "perfectly able to assume all the duties of the office of Examiner," he realized that "Political capital is not gained by helping 'insiders'."[47] And Gale, after seeing two capable assistants lose out to an inexperienced youth for a vacant examinership, lamented the ruinous effect political interference had on "the stability of the Office."[48]

Examiners who conceived of themselves as disinterested professionals—surely the vast majority of those contemporary with Page—were continually distraught by the obtrusion of partisan politics. In 1852, for example, Page wrote Bache that Lane had decided to have done with the *"very public* position of an Examiner,"* and inquired about the availability of "a *good* Office on the Coast Survey."[49] Bache had nothing open at the time, and five years passed before Lane got the opportunity to pursue "an occupation of a more quiet character"—ironically, because he was forced out of his job during what has generally been interpreted as a political purge set in motion by President Buchanan in 1857.

Political interference, or rumors thereof, was bound to keep the examining corps in a state of agitation. Political indifference had the same effect upon inventors. Each year, the anomaly of devoting the *Annual Report of the Commissioner of Patents* largely to agriculture became less palatable. Commissioner Ewbank assumed office with great ambitions. In his first annual report he addressed himself at the very outset, not to agriculture, but to "the objects for which the Patent Office was intended." Vigorously protesting the diversion of receipts to purposes he considered inappropriate, he requested priority funding not only for annual publication of patent specifications and drawings, but also for compilation of a definitive index to inventions. Furthermore, he proposed "the institution of national premiums for new discoveries of transcendant value and enduring beneficence." As a start, he urged Congress to set aside a permanent "Inventors' Premium Fund," the interest from which would be distributed in amounts ranging from $10,000 "for an invention whereby land can be watered without animals," to $100,000 for the rendering of electricity available "as an economical, efficient, and general prime mover."[50]

The patent lobby had mixed feelings about Ewbank. *Scientific American* liked him at first, although dubious about encouraging the "quacks" who infested the science of electricity.[51] Others thought him all wrong for the job. There had been a protracted deadlock over his confirmation. And there was another suggestive incident. Congress had slipped into the habit of neglecting to appropriate funds for publication of the commissioner's report until long after receiving it—part of Burke's for 1848 remained in manuscript as late as 1850. When the House at long last entertained a motion to have Ewbank's first report published, it triggered a debate over the whole system of public printing. One legislator zeroed directly in on Ewbank's report,

124

deeming it "an abstract treatise on abstract science and philosophy," and demanding to see instead "the right kind of Report—something practical and not speculative."[52] This sort of talk clearly indicated that Edmund Maher and Junius could rest assured of the presence of kindred spirits on Capitol Hill. True, they never passed any large-scale reforms. Except for creating the Department of the Interior, Congress was unwilling to sanction any major administrative restructuring at all during the antebellum period—and even Interior was reviled by Southerners as "monstrous." Nevertheless, many legislators were sympathetic to the cause of "liberalization," and they helped it along in various subtle ways.

As for the major source of lobbying pressure, *Scientific American* often reiterated that the patent law of 1836 would be difficult to improve upon. The matter about which it was most concerned—the rendering of judgements concerning novelty and utility—seemed extremely difficult to deal with objectively, and consequently it wavered for some time before resolving its stance on the matter of "liberalization." Finally, however, it was compelled by the demands of its constituency to call unequivocally for a halt to "the custom of the Patent Office to throw every doubt in the scale against applicants."[53]

Thenceforth, *Scientific American* never voiced approval of "liberalization" in terms any less emphatic than this, and occasionally it struck a posture as radical as that of Junius Redivivus. This it did, for example, in its response to an allegation that charges of favoritism in the Patent Office "mainly emanated, not from inventors, but from agents and patent pirates." By 1850, Messrs. Munn, Wales, and Beach had also become the operators of the largest patent agency in the world. Such talk was bound to incur their wrath, and a week later they lashed out at "the biggest pirate of all":

> There is abundant evidence to prove the Patent Office guilty of injustice, recklessness and partiality. The business of the Patent Office, as it respects decisions upon its applications is conducted upon a system of erratics. Applications are granted or rejected, according to the *state of mind* the examiners may be in. There are four chief examiners in the Patent Office, each a feudal baron in his own domain. . . . One has acquired for himself the glorious title of 'the guillotine.' He knows every thing that was, is, and is not, and never will be. It certainly looks singular to see men making

125

decisions, which resemble a dance of crooked sticks. Decisions are sometimes made in the Patent Office, which amount in substance to boxing the bones and throwing the compass overboard.

It is time that there were some uniform rules and regulations for *all cases* in the Office. One applicant will be rejected this week upon some shallow plea, when lo and behold another will receive a patent next week for something which has far less claims to patent protection.[54]

Such intemperate language was atypical of *Scientific American,* though not of some of its regular contributors, and Junius pounced upon the implication of partiality with undisguised relish. He likened the examiners to a "sort of 'Privy Council' from whose decision no appeal may be taken, without a great deal of expense." As a consequence, truly new and useful inventions had been deprived of patent protection, while "schemers, backed by good friends, have got patents for what was worthless and old"— on occasion, "as old as the ruins of Ninevah."[55]

Now, it was one thing to accuse the examiners of being too "scientific," and quite another to impugn their integrity by charging them with favoritism. The latter remained but an undercurrent in the rising swell of criticism directed at the Patent Office. The former, on the other hand, became the very heart of the case against the way the examiners behaved. Too "scientific" an attitude was conducive to an "illiberal spirit," a trait repeatedly condemned:

> Some of the oldest and most experienced among the examining officers ... are, to their discredit, the most illiberal in their feelings towards inventors and in their interpretation of the Patent Laws. ... conceited, crabbed, mulish, illiberal-minded individuals—men who never see anything new— who are always prone to regard one device as but the mechanical equivalent for another. ...[56]

As for Page, while he sometimes was reprimanded for conducting his examinations with excessive stringency—and, of course, *Scientific American* adamantly disputed the propriety of giving anybody public money to finance a private enthusiasm— never was he accused of anything unethical, not after he lowered his profile *vis-à-vis* Professor Morse, at least. Besides, right around mid-century his "spirit" seemed to undergo a metamorphosis, as did his scientific precepts—especially the way he reacted to the

126

notion of "one device as but the mechanical equivalent of another." In the fall of 1850 *Scientific American* reprinted approvingly an article from the St. Louis *Reveille* which, although it lamented that "a herd of worthless fellows had worked into the [Patent] Office," noted a few exceptions, Page included, as "men creditable to any station" under whom it should be possible "confidently to look for the long expected reform."[57]

The *Reveille* left no doubt about what it meant by *that* phrase—"liberalization," nothing else. It also thought Renwick, "with a little improvement," might be counted on the side of the angels. About this possibility *Scientific American* was not so sanguine, implying that Renwick lacked "a candid and liberal mind," and accusing him of rejecting many applications because he "thought he saw resemblances to old inventions, when no resemblances were apparent to others."[58] It was not Renwick for whom the patent lobby felt the greatest antipathy, however, but the employee with the longest tenure of all, Fitzgerald. When explicit attacks on individual examiners first became commonplace on the pages of *Scientific American,* Fitzgerald drew by far the heaviest fire. The reason was obvious—only one-fourth of the applications he examined ever eventuated in letters patent. While the editors themselves took only an occasional pot-shot, major assaults appeared in correspondence received (presumably) from ordinary readers, albeit readers who often affected some Latinate *nom de plume.*

Junius, for example, called Fitzgerald a practitioner of "the cut and thrust system of Hungarian exercise," the basis of both his "skill of fence in warding off the claims of applicants" and his "very bad name."[59] Then, at the end of 1850, one "Daclede" launched a long diatribe commencing with the observation that Fitzgerald had "failed signally in obtaining the countenance of inventors—the patrons of the office." "However well informed he may be in many parts of the routine of his business," Daclede continued, "he evidently does not possess that first of all important qualifications,—a knowledge of his proper relation to us, as inventors." Fitzgerald, recall, not only was a lawyer, he had also stood first in his class at West Point in mathematics and natural philosophy. But, criticism such as Daclede's often carried a powerful aroma of Jacksonian anti-intellectualism:

> Mr. F. evidently possesses no feeling in common with inventors, hence he can never be a man acceptable to them. ... Give me a vacillating simple headed enthusiast, in fact,

anybody, to reason with, in preference to a dogmatic examiner. . . . As an inventor, I do not pretend to disguise the fact that I want to see Mr. Fitzgerald dismissed from the office and a *practical* man—a man of known feeling and community of interest with us, appointed in his place.[60]

One can almost sense the specter of Old Hickory standing by, saying, "The duties of all public offices are, or at least admit of being made, so plain and simple that men of intelligence may readily qualify themselves for their performance. . . ." "A man of known feeling and community of interest" with inventors (much less a "simple headed enthusiast") was no longer likely to enjoy much status with the Washington scientific establishment, which was assuming an ever more elitist stance. But, then, what a change had taken place since Commissioner Burke declared that the great majority of inventors desired only men "of the highest order of talent and scientific qualifications" in the Patent Office, or since *Scientific American* had estimated that there were "but few men in the country" qualified to act as examiners!

While Fitzgerald took the worst drubbing in print, it was Page who was most deeply impaled on the horns of a dilemma. As a scientist, his attainments outmatched those of any of his Patent Office colleagues. Yet, Daclede proceeded to single him out and, in effect, praise him with faint damnation: one of his observations is quoted at the beginning of this chapter. Daclede attributed Page's potential "conversion to right" to his having "become an inventor himself, and [to knowing] what it is to be hung between hope and fear (the inventor's greatest fear is of the Patent Office)."[61] In one sense, of course, Page had been an inventor since he was a boy, and he had long been on record as one who gloried in the "proverbial genius" of American ingenuity.[62] Moreover, his travails in getting his locomotive together no doubt had reinforced his sympathy for the concerns of the ordinary patent applicant. Yet, what Daclede perceived as his "conversion" might well imply to others an abandonment of the methodological circumspection by which any trained scientist was expected to set high store.

As of 1850, a strong bond of friendship and mutual loyalty still existed between Page and such scientists as Peirce, Silliman, and Henry. It was simply impossible, however, for anyone to remain in equally good standing with a Daclede and with Joseph Henry or Benjamin Peirce. When it became clear that Page had indeed become a proponent of "liberalization," most of his scientific cohorts assumed he had turned his back on them. After all, those men who called themselves "Daclede," "Junius," and so on, not only abhorred the presence of "scientific men without practical experience" on the staff of the Patent Office, they quite transparently thought ill of scientific men in general.

By no means is it simply fortuitous that in the Smithsonian Institution Archives there are preserved some two-dozen letters between Page and Henry dating from Henry's first four years in Washington, while in the following 18 years the total can be counted on one's fingers. This development was not without a tragic aspect, since Page had no intention of cutting himself off from his friends and associates in the scientific community. It seems to have escaped him that ultimately the choices confronting him were mutually exclusive. Even while aligning himself with the proponents of "liberalization" and criticizing the disposition of the examiners to reject claims on the basis of "abstractions and metaphysical refinements," he was still seeking to solidify "the community of interests between the philosopher and the practical man, the man of science and the artisan." [63]

Yet, whatever unity of outlook and purpose had once overlapped these realms was rapidly disintegrating by the early 1850s, with recriminations between "the practical man" and "the man of science" becoming ever more frequent. Two months after Page expressed his optimistic prognosis for "the reciprocities of Science and Art," Joseph Henry addressed a convocation of Washington inventors in the new Seventh Street wing of the Patent Office and observed that the records stored there testified to "the immense expense of time and money lavished on futile attempts to innovate and improve." Henry felt he could "safely venture to affirm that out of fifty propositions for improvements in arts or mechanics forty-nine at least are either useless or old." [64] Along with other scientists, Henry had sometimes been asked for an opinion about patentability; yet, in suggesting that no more than two percent of all patent applications warranted approval, he of course located himself ideologically on the nether fringe of the "illiberal" school. Even if he *was* its president, it seems a wonder that he could feel "safe" in saying this before the Metropolitan Mechanics' Institute of Washington, or even in asserting that "The inventor, to insure his success, must consult the discoverer [i.e., the scientist], and the practical skill of the one be directed by the theoretical knowledge of the other." [65]

Those who spoke for the inventor were not about to take that kind of talk lying down, not even from Joseph Henry. *Scientific American* wanted to know what exactly was being accomplished at Washington's great institution for the discovery of "theoretical knowledge." So little, it seemed, "that if Smithson were to rise from the dead, his first object would be to try and get the funds he bequeathed to our nation . . . removed from the guardianship of our government at Washington."[66] And this variety of criticism was literally benign compared, say, to what appeared in the Albany *Knickerbocker*, which called Henry and his cohorts "a lazy set of professors; too deficient in talent and industry to obtain situations in colleges,"[67] or especially to what Greeley printed in his *Tribune*. Read, for example, this declamation about the Smithsonian's "vicious system of publication:"

> Books which have so little real value that they could not find a private publisher—works on the minutiae of ichthyology, geology, antiquities, or whatever other subject—are to be printed in small and costly editions for distribution among European libraries, possibly endorsing one or two names with a sort of remote eclat, but genuine science will be as little advanced by them as by their predecessors. In a word, the Smithsonian Institution is to remain a sort of lying-in asylum for luxurious authors, where their still-born off-spring are arrayed in useless splendor at the expense of a fund given for no such purpose.[68]

Greeley probably never did understand what Henry had decided about the "purpose" of the Smithsonian, or even have a clear concept of what he himself thought "genuine science" was. With regard to this particular attack, moreover, even *Scientific American* had to allow that it was "somewhat violent," that by 1855 the Smithsonian had in fact published some works of considerable value.[69] Nevertheless, kind words for the Smithsonian had been scarce in that periodical from the very beginning, when it described the Secretaryship as a "fat office of eleven dollars a day, and not much to do." At one point it even declared that "The American Academy of Arts and Sciences . . . a voluntary unendowed Association, does ten times more for science every year than the Smithsonian Institute."[70]

With such rhetoric poisoning the atmosphere, Page's hopes for "the community of interest" between scientist and inventor scarcely had much of a chance. For a time, it may have seemed as if the American Association for the Advancement of Science could provide a common forum. Page took an active part in the affairs of that organization at the beginning and kept up his membership until 1854. But the AAAS never met with unreserved enthusiasm from professionalizers skeptical of "a semi-popular organization, in which papers might be presented and membership allowed without stringent discrimination," while from the other side it was excoriated because of "the undue prominence . . . given to papers upon merely speculative subjects." [71]

Like it or not, Page was stuck with the fact that no tenable middle ground existed. By embracing the "liberal" position on patents, he had in effect switched teams, although neither his personal nor his professional relationship with Henry terminated all at once. Henry penned him a respectful note of thanks when he donated his large magneto to the Smithsonian in 1852. That same year they went to New York together, and in 1853 Page enlisted Henry's counsel in preparing a book exposing the notorious Fox sisters of Rochester. Indeed, Page was moved to write such a book precisely because he believed the sisters defamed science "to account for modern sorceries." Moreover, he was appalled at the idea that people thought fraudulent "wonders of knocks and table movements" derived from "electricity or magnetism in some shape." [72] This book reveals several things about Page: first, his personal reverses had left his sense of humor intact (if mediums really could levitate tables, he suggested, "they should be in great demand for mechanical purposes"); second, he was perfectly capable of producing a lengthy disquisition, at once closely-reasoned, convincing, and thoroughly entertaining (it remains quite readable even today); and third, he remained every bit as anxious as Henry or Bache—or Michael Faraday, who was also at pains to expose "rappers"—to dissociate the pursuit of science from charlatanism. "We must put down quackery or quackery will put down science," Bache had been fond of remarking. "A quack will draw crowds around him where a truly learned man could not get a foothold," was the way Page put it. [73]

Ultimately for Page, however, this kind of concern for the integrity of science was not enough. To most of the men committed to uplifting the image of science as a professional pursuit in America, the enormous amount of time and money he poured into his locomotive suggested that his judgement was faulty, and his pronouncements on the patent system made him ideologically suspect. He never became an out-and-out enemy of Henry, Bache,

131

Peirce, Agassiz, Charles Henry Davis, and the others "united in close ties of friendship and mutual admiration,"[74] who constituted themselves the *Scientific Lazzaroni* and guardians of proper professional decorum. But, whereas it is conceivable that he might have been admitted to this little clique had it been established earlier, now there was no chance at all. He was never condemned overtly, as was Matthew Fontaine Maury. He was simply ignored.

In the technological community, on the other hand, the "conversion to right" of such a celebrated scientist as Page assured him—just as Daclede had promised—of a hearty welcome. Welcome turned to endearment when soon enough Page showed no compunctions about disputing the validity of "certain opinions recently advanced by some eminent men of science in this country, which . . . might exert an unfortunate influence upon a particular class of inventors, and operate to the prejudice of our patent system."[75] One such "eminent man of science" he then proceeded to indict with no further ado was Joseph Henry himself.

Chapter Seven
Dignity of Patents

> I left to others what I considered in a scientific point of view
> of subordinate importance, the application of my discoveries
> to useful purposes in the arts. . . . I partook of the feeling
> common to men of science, which disinclines them to secure
> to themselves the advantage of their discoveries by a patent.
>
> *Joseph Henry, 1850*

> Prof. Henry . . . was in error in assuming that the feelings
> which actuated himself [are] '*common* to men of science.'
>
> *Charles Grafton Page,*
> *"Dignity of Patents," 1853*

> . . . we now occasionally hear it said that the scientific do not
> patent. This, however, is a sad mistake, and we would call the
> attention of the timid aspirant for scientific fame to the bright
> galaxy of names upon the patent rolls of all countries, to
> encourage him, if he makes a discovery worthy to class him
> with a Davy, a Watt, a Hare, a Morse, or a Page, that it will
> not tarnish his laurels to secure, not only its benefits to
> himself, but to place it beyond the possibility of being lost to
> his fellow men by patenting it.
>
> *John J. Greenough, 1854*

The year Page finally unveiled his controversial locomotive, 1851,
a veritable storm of controversy engulfed the Patent Office too. At
the beginning of the Ewbank regime there had been an apparent
shift toward a more liberal policy, but subsequently the percent-
age of acceptable applications had skidded from 50 in 1849, to 40
in 1850, to 33 in 1851. At that rate, alarmed inventors and agents
foresaw the impossibility of getting any patent at all. Moreover,
out of a confused babble of reform proposals, at least one of them
aimed not at restricting but rather at *augmenting* the staff's
discretionary latitude and quasi-judicial power. The sponsor of
that legislation was Jefferson Davis, and it did not escape notice
that he and Fitzgerald were old acquaintances. Senator Davis's
bill came to naught, as did the others on the Congressional
docket. But the pot was kept boiling, as the proportion of
successful applications slid to an all-time low and persuasive new
proponents of liberalization condemned Ewbank and his examiners in the strongest conceivable terms.

Meantime, of nearly as serious concern to the patent lobby during the Fillmore Administration was another sort of "usurpation"—the progressive takeover of space in the Patent Office itself by the Secretary of the Interior. Here was Alexander H. H. Stuart, "the gentleman who considers himself the head of the Patent Office," shamelessly diverting it from "its legitimate and original purpose," while Ewbank did not even appear to be putting up a fight.[1] Overcrowding had started to become evident long before, as early as 1844. In his last annual report, Commissioner Ellsworth had indicated that he was having trouble keeping the models properly classified and displayed, and proposed enlarging the building in accord with the original plan. He requested an appropriation covering the cost of erecting two wings, east and west. Although he was unsuccessful, his successor Burke kept pestering Congress and finally in 1849 it earmarked funds for the wings. The following year, after passage of an additional appropriation bringing the total to $140,000, construction commenced on the Seventh Street side.

At that point, however, Ewbank announced that the additional room was not really needed, not for patent business anyway. The Senate Committee on Finance responded by rescinding the second appropriation. Although the Senate as a whole overruled the committee and work proceeded, Ewbank's disclaimer remained a matter of record and Stuart was naturally determined to take full advantage of it. Early in 1851 he asked to be given a free hand in assigning space in the wings to other bureaus. Opponents of this perceived that even if the Patent Office did not presently require more space, getting it back when it was needed would not be easy. Already, part of the splendid model gallery had been walled off into small offices, an offense that *Scientific American* equated with "Gothic pillage." This had made it necessary to relegate many of the models to the leaky and poorly lit basement. The whole idea behind keeping models was to make them readily accessible to public scrutiny and thus help inventors avoid covering old ground. Week after week *Scientific American* hammered away at the point that "the Patent Office was never designed nor intended to be degraded to any other purposes than those connected with patents."[2]

This probably *had* been the intention in the 1830s, but the federal establishment had expanded considerably since then, while little attention had been devoted to its physical accommodations. As one of the four major public buildings in Washington, it was simply inevitable that the Patent Office should attract covetous bureaucrats. On the liberalization issue, the patent lobby was beginning to command more than passing notice on Capitol Hill, yet when it came to bureaucratic infighting this influence virtually evaporated. The Commissioner of Patents was of course subordinate to the Secretary of the Interior. But there were those—Edmund Burke for one, and later Page—who insisted that Ewbank had foolishly surrendered some of the legitimate prerogatives of his office, thereby adding insult to the injury already done American inventors by treating applications with an "elaborate reasoning" that was wholly uncalled for.

Besides Ewbank's illiberal temper and Stuart's imperialistic designs, there was much else to worry inventors and their partisans during the early 1850s. For one thing, the Patent Office was once again falling seriously behind in its examinations, with some classes five months or more in arrears. For another, certain disclosures had deeply eroded confidence in the integrity of the professional staff. In the most sensational instance, Edmund Burke had revealed an episode which cast considerable suspicion over the conduct of the agent and the examiner in a case involving re-issue of the famous patent on the Woodworth planing machine, a patent valued at several million dollars by its owners. The agent was Keller, the examiner his former assistant, Fitzgerald. Burke, who evidently had never forgiven Fitzgerald for partially sustaining some of the charges preferred by T. G. Clinton in 1848, called the re-issue "a fraud upon the public."[3]

While no such allegation was ever proven, the manner in which Fitzgerald conducted his routine examinations continued to draw heavy fire. *Scientific American* commented at length on the commissioner's report for 1850, especially on Fitzgerald's write-up. "Like Atlas," he portrayed himself bearing "the whole Patent Office on his shoulders." By this time—the report was not published until September 1851—*Scientific American* thought little more of Ewbank than it did of Fitzgerald, observing that he must have "a very insignificant view of his own place and office, to have allowed some parts of [Fitzgerald's] Report to appear before the public, for he (the Commissioner,) appears to be a cypher—Examiner Fitzgerald, the head of the Department." Worst of all, Fitzgerald seemed to regard almost every applicant "as a rogue or a fool."[4] The next most illiberal examiner was Renwick, who compounded his effrontery by being "savage" to anybody who complained. Gale's report was summarized without comment,

135

but Page's was deemed "chaste" in its language and "excellent" in spirit.[5]

No doubt about it, Page had become the favorite with the patent lobby. This was clear from the reaction to an episode involving Dr. Charles T. Jackson, one of the parties to the tangled controversy over the discovery of etherization. Jackson had once held a ten percent interest in W.T.G. Morton's patent, but had ostentatiously "renounced" it before a meeting of the Massachusetts Medical Society, then gone Henry one better by declaring that "no true man of science" would ever "disgrace himself" by seeking a patent. Naturally incensed, *Scientific American* wanted to know what Jackson's notion of a "true man of science" was. James Watt had taken out patents. "As a man of science he was certainly superior to the learned Doctor [Jackson]." And was not "Dr. Hare, of Philadelphia, a scientific man?" Jackson obviously had "a wrong idea of men and things," for many scientists had secured patents—surely not the least important being "Dr. Page, of the Patent Office, & c.—to whom the remarks of Dr. Jackson do a great injustice."[6]

While *Scientific American* might thus find cause to compliment Page individually, its general opinion of the Patent Office had sunk very low indeed. Nearly all the examiners, it seemed, looked upon applicants "as dishonest men" and operated "in Star Chamber fashion." Of utmost concern to Munn, Wales, and Beach was their apprehension that the office, especially under Ewbank, had set out "to destroy the business of regular and respectable Patent Agents" by claiming to be more lenient about passing applications from inventors who prepared and submitted their own.[7]

Soon, Page would also take up the cudgels against this policy. He became free to do so in 1852, a year that began with the office more deeply embroiled in controversy than ever. The dispute involving the Woodworth patent flared intermittently. And, for the first time in several years, advocates of total abolition began to command attention. *Scientific American* had to spring to the defense of the patent system (and its own self-interest) by emphasizing that necessity was not always the mother of invention, and that the rewards the patent system made possible were essential to "excite inventive genius."[8]

Since Page well knew that patents were not the *only* conceivable way of encouraging innovation, he might or might not have agreed. By the spring of 1852, however, he could regard such

136

matters from a new perspective, if hardly any more disinterested. For, in April, just short of his tenth anniversary as an examiner, he handed in his resignation. While his reasons were no doubt complex, he must have watched with increasing envy the success of his former colleague, Charles Keller—not to mention Munn and Co., which handled hundreds of applications every year. No other agency was nearly as popular. Still, invention and patenting were obviously on a steep upward trend, and Page clearly perceived the exponential character of technological innovation. Years before he had written that "the offspring of each distinct and notable invention may be hundreds, or even thousands. . . ." It seemed an auspicious time, the 1850s, to get into patent soliciting. Of upstarts there were many, of men with the sort of qualifications Page possessed, few others.

While Page's government salary would have been the envy of virtually every college professor in the land, his personal financial burden was exceptionally heavy. His daughter Emmie was almost 7, Charlie was $4\frac{1}{2}$. There was also a new baby, Harriet, less than a year. An infant son, Howard, had died in 1850. Priscilla's mother lived at Grafton Cottage, and there was talk of his parents moving in too, along with his handicapped, 35 year-old brother Henry, who, though he occasionally worked copying patents, could not support himself. On top of that, Page still owed much of the $6,000 he had borrowed in order to finish his locomotive. Monetary considerations alone might well have sufficed to induce him to strike out on his own, and he had good reason to feel confident of success in private business.

Besides that, however, he had also become increasingly dissatisfied with the way the Patent Office was run, and with its continual involvement in rhetorical warfare. Indeed, dissatisfaction was endemic. Not only did Page resign in 1852, so did Commissioner Ewbank, and Fitzgerald, Renwick, and one of the other principal examiners, Samuel Cooper. The number of examinerships was then six, two more having been created in 1851, one of which went to Lane. But losing two-thirds of the examining corps and the commissioner in a single year left things in serious disarray. Gale complained privately to Morse about the "bad management" of Ewbank's successor, claiming he had appointed "the youngest assistant examiner in a place he had no experience to fill," thereby compounding the instability occasioned by the rash of resignations.[9]

Shortly, Gale feared, there would be "little honor" in working for the Patent Office. He told Morse, nevertheless, that he would not leave until he saw "a palpable necessity for it." Most men could put up with a lot for $2,500 a year. As it turned out, Gale stayed until 1857 and then went unwillingly—peremptorily fired with no honor at all. During that five-year interval, particularly towards the end, the internal policy of the office underwent a transformation nothing short of revolutionary. This transformation represented the fulfillment of demands by the patent lobby that applications be treated more liberally, and that examiners who would not conform be thrown out.

Page played no small role in fostering the climate of opinion that ultimately led to the achievement of this aim. For, not only did he set himself up in a new profession, he also became a vocal proponent of the liberal philosophy. At first he had two partners, old friends both. One was Charles L. Fleischmann. A graduate of the Royal Agricultural School of Bavaria, Fleischmann had once submitted a detailed proposal for devoting James Smithson's legacy to agricultural education.[10] He was also a popular author and illustrator, and had worked for the Patent Office as a draftsman as far back as 1836. His supervisor then had been John J. Greenough. And it was Greenough, who had established himself as an independent agent in New York City after dissolving his partnership with Keller in the late 1840s, who became Page's other partner.

Munn, Wales, and Beach had been eminently successful in linking the publication of a periodical for inventors with the operation of a patent agency. None of the several attempts to emulate this combination had succeeded, but prospects for Page, Greenough, and Fleischmann appeared excellent. All three knew the Patent Office intimately. Page had served more time as a principal examiner than anybody else. Greenough could boast just about the longest tenure of any agent still active, having been in the business since 1839, and the years he spent in association with Keller had given him invaluable experience. Besides, he was quite a successful inventor in his own right. While nothing had ever come of the sewing machine he patented in 1842—the first in America—he did well with machinery for shoes, plate glass, woodworking, and much else. Like Ewbank, he was an authority on the history of technology. As for Fleischmann, he had served as the American Consul at Stuttgart, was a linguist, and maintained the sort of connections that would enable them to handle foreign patents, a field theretofore virtually monopolized by Munn,

138

Wales, and Beach. Even the name of the new firm had a similar pleasing cadence.

The *American Polytechnic Journal,* however, represented no deliberate attempt to imitate *Scientific American,* as did such periodicals as the *American Artisan,* begun by a Philadelphia patent agency later on. First, it was a monthly, with a format and content that bore distinct resemblances to the *Journal of the Franklin Institute* and even to *Silliman's.* The cover proclaimed its devotion "to Science, Mechanic Arts, and Agriculture" (see plates). Each editor took responsibility for one of these fields. Page published many articles on electricity, and Greenough wrote about a multitude of mechanical topics. Both of them also devoted close attention to matters of Patent Office policy.

Greenough addressed himself mostly to such perennial controversies as the stinginess of Congress. The commissioner's report for 1851 did not appear in print until 1853—a delay which guaranteed, in Greenough's word, its "worthlessness." He lamented Ewbank's "lax management" and his acquiescence in the impositions of the Secretary of the Interior. And he echoed *Scientific American* in assessing the examiners as "hypercritical," an attitude that was most pronounced in their peculiar flair for perceiving far-fetched analogies between the components of entirely different apparatus.[11]

That was one of Page's main bugaboos, too. But what personally distressed him more than anything else was the growing currency of the notion that "the scientific do not patent"—a notion nurtured by a clique that claimed to speak for all true scientists. Page was extremely anxious to show that by no means did *all* scientists feel this way. He himself then held only one patent, an English one on his axial engine. In general support of his views, though, he cited:

> The distinguished Liebig, who has taken out a patent for a manure of his own invention,—Sir David Brewster, preeminent for his physical researches, multiplied discoveries, and inventive genius, whose name appears often upon the patent-roll,—Wheatstone, a prince among practical philosophers, abounding in patents,—Bramah, Watt, Barlow, Stephenson, Lardner, and many others of distinction, as bright examples among foreign patentees, and in our own country among the many patentees, we notice Prof. Hare, Prof. Locke, Prof. Maury, Prof. Horsford, Prof. Olmsted, Prof.

Renwick, Prof. Johnson, Prof. Espy, &c., &c. With the countenance of such distinguished men, surely we need no reinforcement.[12]

Yes, there had been instances of "open hostility to patents from the scientific profession in this country"—Jackson's "tirade," for example. Page affirmed his "high personal and professional respect for Dr. Jackson," and felt "at a loss to account for his sallies."[13] Jackson was a notorious eccentric, however, so perhaps there was really no need. On the other hand, for Page flatly to dispute Joseph Henry's assertion that his own feelings about patents were "common to men of science" was virtually to invite ostracism by the Washington-Cambridge clique that was rapidly appropriating authority to determine just who was a man of science and who was not. Moreover, Henry was exceptionally sensitive about being contradicted, as Page well knew. Gale, for instance, had found him "as cold as a Polar berg" ever since the two presented "incompatible" testimony in one of the telegraph suits.[14] He may not have reacted quite so strongly in Page's case, yet the fact remains that from this time until after the Civil War, for a period of more than a dozen years, all correspondence between the two erstwhile comrades appears to have ceased. Quite simply, Page had taken a different road from the one prescribed as proper by Henry and his cohorts.

As for the American patentees Page cited, what is most significant is that not *one* of them ever received the imprimatur of the *Lazzaroni*. Johnson was dead. Most of the rest were either aged or discredited or both. Horsford and Maury, the youngest, both had substantial reputations—well earned for the most part. About Maury it has been said, nevertheless, that his lack of acceptance stemmed from his "failure to measure up to a set of ill-defined and largely unspoken standards of behavior, often manifested in matters of style and tone, but derived from a concept of the ideal scientific life."[15] This observation, I suggest, applies equally well to Horsford and Page. There were many "matters of style and tone." Maury continued to think of science in democratic terms, while the professionalizers were working to define it as an elite enterprise. Horsford liked to make money, while the professionalizers kept insisting that a true scientist's first duty was public service.[16] Page was guilty on both counts, and besides he was adamant about patents *not* being of "subordinate importance." All three men were something less than subtle about their style of self-promotion.

140

Ironically, in the end Page's effort to bolster his *scientific* image by exploiting the *patent sytem* in an extraordinary manner proved terribly damaging both to the "dignity of patents" and to assessments of his "career of science." Long before that, however, this man who ranked second only to Henry as a pathfinder in the specialty they shared, and second to none in his ingenuity as an experimentalist, had been tacitly dismissed by the minions of "true science."

Chapter Eight

Liberalization

> With but few exceptions the examiners in the Patent Office appear to be *entirely unfit* for their situations.
>
> Charles Grafton Page, 1853

> The patent laws . . . were enacted for the government of an office whose range of action is altogether above the barren field of mere technicalities. That office, in my judgement, would be forgetful of its mission, and disloyal to one of the highest interests of humanity, were it to permit itself to be entangled in a mesh of mere words, or palsied by doubts born of intricate metaphysical disquisitions.
>
> Joseph Holt,
> Commissioner of Patents, 1857

> The inventor is now received beneath the roof of the Patent Office as a friend and patron in the frank and free conference.
>
> Scientific American, *1858*

When he left the Patent Office to go into business in 1852 Page was 40, an age at which men and women often feel compelled to take a critical look backward—at the disparity between youthful aspirations and their fulfillment. People may fix on some key event and treat it as proof either of personal affirmation or of failure. Anxiety may profoundly upset perceptions, values, and loyalties. Individual responses to this "mid-life crisis" (lately so-called) range from a relatively quiet internalization of some new reality, to the most explosive possible. Poe, a favorite of Page's, was 40 when he killed himself in 1849. Other contemporaries sought salvation in remaking the world—Julia Ward Howe was 41 when she took up anti-slavery, Dorothea Dix 39 when she threw herself into reform with ferocious dedication. Still others became obsessed with their place in history—Charles T. Jackson was 41 when he began waging his vindictive priority fights. And still others radically reoriented their career—Louis Agassiz, say, or Morse.

Page's new goals and motives were both mundane and idealistic, but the chief outward manifestation was his abandonment of a well-established station to risk a whole new beginning. Joseph Henry, when somewhat older, had done the same, though

142

the final outcome was far different. Like Agassiz, like Morse, his fame and prestige waxed continuously for the rest of his life and beyond. With Page it was the opposite. After a few years his notoriety had receded from the popular consciousness, and understanding of the basis of his once-substantial repute had become badly blurred.

In 1867, in a last-ditch attempt to recoup, he published a book recounting his most important work in electrical science. One of that book's most salient characteristics, unfortunately, was its lack of modesty—a trait the professionalizers might overlook in a Peirce or an Agassiz, but not in a Maury or a Page. Yet, it also clarified his genuine importance in the history of science, something which might get blurred but could hardly be erased. Like his 1867 book, Page's articles on electricity in the *Polytechnic Journal* were self-consciously historical. The most important was a series on "Electro-Mechanics," wherein he set out to "describe and illustrate the various inventions in which mechanical operations are effected through the agency of electricity and magnetism, for the purpose of showing how far this subtile agent has already been made subservient to the mechanical necessities of man."[1]

Other descriptive papers ran a gamut from utilitarian apparatus such as an invention for use in telegraphy he called a "compensated armature," to instruments such as a thermogalvanometer based on the principle of Regnier's metalline thermometer, to purely didactic devices he had contrived for class demonstrations during his years as a professor. A favorite was made from two dissimilar metallic bodies, one of them wired to a galvanic battery. Due to differential rates of expansion, the superposed bar would rock to and fro whenever the circuit was closed.[2] While it was possible to illustrate this phenomenon simply with a plain chunk of lead and a brass bar, how much more amusing to do so by means of a "galvanic see saw"! (Fig. 13).

That was Page the showman, the same Page who once had demonstrated the way his helices worked with a "magnetic gun" that shot a metal bar 50 feet through the air. There was also Page the philosopher: "When an isolated principle or truth in any branch of science is discovered," he wrote, "the question is immediately asked, *cui bono? quid utile?* of what use is it? Franklin answered this question for all time by asking another, viz., 'What is the use of a new born babe?'"[3] Page made it clear

143

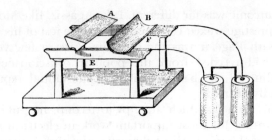

Fig. 13.   *Apparatus for demonstrating vibrations of "Trevelyan's Bars." (From*
AMERICAN POLYTECHNIC JOURNAL 2 [1853]: 316, 317.)

that he still regarded the sort of research he had pursued in the
1830s as eminently worthwhile. In part, this was because even
"the most obscure . . . scientific propositions" might eventually
bear practical fruit. Such a proposition was Etienne Malus's, that
a ray of light had different properties according to its plane of
incidence. In the years since the discovery of polarization in 1810,
Page noted, that phenomenon had yielded a veritable treasure of
practical applications in fields ranging from navigation to stress-
testing—all from a finding which, at first, could only raise the
question, *cui bono?*[4]

One could scarcely expect to find a nicer defense of the virtues
of basic research. Yet, as far as Page personally was concerned
with electrical science, fundamental new discovery was beyond
his ken. He still retained his affection for experimentation,
though, and found a sufficient outlet in another field whose
cultivation he had long enjoyed, floriculture. Indeed, he now
transcended the status of a mere "cultivator," by publishing his

experiments and thereby becoming a "practitioner."[5] His sophistication was evident in his work on artificial fecundation, during which he performed thousands of experiments in cross-fertilization. Moreover, he had not lost his knack for perceiving interesting analogies, as between grafting and "surgical subjects."[6]

Nevertheless, Page's turn to floriculture clearly defined his new position *vis-à-vis* the world of science. For all its subtleties, it was hardly a subject that demanded a large store of abstruse knowledge. This is by no means to speak condescendingly about papers with titles such as "Successful and Easy Mode of Preventing the Ravages of the Peach Insect," or "The Petunia;" his experiments not only served as a means by which he could continue to satisfy his "love of novelties,"[7] they also proved useful to others. As for electrical science, perhaps suggestive of how he perceived his own situation was his protest against "the attempt to lug into scientific communications the word *physicist*." The English language, he felt, was "sufficiently charged and chargeable with hissing, without affecting more of it; and if any man can pronounce *physicist* without a perfect *phiz of sibilation*, we will procure him a patent for liquidity of articulation."

For all its facetiousness, this amounted to a tacit confession. "Everybody understands what is meant by philosopher," Page wrote,

> and we have great respect for the cognomen. It is sententious, euphonious, and full of meaning; not so much, perhaps, from its etymology as from association and logical import. A philosopher must be a lover of science, and a *real lover* of science must be a philosopher.[8]

Page still conceptualized himself as a natural philosopher, but the day of the natural philosopher as electrical scientist was over. The stage was now commanded by the physicist, more precisely by the mathematical physicist. Despite his persisting interest in peach trees and petunias, Page's "career of science" was over.

Yet, it was not because of this that he became an outsider in an institutional sense, too; Henry's truly important contributions were long past by the time he settled in Washington, and some of the leading professionalizers had *never* done any significant research to speak of—Professor John F. Frazer of Philadelphia, for one. Page's reputation might have survived the locomotive debacle—others such as Benjamin Silliman, Jr., weathered worse

145

mistakes. But what clinched Page's fate was the sort of thing he began saying when he addressed himself to the policies of the federal bureau he had recently left and with which he now dealt almost daily as an outside party.

Most significant was a series titled "The Patent Office," which he prefaced with these remarks:

> We propose, under this caption, to consider the Patent Office in all its relations; to furnish a full and particular account of the method of conducting business in the office, to advert historically to whatever, in our judgement, will be interesting to our readers. We shall also have occasion to comment on some of the defects of the existing laws; and upon one topic we shall be free to dilate, enabled as we are to speak *ex cathedra* from our long official experience in the Patent Office. This topic relates to the principles upon which the patent laws are administered. . . .[9]

Page regarded the law of 1836 as basically sound. The necessity for certain changes, however, he thought obvious—for example, some routine mechanism for publishing patents with illustrations. While this had been continually urged—by Ellsworth, Burke, and Ewbank, by Secretary of the Interior Stuart, even by President Fillmore—Congress had never appropriated funds. Page related that he had once been asked to see how publication was handled in other countries. He liked the English private-enterprise system best. And, when he, Greenough, and Fleischmann issued the prospectus for their *Polytechnic Journal* they indicated their intention "to undertake this laborious, responsible, and expensive work, at their own risk."[10] Clearly they hoped to obtain a federal subsidy, but otherwise this was hardly a controversial matter. Beyond that, however, Page purposely began to ruffle some feathers.

The Patent Office, he noted, periodically published a circular that outlined current regulations. While praiseworthy in intent, the issuance of these publications tended to convey a false impression that they were "all sufficient." On the contrary, Page wrote,

> Hardly a week passes in which questions of practice do not arise in the Patent Office among the examiners and others which are settled according to the memories solely of the older *employees*. Technical and professional knowledge is of all kinds the most fugacious, and the Patent Office has been

146

often awkwardly placed, in consequence of either uncertain memories, conflicting precedents, or the absence of its older officers. Every conclusion upon a mooted point is of importance as a precedent; and if some regular system of commitment to paper of these important points, as they occur, should be adopted, the office and the public would be mutually guarded against error and uncertainty.[11]

Here, Page was echoing the longstanding complaint that examiners often seemed to act arbitrarily. The reason was simple: "Many and very important rules of the Patent Office are unwritten." Yet, there was considerable irony in Page's addressing himself to the matter of "unwritten rules," since it was obvious that the formal *modus operandi* of the office was merely sketched in the law of 1836, that many policies *had* evolved in an *ad hoc* manner, and that Page had been the key figure in this. Indeed, Fitzgerald had once testified formally, "I think Dr. Page had much to do with drawing up a good many of the rules."[12] Now, however, Page was afraid that some of the rules, whether simply tacit or printed, tended to demean the dignity of patents. The office felt constrained to "parade" its own "integrity, impartiality, and incorruptibility," for instance, to emphasize that patents were granted only "upon the merits of the cases presented," and to insist that it was impervious to "offers of money, or payment of the same to third parties." After ten years with the office, Page felt he could personally testify to the probity of its officers. Thus, "such ostentation of moral purity" was "in bad taste, to say the least."[13]

Far worse were the rules regarding agents, something that had long perturbed Munn and Co. Page conceded that, while there had been dishonest agents, most of the more flagrant abuses had been squelched during Burke's regime. Nevertheless, the current circular stipulated that the office would "decide questions of novelty and patentability upon papers imperfectly prepared, if sufficiently perspicuous to be understood, *when such papers are prepared by the inventor himself.*" On the other hand, if an agent were employed, he was presumed "qualified for the business he had undertaken" and adherence to all technical requirements was to be strictly enforced. Page went on to cite other examples of "a spirit of partiality and unwarrantable discrimination" against patent agents, and concluded darkly that such a policy "was made to serve some personal ends."[14]

Whatever those "ends" may have been Page did not say. Yet

pension agents, who had been around Washington a long time, did not as a whole have the most savory of reputations—and some of this had definitely rubbed off on patent agents. Thomas Ewbank had gone on record as taking a rather dim view of the whole genre. Page, for his part, considered Ewbank a fraud, since he had not really done anything "to aid the cause of the *inventors*, for whom he proclaimed so much sympathy in his reports, *passim*." On the other hand, he was pleased with Ewbank's successor, Silas Hodges, who had *"courteously* and *sagaciously"* submitted a revision of the information circular "to persons outside, having experience in business with the Patent Office, for suggestions, objections, or amendments."[15]

This led Page to speculate about the sort of individual best qualified to serve as commissioner. Ewbank unquestionably had the most impressive technical background, yet Page regarded him as the worst of all. Both Hodges and Burke, on the other hand, were lawyers, and Page thought that each had done a good job. (He could say this about Burke *now*, although he had felt differently when Burke cracked down on him for failing to devote full time to his official duties.) He recalled a conversation with Daniel Webster during Ewbank's regime, when Webster told him that "if he had it in his power he would put a good *lawyer* at the head of the Patent Office." He had answered that it might be difficult to get a good lawyer to work for the salary. To this Webster had replied: *"Then give him five thousand a year and I wouldn't care if he never saw a cog-wheel in his life. Your examiners have, or should have science enough, let them report to the commissioner for his decision."*[16]

Page averred that he was "inclined to go even beyond the commissionership with [his own] legal preferences." Recalling his years in the office, he noted that there was only one examiner who was a lawyer (i.e., Fitzgerald), and that his "knowledge and advice was common stock in the office, of daily use to himself and his brother examiners, and on many occasions saved the Patent Office from exposure to public derision." Here was a point on which Page disagreed with reformers such as Edmund Maher. He thought it mistaken to suppose that the prime requisites of a good examiner were either scientific *or* mechanical. They were, in fact, *"Scientific, Mechanical, Legal,* and *Judicial;* and . . . the most extensive and profound knowledge of science or mechanics can never make an *examiner* if he have not a judicial mind."[17]

Page was not suggesting that lawyers be given preference for

148

examinerships over men with scientific or technical knowledge; he merely wished to emphasize that since the commissioner could not possibly decide all questions himself it had "always been the practice for the examiners to decide for themselves." This being the case, he concluded, "the importance of legal knowledge should not be overlooked."[18]

Regarding the propensity of examiners "to decide for themselves," Page well knew—unlike such simplistic critics as Junius—that deciding questions of patentability was "one of the most difficult undertakings within the whole range of jurisprudence." Besides, each examiner was "possessed of different qualifications, of differently constituted minds and temperaments, and each [was] a judge within his own precincts." One had to be "a chemist, another a mathematician and physical philosopher, another a mechanical philosopher, another an engineer, another an agriculturist, another a physician." Indeed, it was necessary to have representation for "the whole range of science and art." With a board so constituted, it was inevitable that there should arise "much contrariety of action in the respective departments," and that the examiners should be "in the habit of applying certain principles of Patent Law with more stringency to one class of inventions than to another."[19]

The responsibility for enforcing some degree of uniformity properly rested with the commissioner. But, Page lamented, "owing to a most unfortunate misconception of the duties of this important office, the employment of the Commissioner of Patents has of late years been mostly that of book-making." As a result, the examiners had become "almost the sole arbiters and expounders of the law." He had personally seen, he said, "examiners exulting in the hope or act of finding something to defeat a claim." This was symptomatic of a deplorable tendency—"too much of a disposition on the part of examiners to *reject* claims," often by resorting to "abstractions and metaphysical refinements." Indeed, it was nothing short of "disastrous" that at least one examiner habitually rejected nine-tenths of the applications that came before him, and virtually all of them rejected too many.[20]

As the months passed Page began to warm to the task of dressing down the examiners for citing the "most remote analogies to prove want of novelty." This, combined with an inexcusable "hauteur, impatience and stringency," laid the Patent Office "open to the charge of *sporting* with the rights of inventors."[21]

149

Page recalled that when he became an examiner, eleven years previously, Commissioner Ellsworth had told him that "inventors or applicants for patents should in all cases have the benefit of any doubts on the part of the office," and that due consideration was to be accorded every inventor's "'feelings'." He had nothing but praise for Ellsworth, particularly his foresight in anticipating "the temptations, tendencies, and dangers of blending executive and judicial powers." While Ellsworth had been determined to prevent the office from becoming "a star-chamber," Page felt that in recent years it had acquired "too much of this odious feature," that the tendency had been toward a regime of "will and whim" with the distinct possibility of the office becoming "a dangerous oligarchy of Examiners." [22]

He conceded that "the disposition to refuse patents [was] not universal with Examiners, nor [was] this research for remote analogies, and 'travelling out of the record' for certain single elements of an invention . . . upon which to refuse a patent." Nonetheless, it was typical, as was the "extraordinary proclivity on the part of many examiners . . . to regard inventors with suspicion, and to make themselves *parties* to every case brought before them." Page then proceeded to offer his startling observation that most of the examiners appeared "to be *entirely unfit* for their stations." [23]

One needs remember that he was referring to a corps comprised of men highly regarded for their scientific and technical expertise—highly regarded by most of their peers, at least. He was talking about his friends, Lane and Gale. He was talking about Peale. And lately added was the eminent George C. Schaeffer, whom Benjamin Silliman, Jr., called a man of "original power" and "one of the best read chemists of his time." [24] (Schaeffer also happened to be the examiner who rejected 90 percent of his cases.) Lane, Peale, and Schaeffer were all closely allied to Henry's circle. As a matter of fact, though, Page seemed bound and determined to alienate an even larger circle. While he professed respect for all the examiners as "intelligent and worthy men," he openly questioned whether scientists, *or* engineers, *or* artisans, *or* even practical mechanics should serve as examiners under the present setup. He had already ruled out lawyers; whom did that leave to choose from? Page recalled another conversation several years previously, the one in which Webster had told him that rather than allowing the examiners so much power *"it would be better to go back to the old system, and give every man his patent."* No matter how Page may have regarded this observation at the time, he now believed that Webster had "bequeathed this text upon which to frame our reform of the patent law": "'You Examiners have too much power'." Let Webster's sentiment "be echoed in the legislative hall, and the jealous eye of Republicanism [will] soon see to it, that there is not *too much power with the examiners.*" Thus, "the great pivot of reform" lay simply in wresting power from the examiners. This done, Page concluded, the Patent Office would become "the palladium of inventors' rights." [25]

Knowing that these remarks might be "unpalatable" to the examiners, he explained that he was motivated not only by a concern for the rights of inventors but also by his regard for the reputation of examiners. The latter, every one of them, were continually being accused of corruption. Page put no stock whatever in these charges, declaring that the corps was comprised of "gentlemen of the highest respectability, integrity, and standing in society." Nevertheless, such accusations stemmed naturally from their "extraordinary and inconsistent" decisions, which led people "to suspect the worst." [26]

Finally, Page outlined his solution, and it was amazing how easily a steadfast Whig could borrow straight Jacksonian rhetoric! First, the examiner's role should be merely *advisory.* After reviewing an application, he would inform the applicant if he had any doubts concerning its novelty. The applicant then could either take a patent or not. If he did so despite the examiner's objections, these would be appended to the patent. "This system appears to us to be the best ever proposed," Page declared, "and as promising as it is novel." He felt that if the examiner's objections were valid, an inventor would seldom take a patent. On the other hand, examiners would become very cautious about registering objections, for these would be open to "the trial of public opinion and the censorship of legal proceeding." In other words, "the *ingenuity* of Examiners would [no longer] be arrayed against the simplicity of inventors, the Examiner would be *tried* in every litigated case, and the verdicts of judge and jury would soon decide his fitness for office." [27]

So it was: Page had gone all the way over to an extreme radical position regarding Patent Office procedure. Having had much to do with shaping policy from inside the office, he also played a crucial role in reshaping it from outside. His plan for making the examiner's role merely advisory, virtually tanta-

151

mount to returning to a straight-out registry, was of course never officially effected. Yet, in a *de facto* sense it very nearly came to fulfillment. There is no inordinate exaggeration in suggesting that by the late 1850s the examiners "seem to have granted about everything that was applied for, without giving themselves the trouble to look up and ascertain whether the thing applied for was new and useful, or whether it had been patented previously or not." [28]

These were obviously the words of someone less than overjoyed by this turn of events. Yet, it needs be noted that liberalization was not something that had been pushed *only* by patent agents and other personally interested parties. Ultimately, politicians and bureaucrats perceived that, after all, more patents meant more federal income. Besides, proponents could be found even among the relatively disinterested. For example, the English engineer and industrialist Joseph Whitworth had wondered "whether too much is not attempted by the examiners in undertaking to decide the important questions of novelty and utility." He suggested that preliminary examination might "be limited to warning an applicant of what has been done or known before, and referring him to authentic sources of information, but allowing him upon such warning to take out letters patent at his own risk." Whitworth's estimate of how this would work out so much resembled Page's that it is fair to assume one man had influenced the other: "In such a case the patent might safely be left to find its proper position and value when brought before the public, and there would be ample opportunity of testing its validity and utility both by public opinion and, if requisite, ultimately in a court of law." [29]

That it should become very much easier to obtain patents was literally intoxicating to inventors—the rank and file, anyway—and certainly to every agent. However, there was one unfortunate concomitant insofar as the examining corps was concerned. A drastic reorientation in its philosophy was required, and it so happened that those examiners least amenable to this were the "scientific men" with whom Page had once enjoyed such a close rapport. "Illiberal" examiners fell under relentless attack by the patent lobby. Not immediately, however, did it get a kindred spirit in the commissioner's office. When that finally happened, though, examiners of the "old school" found themselves without jobs. Most of them made an attempt to earn a

152

livelihood as agents themselves, but rarely was their heart in it like Page's was, and only a few had much success.

As for Page, he stayed in business until 1861, although Fleischmann had gone off on his own within a year, and Greenough not long after. He and Page kept the *Polytechnic Journal* going for a total of two years, but the amount of original material fell off to almost nothing and they folded at the end of 1854. Page the reformer no longer had his own forum, but perhaps felt he no longer needed one, having had his say. The final issues were devoted almost exclusively to publishing patent specifications with engraved illustrations, and that became a superfluous undertaking after the office began buying their plates for the commissioner's report. This was a solid accomplishment about which Page and Greenough were justly proud.

Despite the controversial preachments that emanated from the office of the *Polytechnic Journal,* its two years were relatively quiet ones across Seventh Street at the Patent Office. Significant changes did occur, however, one being the new illustrated annual reports. This was an innovation attributable to Charles Mason, the appointee of President Franklin Pierce. Mason was certainly the most versatile and urbane of all the antebellum patent commissioners. He had graduated from West Point in 1829 at the top of his class, a step above Robert E. Lee. He served two years with the Corps of Engineers, resigned to study law, passed the bar and practiced from 1832 to 1836, ran the New York *Evening Post,* then went to Iowa where he became a railroad entrepreneur as well as serving in numerous official capacities including Chief Justice of the Supreme Court. No previous commissioner could boast of such broad experience as Mason had when he took office on March 24, 1853.[30]

Mason quickly ascertained that the bounds of his authority might be stretched considerably. One of his first official acts was to convert six of eight clerkships recently authorized by Congress into slots for a new class of employee, "second assistant examiner," a sort of apprentice. Subsequently he became highly adroit at wringing funds out of Congress for augmenting his staff. Before the end of his first year he had 30 full-time employees; by 1855 he had managed to double the number of principal examiners; and by 1856 he had fully 36 staffers at the level of assistant examiner or above (recall that two decades previously there had been exactly *one* examiner), plus at least that number of other employees. He was especially effective at exploiting a loophole in the law of 1836 which authorized the commissioner to employ an unlimited number of "temporary clerks." Another of his innovations was to hire several women, one of whom was Clara Barton, to copy patents and handle official records.

Old points of contention such as the Department of Interior's appropriation of space had by no means just disappeared. Still, Mason's first two years were a period of comparative calm during which he was able to accomplish a great deal in the way of catching up and rationalizing procedure. He inspired reverence for having extricated the Patent Office from the effects of

> years of ignorant and imbecile management, occasioned by the appointment of officers wholly unfit for their stations, not only in the executive but in other branches of the establishment, [who] had heaped up a mass of rubbish in the shape of abuses, errors, absurd rules, complaints, unfinished business, and the like, that had nearly crushed out the vitality of our patent system.[31]

The New York *Tribune* called Mason "undoubtedly the best, the ablest, and the most successful man that ever stood at the head of this highly important department, and probably the most efficient officer the present government has had to boast of."[32]

But Mason kept his admirers continually on edge as a result of recurrent rumors that he was on the verge of resigning. In July 1855 he actually did and went off to tend his affairs in Iowa. His post was left vacant, though, because of other rumors that he intended to return in the fall when Congress reconvened. He did, but during his four-month absence Secretary of the Interior Robert McClelland dismissed the temporary clerks and undermined many of his accomplishments. While McClelland had never been known as a friend of the Patent Office, it is not entirely clear why Mason should have escaped criticism for abandoning his post, thereby permitting McClelland to commit his "outrages."[33] As he prepared to return, Mason expressed regret that the secretary had "given umbrage to the class of inventors and their organs," although his major concern seems to have been that McClelland felt "rather sore in consequence of some strictures on his course contained in the Scientific American."[34] Nevertheless, Mason immediately attended to reinstating the temporary clerks. Clara Barton remained on the payroll until dismissed in May 1857. An ardent Frémonter might survive in such a position during the Pierce Administration, but hardly under James Buchanan.

Commissioner Mason lasted only a little longer than Miss Barton. When the Patent Office was part of the State Department, Webster and the other secretaries had limited themselves to reviewing personnel nominations. Still, the Secretary of the Interior was perfectly within his rights to oversee its day-to-day affairs, and, upon finding it impossible to get along with Buchanan's appointee, Mason resigned. His had been an interesting term. While he definitely favored loosening up examinations, his years were not marked by any sustained increase in the ratio of patents to applications. It did rise sharply between 1853 and 1854, from 32 percent to almost 53 percent. In 1855 and 1856, however, it slipped below half. Not until after 1857 did the ratio show a truly dramatic jump, topping two-thirds in 1859. The *sine qua non* for this degree of liberalization was the appointment of a commissioner willing and able to demand absolute compliance from the examiners, or else. Mason often reversed his examiners, but he did nothing about removing any of the "old school."

The fact was, he had a great deal of respect for his "scientific men" and even hired more of them. As of 1856, his last full year as commissioner, the 12 principal examiners included Gale, Lane, Schaeffer, Peale, Foreman, and Everett. There was also Alfred Herbert, a talented engineer, and William Chauncy Langdon, formerly a professor of astronomy at Shelby College in Kentucky. Most of the examiners had been promoted from assistantships, and the assistants' ranks were loaded with talent too: there was Thomas Antisell, who had begun his distinguished career with a Continental education under Dumas, Biot, Pelouze, and Berzelius; William B. Taylor, a man "widely informed on all the deeper topics of general science;" Samuel Coues, whose son became America's preeminent ornithologist; and Daniel Breed, a former student of Eben Horsford's and translator of Heinrich Will's *Outlines of Chemical Analysis*. The Patent Office still employed a number of men who took pride in their scientific erudition, and who presumed that their capacity for drawing fine distinctions constituted a prime tool of their trade. Within two years, most were gone.

Mason's successor believed simply that the Patent Office must not discourage inventors by confronting them with "subtle distinctions." Its right and proper role, instead, was in "kindly taking them by the hand, as the benefactors of their race, and

155

strewing, if possible, their pathway with sunshine and with flowers."[35] The man who penned these words, part of the same passage quoted at the head of this chapter, was Joseph Holt of Kentucky, named commissioner by President Buchanan in August 1857. Although Holt had practiced law for many years, this was his first public appointment. It was a memorable one. Very soon it became apparent he was not going to countenance any "hairsplitting niggardly system of examination," and rumors began to fly that he contemplated a purge of illiberal examiners. *Scientific American* immediately suggested one who merited top priority, Schaeffer. While Schaeffer's *"educational* competency" was beyond question, he was not *"adapted,* in every sense of the word" to perform his duties properly. As public servants, examiners were "bound to show a liberal discrimination in their official acts." Schaeffer did not and was therefore not fit to fill the post he occupied.[36]

For the patent lobby, Holt's appointment was a dream come true. By now *Scientific American* believed it "folly to suppose that *too many* patents can be granted."[37] Among the examiners, only those it characterized as "old fogies" still held contrary notions, and Holt soon began to dispose of them. Of the 12 principal examiners in the office when Holt took over, five had been removed by early 1858. Even those directly affected thought the motivation was political and the impetus came primarily from Jacob Thompson of Mississippi, the new Secretary of the Interior (whom *Scientific American* actually liked!).

The first to be fired was Lane. In a letter to Ari Davis, he outlined his impression of what had happened:

> Myself together with Drs. Gale and several other Examiners, have been dismissed by order of Secretary Thompson of Mississippi. Of this you may have heard. When Thompson came into office he undertook to take the Patent Office into his special keeping. Commissioner Mason however resisted the attempted encroachment and refused to make removals or to be dictated to in other things which the law places in the Commissioner's hands. The contest between the Commissioner and Secretary continued till August when the Commissioner . . . resigned his office. After a time Mr. Holt of Kentucky was appointed for the new Commissioner and he has shown himself the willing tool of the Secretary. On the 1st of October [1857] Dr. Gale and myself and a number of others in lower places were removed. A short time before, all

156

the *colored laborers* but two or three had been dismissed. Not long after Dr. Gale and myself, Capt. Herbert followed. During the winter Dr. Everett, and in March [1858] even Prof. Schaeffer, by all odds the most learned and able man of all the Examiners, was dismissed, though with a numerous family on his hands and no other means then present of supporting them. The pretext in this case was retrenchment of expenses, no successor being *then* appointed, but the absurd selection of such a person as the one to be dropped gives the lie to that plea. In fact, a recently appointed assistant Examiner represented to be utterly unqualified, has since been promoted to the place of Principal Examiner.[38]

Lane, who admitted to being a "Black Republican," obviously believed the purge was partisan. Journalists and historians who have noted this episode have generally concluded likewise.[39] There is, however, something more to the story. Lane and Schaeffer were not open partisans, but they *had* become prime villains to the patent lobby. It is true that inventors' journals were not quite unanimous in approving Holt's purge. When Everett showed an inclination to accept a professorship in Ohio on account of intimations of his impending removal, a periodical called *The Inventor* protested that he was "almost a *necessity*" in the office because he commanded such a "thorough knowledge of patent law, intimate acquaintance with the details of his department, and a memory that we have never equaled."[40] Even *Scientific American* respected Everett, yet there is very strong presumptive evidence that Holt's removals resulted largely from pressure by Munn and Co. and other patent agencies.

There is a suggestive comparison in the number of patents approved by various examiners. During a four-month period in 1857, two of them, Foreman and James Henry, passed more than 100 apiece. Holt kept them. Gale and Herbert approved considerably fewer, around 70. Everett approved only 46, Lane 29, and Schaeffer all of ten—in four months! Naturally, certain classes attracted more applications than others, so some disparity would be inevitable. Yet, it so happened that Schaeffer had charge of the class comprehending all land conveyances, a field being assiduously cultivated. *Scientific American* declared it had recently been advising would-be patentees of railroad improvements not even to bother applying until Schaeffer was ousted.

This is not to say that Holt's removals did not embody an element of traditional spoilsmanship. Nearly all the new appoin-

157

tees were Southerners. (Schaeffer's successor, Rufus R. Rhodes, later headed the Confederate Patent Office in Richmond.) Still, it needs be emphasized that the motivation was not *purely* political. After Holt's arrival a new spirit pervaded the Patent Office: between 1857, 1858, and 1859, the number of patents increased from 2,910 to 3,710 to 4,538. But more significant was the *proportion* of applications approved: 67 percent in 1859, as against 47 percent in 1856, and 31 percent in 1853. And this was because it was clearly understood that examinations were *not* to be conducted with an eye to physical analogies. *Scientific American* saw the golden age at hand. When Holt's first annual report appeared, it was literally beside itself in praise of "this admirable document—so frank, so manly, and so outspoken in support of the high claims of inventors." He was encouraged to go forward with his purge of the "refractory element;" "two heads" then remained to be "lopped off" (Everett's and Schaeffer's) and soon they were.[41]

Having apparently set everything right with the Patent Office, Holt resigned in March 1859 to become Postmaster General.[42] His successor was a young ex-Congressman from Connecticut named William D. Bishop. Bishop started out under a considerable disability, being admonished that filling the place "of so gifted a man as Mr. Holt is no easy task," and he never impressed anyone very much. Neither did Philip F. Thomas, who came next. In October 1860, Thomas appointed a "Censor" charged with ferreting out errors in the examiners' decisions. Holt had created a permanent Board of Appeals to review *rejected* applications. But the review of *approved* applications was something else, especially since Thomas gave the post to William B. Taylor, a man who moved freely among Washington's scientific elite, but was scarcely the most popular examiner among patrons of the office.

Thomas subsequently modified his initial plan by setting up a Revising Board comprised of Taylor and Peale. A *Scientific American* correspondent who signed himself "Liberal" wrote that these two had both "been educated in the illiberal old school practice of the Office, which prevailed as far back as 1850, '51 and '52, when terror to the inventor reigned triumphant." "Liberal" feared they would "unwittingly return to their early proclivities."[43] Fact was, Taylor had been hired by Mason in 1854. Small mistakes aside, Munn and Co. likewise feared that a "retrograde movement" was in the offing. Thomas showed no particular devotion to "that essentially American policy which welcomes the inventor, and kindly and anxiously sifts from his invention its minutest patentable details." Besides, "some of the older examiners" now appeared to be trying to reverse the policies "so eloquently enforced by Commissioner Holt." [44] During late 1860 the ratio of successful applications slipped noticeably, while a fretful debate over the Revising Board continued. Soon, however, all else became overshadowed by the specter of disunion.

Ultimately, for all the fear that the office was headed back towards the Dark Ages, Thomas's policies had little effect. Lincoln's commissioner, David P. Holloway, immediately abolished the Revising Board, thereby depriving Taylor and Peale of the opportunity to spread their allegedly "antiquated views," and the ratio of patents to applications returned to about two-thirds. It stayed there for the duration of the Civil War.

As for Page, while he had been a patent agent throughout the regimes of Mason, Holt, Bishop, and Thomas, their policy changes do not seem to have affected him much personally. His most prosperous years, 1853, 1854, and 1855, roughly coincided with Mason's tenure. His best was 1854, when he handled more than 50 successful applications. He had several clients on whom he could rely for a certain amount of business every year, as well as a few rather illustrious ones—Professor Horsford, for one, and Walter Hunt, inventor of the safety pin. Page also handled a sewing machine for Theodore Weed, various machine-tool attachments for Thomson Newbury, paper folding apparatus for John North, all manner of mechanical devices for Birdsill Holly, and hydraulic paraphernalia for Lysander Button and Robert Blake, who dominated the American fire engine business for many years. He acted as counselor to a number of old friends, including Ari Davis, whose profitable inventions included woodworking machinery and a popular electrotherapeutic device. (Page endorsed this gadget publicly, something the professionalizers no doubt regarded as on a par with Professor Horsford's turning a commercial profit from what he learned at Giessen.)

Yet, ironically, Page himself did not profit much from the triumph of liberalization. In 1856 he had a very bad year, and during the next three the number of patents he negotiated annually remained static at about two dozen. Even when he failed to get an application passed he still kept his fee; it was generally considered unethical to make any of the fee contingent, since this tended to foster undue constriction of claims. He also received fees

159

for patentability searches, and for other advisory services not necessarily resulting directly in letters patent. His client Hunt, for example, was a major party to the complex of sewing machine suits involving Elias Howe and Isaac Singer. Nevertheless, on a month-to-month basis, it seems unlikely that Page's income matched what the Patent Office had been paying him when he quit.

Beyond doubt, Page knew his business. But during the 1850s the business of patent soliciting became extremely competitive. By 1860 there were nearly three-dozen agencies in Washington alone, and at least twice that many throughout the rest of the country. The standard fee for securing a patent ranged from $25 to $50; the better agents could command the higher figure, and Page usually got something close to it. But many of his rivals were quite capable men, including Fitzgerald, Everett, Gale, Breed, Cooper, Renwick, Schaeffer, and others who knew the Patent Office from the inside too. Charles Mason became chief legal consultant to Munn and Co., which handled over a quarter of all successful patent applications, more than the next 15 firms combined. The only other agents with even a two or three percent share of the market were one in Philadelphia, Henry Howson; two in Boston, Cooper and Richard Eddy; and three in the capital, C. M. Alexander, A. B. Stoughton, and Anthony Pollok.

During early 1861, despite Page's desperate effort to show that there was actually no better time than the present to apply for a patent,[45] his volume of business would not have been sufficient to support a household as large as his—Priscilla, three sons, two daughters, his parents, his brother, and Priscilla's mother. He did have a few patents of his own which may have yielded him some income, including an acoustic hearing-aid, door bolts, an ice-box, and a pipe coupling. The latter, apparently a by-product of his association with Button and Blake, probably paid him some dividends. On the other hand, for some reason he also patented a "combined umbrella and head rest" (see plates), a classic piece of "patent nonsense."[46] His refrigerator patent dated from April 2, 1861, exactly 30 days after Lincoln's inauguration and ten before the attack on Fort Sumter.

The Lincoln Administration turned the Patent Office literally topsy-turvy. Since the President had been a patentee himself, there was hope that he would not put the office to partisan ends. As it turned out, though, Holloway wielded the sword of patronage far more ruthlessly than any of his predecessors ever had, and

160

within three months no less than eight of the twelve examiners were gone. A ninth went in 1862 and a tenth in 1863. Yet, if Lincoln's inauguration proved a personal disaster for most of the incumbent examiners, it was a blessing for Page: amidst an enormous hoard of office seekers who descended upon Washington in 1861, he could still mobilize a sufficient amount of political influence to get himself reappointed. Thus, after nine years on the other side of the counter, Page had ended up right back where he began. While he was extremely fortunate to have managed this, by and large his last few years were to be a period of adversity and finally tragedy. The ultimate wish of his brother Jery—"may you have a long and happy life, and may the promising appearance of your early younger years never be blasted by any of the storms of this frail life"—was a wish that in the end went unfulfilled.

Chapter Nine
An Outrage on the Public

> ...Ruhmkorff was not the originator of any invention, discovery, principle, or improvement connected with the induction coil bearing his name. ...
>
> *Charles Grafton Page, 1867*

> ... in view of the fact that a foreigner now unjustly reaps a reward that belongs to Dr. Page, it would seem but just to allow him to apply for a patent without regard to the intervening time, and your committee recommends the passage of an act for that purpose.
>
> *Leonard Myers (R-Pa), 1867*

> The passage of such a law shows how careless and stupid our legislators at Washington have become since the small amount of brains they possess has been muddled up by the impeachment. ...
>
> *New York Herald, 1868*

> ... the patent is an outrage on the public. ...
>
> *The Telegrapher, 1868*

> Page had nothing to do with the invention of the Ruhmkorff coil. ...
>
> *Jerome Kidder, 1876*

The Patent Office to which Page returned in May 1861 was very different from the place he first had known nearly 20 years before. There was the pervasive partisanship and throughout the summer hardly a week passed without one employee or another being handed his walking papers. Men the patent lobby liked, as well as men it did not—dismissals stemmed from pure, unalloyed political motives. While the Republicans had good reason to fear disloyalty in the civil service, Lincoln's mass purges were terribly disruptive. Only a few of the old examiners were regarded as fully trustworthy. Peale and Taylor both stayed on. Thomas Antisell was promoted, but soon left to enlist as an army surgeon. His place was filled by Benjamin S. Hedrick, whose comradeship Page must have appreciated, for he too, like Antisell, was a distinguished chemist—a Republican chemist, naturally. In 1856, Hedrick had been forced to flee North Carolina, where he was a professor, on account of his support for John C. Frémont. At the

Patent Office in 1861, on the other hand, being a *Democrat* was definitely fatal. Holloway, the commissioner throughout the war, had been one of the first men ever elected to Congress as a Republican, and once had introduced legislation to establish a department of agriculture. Previously he had been a printer, and then a newspaper editor in Indiana. Aside from that, there was not much else to be said about his background except that he was more than equal to the task of turning the Patent Office "into a guillotine to behead faithful men for mere differences of opinion." [1]

The war upset the office even more seriously than the administration did. Incoming applications, 7,653 in 1860, fell 3,000 during the first year. Since the office was required to be self-supporting, many of the employees Holloway dismissed were simply not replaced. Even though the law authorized 16 examiners, he left more than half these positions vacant. In another austerity measure, he demoted the examiners and paid them the salary for assistants. Yet, after the initial downturn, the number of applications began to pick up, and quite rapidly. In 1864 the total came within 800 of the pre-war high, and surpassed it by 3,000 in 1865. Many of the staff positions remained open, however, so that each examiner had to contend with a work-load about three times greater than during the 1850s. Careful examinations were out of the question. For merely fortuitous reasons, if no other, a liberal policy prevailed until the end of the war.

This was not the happiest of times for Page. For one thing, the Patent Office was partly converted into an army hospital, so that the horrors of the war were literally right outside his door. Business did go on, but Page could not get enthusiastic about many of the inventions he saw: fully a third were churns and washers (the two devices were often identical in form), a quarter were woodworking machines, and only a fifth were philosophical or electrical apparatus. He passed almost everything assigned him, usually without even going through the motions of requiring the rewording of claims. Congress finally authorized a supplementary appropriation, and the number of examiners was increased to 12. Even so they remained far too busy to make critical examinations. Action on their pay was continually put off, and Page was hard pressed to provide for nearly a dozen dependents on a monthly income of $150. In 1862 he wrote Lane:

> ... I thank you for your interest in my appointment and I wish I could have influence enough to bring you back here to

163

your old place. We have been getting short pay for eight months past and it goes hard with me. $1800 is the Examiners pay and $1400 asst's pay. It is an illegal proceeding but we must make the best of it, and I doubt if we ever get the back pay allowed us, though it is promised. My family (lately increased by one little girl) is well and I am trying hard to sell my place and move to the city. . . .[2]

Page was mistaken in fearing he would never get the money owed him, for in May 1863 Congress authorized Holloway to make it up retroactively. On the other hand, he could not sell his home right away, and the upshot was a personal disaster. After the outbreak of war, the entire neighborhood of Grafton Cottage was turned into a staging area for Union troops. Confederate sympathy was rife among the local residents, and in early 1863 a mob of soldiers broke into an outbuilding containing Page's laboratory and destroyed everything. Lane was outraged at the barbarity of this act, which seemed much the more senseless since Page "was as good a friend as our government ever had." In her autobiography, Priscilla Page only mentioned that they left Grafton Cottage after it "became undesirable on account of its proximity to camps and hospitals."[3] Either she found the details too painful to recount, or, more likely, she simply did not comprehend how catastrophic this must have been to her husband. Indeed, in his last years Page's relationship with his wife seems to have lacked much warmth. She apparently never adjusted happily to the routine drudgery of homemaking; after his death she immediately plunged back into the social whirl she so loved before her marriage. She neither made any effort to understand his work, nor does she seem even to have known what his strongest urges were. He drifts into her book, then out 30 pages later, as a sort of odd interlude separating two vivid epochs of parties, travel, and gaiety. She and Charles evidently had a life that was magic only briefly, then no more than stable and superficial afterward.

Lane was one of Page's few comrades from the past whom he could still address as "truly your friend." Greenough and Henry Oliver were others, but he rarely saw either of them. He remained close to his two brothers-in-law, Harvey Lindsly and Peter Parker, but figuratively distant from the Washington scientific community. Although Parker was an active member of a social group calling itself the Scientific Club—as were Henry and Bache, Lane, Schaeffer, Taylor, and Peale—Page apparently did not participate. Daniel Webster, Choate, Benton, and other political luminaries with whom he had once hobnobbed were dead. So was his best partisan overseas, William Sturgeon. So was Alfred Vail. As for Morse, he and Page had had an especially bitter falling out.

The patent commissioner was legally empowered to extend the life of a patent from 14 years to 21 if, in his judgement, the patentee's remuneration was substantially less than it ought to have been, considering the "time, ingenuity, and expense" he had bestowed on his invention. Of all the very subjective decisions the office was called on to make, this was one of the most troublesome. Such petitions came in almost every day, however, and in 1860 Morse applied for an extension on his second patent, the one dating from 1846. His senior counsel was Charles Mason, his star witness Leonard Gale. His principal opponents included Henry O'Reilly, an old foe from previous litigation, and—to the surprise of most who knew them—Page. The patent Morse was attempting to keep in force covered the miniaturized form of receiving magnet Page had helped develop. For this Morse had paid, and in return Page had eschewed any credit, writing to Amos Kendall in 1848, "I will state briefly that I have never claimed that invention publicly or privately, directly or indirectly." [4]

Nevertheless, in March 1860 a printed flyer began to turn up around Washington titled, "Invention of the Magnetic Telegraph," with Page's name at the bottom. In essence, it charged that Morse had greatly exaggerated his due share of the credit for the telegraph, that much of it actually belonged to others, including Charles Wheatstone, Henry, and Page himself. Regarding his own contribution Page wrote,

> The first step towards the introduction of a wire for the receiving magnet *smaller* than the circuit wires in the Morse telegraph was made by myself while Prof. Morse was in Europe. I substituted for the cumbrous Morse magnet a small receiving magnet which occupied about *half a cubic foot* space. I was not [then] aware of what Prof. Wheatstone had done in Europe.

Page went on to state that, by denying the key significance of the "Wheatstone receiving magnet," Morse was guilty of "the most extraordinary fatuity that has ever come under my observation." [5]

Strong words—yet Morse and his associates should not have been too surprised, for as early as 1847 Page had emphasized that

165

Henry's basic discoveries were crucial to the practicality of Morse's telegraph. As for "Page's Manifesto" of 1860, it came to the attention of Morse's chief lobbyist in Washington, Amos Kendall, on April 1. The next day he posted the following letter to Page:

Prof. Chas. G. Page
    Dear Sir,
    I received yesterday a printed slip under a blank envelope through the Post Office with your name appended to it, the object of which appears to be to disparage Prof. Morse and his claims as Inventor of the Electro-Magnetic Telegraph now in general use.
    The object of this note is to ask whether this slip be your production, and if so, for what purpose is it printed and circulated at the moment when Prof. Morse is applying for an extension of his second patent?
    I make this inquiry as a friend of Professor Morse and of truth, and in view of the probable necessity of some commentary upon your statement.

Yours very respectfully

Amos Kendall[6]

Page received this on the 3rd, and the next day replied thus:

Hon Amos Kendall.
    Dear Sir,
    It is hardly necessary for me to reply to your letter of the 2 except for the sake of courtesy.
    I have not published the letter [i.e., the printed flyer] but hope at some future time to lay the subject more fully before the proper tribunal and shall be very glad to see it discussed with a view only of eliciting the truth and for this purpose alone.
    I rejoice at Morse's success with his patent of 1840 but there is no merit in this Patent of 1846 and whether extended or not credit must and will be given where credit is due. The facts have not all transpired, but I think enough to show conclusively that the Invention claimed under the Patent of 1846 is not Morse's and further that he is entitled to no credit whatever in this connection.

Yrs respectfully

Chas G. Page[7]

Kendall answered this at once, with considerably less courtesy:

Chas. G. Page, Esq.
Sir. I received this morning your letter of yesterday.

You do not respond to the inquiry contained in my letter of the 2nd inst. but adopt the printed slip therein referred to and substantially reiterate its contents. And by the statement of the Commissioner of Patents this day, it appears that a copy of the slip was sent to him, while Mr. O'Reilly denied that you had been employed in any way by him.

Now Sir, this gratuitous interference on your part, apparently without motive, is in itself very extraordinary, but it becomes astounding when it is remembered that once certainly if not twice, the claims of Prof. Morse in his Patent of 1846 have been passed upon by you as a sworn Examiner in the Patent Office, and that your testimony affirming them is spread upon the Records of the Court of Justice.

Yet, you may now say that "the invention claimed under the Patent of 1846 is not Morse's and further that he is entitled to no credit whatever in this connection"!

I can only put a copy of this correspondence into the hands of Prof. Morse and until shown how your course in this matter is consistent with honor and integrity sign myself yours with due respect

Amos Kendall[8]

The exchange concluded with Page's reply dated April 7:

Hon Amos Kendall
Dear Sir. In reply to your note of yesterday I have briefly to say that I was not employed by Henry O'Reilly and I say it only in justice to that gentleman.

Please examine carefully my testimony in the French vs. Rogers trial where the Morse party had the indelicacy to call me. . . . Whatever doubts I may have entertained at that time, were long since dispelled by the firm conviction that Morse is entitled to no claim or credit whatsoever in connection with the receiving magnet or the use of main and local circuits, and if the Commissioner of Patents should fail to see this from the evidence before him, the world will ere long see it in unmistakable truth in imperishable type and I shall be most glad to offset the report of Examiner Page with my present opinions on this subject and to acquit myself as early as

167

possible from any part in the perpetuation of the monstrous error that Morse first invented the main and local circuits or the receiving and local magnets or that he is entitled to any credit whatever for appropriating in his telegraph the inventions of Wheatstone. In regard to my "motives," "my honor" and my "integrity" pardon me for saying that I shall endeavor to take good care of them in this matter.

Yrs. Respectfully

Chas. G. Page.[9]

Though Page clearly indicated that he had simply changed his mind since testifying on Morse's behalf a decade earlier, Kendall could not understand why he would attempt "to prove himself a perjured Examiner in the Patent Office without any apparent inducement."[10] As for Morse himself, he first became aware of Page's missive on April 3. He composed a very long letter to Page, whose tone was that of a man who felt deeply wronged:

Sir,

On my arrival on the 3d day of April (this month) to attend the hearing before the Commis. Patents in the case of my Petition for Extension of my Patent of 1846, Mr. Kendall showed me the extraordinary printed article dated March 26, 1860 with your name appended which you sent to him and headed "Invention of the Magnetic Telegraph." The gross misstatements of that article, to use the mildest terms, and its undisguised hostile tone, led me in the first moments of surprize to doubt its genuineness as coming from you. Subsequent events have dispelled this doubt. . . .

As a solution of your strange conduct it was suggested to me that [you] were perhaps [acting] as the legal counsel of my opponents. This indeed would explain the sudden change from friendship to opposition in your relations with me, an opposition which so long as it should be courteously and legally carried on in discharge of professional duty, could not and would not have been objected to by me. But this position would not explain the furtive mode of influencing the Judge in the cause, by sending him an exparte statement outside the legal testimony in the case, a mode which no one better than yourself knows to be both illegal and dishonorable, false in its details, and false in its conclusions.

168

But even this excuse for your sudden and unprovoked hostility toward me cannot be made. You were not even the Counsel of my opponents; they declare before the Judge that you were not in their employ. You have volunteered your opposition unsolicited so far as I can discover by any one, and why? You were impelled to it, you say in your letter of 4 April to Mr. Kendall, by your regard for *truth* alone. Now sir I take issue with you on this ground in the whole and in all the parts of your article and call upon you to justify your assertions and statements. I confess to deep mortification the discovery that I had looked upon you as a personal friend, you were one whom I had always befriended, and with whom I had even been on terms of confidential intercourse, one to whom I had never by thought or word or act done any injury, and now without the slightest warning, you throw off the mark & stoop to the use of means to injure me so dishonorable, which no man of character can possibly approve. . . .

Morse went on to relate his own version of how the miniaturized receiving magnet was incorporated into his telegraph system. While he characterized Page's sketch as an "extraordinary tissue of misstatements," actually the two versions jibed on most points. Nevertheless, he concluded by declaring that if Page was not familiar with the story as he had presented it,

it is unpardonable ignorance in a man of your position and experience as an Examiner, and shows your unfitness as a critic. If you do know it and have deliberately stated what you know to be untrue to effect some purpose of your own I shall leave others to characterize your conduct as it deserves. I have done for the present with your article. When you next attack me, I trust for your own sake it will be in some more open and honorable manner than that you have at present chosen. The cause of *truth* which you have so ostentatiously and gratuitously volunteered to espouse, requires neither falsehood for its support nor the violation of law or honor nor the arts of the detractor for the dissemination of its triumphs.[11]

The upshot of it all was that Morse failed to get his extension, and naturally he held Page largely responsible. Now, the question is, why should Page deliberately have chosen to alienate this man who had been among his closest friends? Plausible explanations are manifold, ranging from a payoff by Morse's opponents, to a guileless wish that credit "be given where credit is due." By no means would it necessarily be naive to assume the latter. Page actually claimed very little personally. Yet, he certainly knew that he had not been irrelevant to Morse's success. He also knew that he could have patented some of the apparatus he had devised for Morse, had the law permitted it. Instead he had settled for a few paltry handouts. Finally, he was faced with the fact that Morse—a man of relatively meager scientific capabilities—had become rich and famous. In contrast, he himself was stuck in a humdrum occupation, and as an inventor had ended up patenting trivia. His one truly noteworthy innovation had proved totally unattractive commercially. Indeed, while his friend Greenough might try to link him with Davy, Watt, Hare—and Morse—among the "bright galaxy of successful inventors," Page must have perceived that so far as the public was concerned he was far less successful than Greenough himself, or than some of his clients from the 1850s such as Eben Horsford. And he was not even in the same league as Elias Howe or Isaac Singer, Samuel Colt or Oliver Winchester, Cyrus McCormick, Elisha Otis, George Corliss, or Richard Hoe. These men were all close to Page's age, born between 1809 and 1819. None was in any sense a "scientific man," yet each had begun to assume a popular stature commensurate to that of Fulton, Blanchard, Whitney, and our first generation of national hero-inventors.

As a scientific man rather than an inventor, Page's reputation was at best mixed, as it has been ever since. In the preface and first chapter I quoted people who thought he was of first rank in American science. But no informed contemporary would have ranked him with Foucault or Fizeau, Bunsen, Becquerel, Regnault, Jamin, Geissler, Mayer, Rankine, or Joule—all, again, men born in the second decade of the 19th century. True, no informed contemporary would have ranked *any* American physical scientist with these men. Yet, when Bache and Agassiz and a couple of others sat down in 1863 to pick the charter members of the National Academy of Sciences, Page likely received about as short shrift as Matthew Maury. While he was not a literal traitor like Maury, he was a traitor in "style and tone"—in much the same way as the manufacturer of "Rumford" baking powder, Professor Horsford. In any event, scientific attainments did not necessarily have anything at all to do with getting into the National Academy, and Page simply had not cultivated the right scientists as assiduously as he had cultivated politicians—that essentially was the main problem with his "style." The burning

170

of his lab the same year the National Academy was founded was thus an event heavy with symbolic as well as tangible significance.

Page's last years were not without their private joys—a new baby daughter, Lucy, for one. He received some modest public honors, and once-hostile periodicals, *Scientific American* especially, treated him with great respect. He occasionally published a short paper on something he found interesting. He must have been pleased when he and Joseph Henry were able to rekindle their friendship after 1866, to discuss such matters as lighting the Capitol dome electrically. But bad luck always hovered around, its presence epitomized in the destruction of his laboratory, followed by the destruction of the apparatus he had donated to the Smithsonian in 1852. Then, finally, one particular turn of events came to assume in Page's mind the proportions not only of an overwhelming misfortune, but also of an intolerable injustice.

It had its genesis in France long before, ten years before Page was born. In 1802, in the wake of a storied four-month visit by Alessandro Volta, Napoleon Bonaparte announced the inauguration of a 60,000-franc prize to be awarded "à celui qui, par ses experiénces et ses décourvertes, fera faire à l'électricité et au galvanisme un pas comparable à celui qu'ont fait faire a ces sciences Franklin et Volta. . . ." "Le Prix Volta" was presented to Page's boyhood idol Humphry Davy in 1806, and competition resumed. It was not to be awarded again for a very long time—the Volta Prize was one of the many Napoleonic novelties that the Restoration scrapped—but, half a century after Napoleon instituted the prize, his nephew, Napoleon III, revived it. Fifty thousand francs were to be given to whomever devised the most useful application of the voltaic pile within five years after 1852. In 1857 the committee charged with selecting the winner suggested that the deadline be put off. Finally, towards the end of 1864, acting on the recommendation of 13 judges headed by Jean-Baptiste-André Dumas and including Henri Regnault and J. C. Jamin, the Emperor awarded the second Volta Prize to Heinrich D. Ruhmkorff of Paris, for "l'invention de la bobine d'induction." [12]

While official awards and emoluments were commonplace in Second Empire France, the Volta Prize was singularly lavish—"la plus haute récompense national qu'on ait pu lui offrir." [13] Ruhmkorff, by all accounts an admirable individual, had been producing induction coils at his shop on the Rue de Champollion since 1851, and in France the cognomen "Ruhmkorff coil" had already become a generic term. Although this usage was common in Britain and America also, it was well understood there that the invention of the coil actually predated the unveiling of Ruhmkorff's first model by many years.

In 1853, when "Ruhmkorff's Apparatus for transforming Dynamical into Statical Electricity" was first publicized in the U.S., the editors of *Silliman's Journal* had pointed out that it resembled an invention of "Dr. Page, whose apparatus appears to be but little known in Europe." [14] And soon after news arrived of the disposition of the Volta Prize, Salem Howe Wales of *Scientific American* charged that since "the so called Ruhmkorff coil was the invention of Prof. Page," the award "must have been made in entire ignorance" of this fact, "an oversight of American achievements by European savans already too common." [15]

Yet, even American savants had tended to forget Page's achievements—to forget that here was a man whom Henry had first addressed as his "fellow labourer . . . in the cause of American science;" who had done for the electric motor precisely what Henry did for the electromagnet, and who was the only other American besides Henry to pursue a lengthy series of experiments in inductive phenomena; who had devised experimental instruments of unmatched variety and ingenuity, and had published dozens of papers here and abroad; whose discoveries had attracted favorable notice from Joule, David Brewster, Auguste De la Rive, and Faraday himself; who had dealt with American potentates such as Hare and Bache as a complete equal, and who had inspired younger men like O. W. Gibbs and Lane; and about whom William Sturgeon had written at mid-century: "I know of no philosopher more capable of close reasoning on electromagnetic and magnetic electrical physics than Professor Page."

More than anything, Page had decided, he wanted to be remembered for his career of science. Yet it now seemed that the esteem he had built up in the 1830s and 40s was no less ephemeral than the experiment diaries of three decades snuffed out by the vandals who burned his laboratory. One of the vagaries of history, as he well knew, was that men are often judged on their last deeds rather than their best. Tangible and widespread evidence of Page's scientific career did still exist, however, in his publications, of course, and especially in the form of apparatus he had designed, much of which was yet being manufactured by commercial instrument makers. Most noteworthy were the induction coils whose prototype was his Compound Magnet and Electrotome. These had been the means by which a whole generation of American students had observed the effects of high-tension current. In recent years, with the improved apparatus devised by William Crookes and Heinrich Geissler for exhibiting electrical discharge *in vacuo,* the induction coil had become a tremendously exciting tool of basic research in physics. But, now, Ruhmkorff had been given official credit for inventing it by the Emperor of the French, and handed $10,000 to boot.

Notices of the Volta Prize generally pointed out that Ruhmkorff's coil derived from "previous discoveries and inventions," even when they did not mention Page by name.[16] But modest acquiescence in credit by indirection was a luxury Page did not feel he could afford if he were going to establish a secure pinion for his scientific reputation. An old hand at cultivating political favor, he knew that one way to rally support for his cause would be to make it a question not of personal pride but of national honor, to mobilize indignation at "an oversight of American achievements by European savans already too common." (Recall also that French adventures in Mexico during the Civil War had badly strained diplomatic relations with the U.S.) This was an effective procedure, yet ultimately most telling was the fact that Page did not take his case to the scientific community, but rather to a popular tribunal.

The vehicle of redress Page sought was one quite familiar to him—a memorial to Congress. Even here he had alternatives: he might simply have tried to obtain an official expression of commendation, or, as was later suggested, asked for "a liberal sum in compensation for the benefits which the nation has derived from his inventions."[17] But what he went after was a special legislative act authorizing him to obtain a *patent* for his induction apparatus. This was extraordinary for two reasons. The coil had been in public use for almost *thirty* years, and, if that were not enough, the law of 1836 quite unequivocally forbade any employee of the Patent Office to take "any right or interest, directly or indirectly, in any patent." Twice previously he had tried for a patent—in 1845 when he sought a special act waiving this proscription, and again in 1854 when he was refused on the grounds that everybody assumed he had dedicated his invention to the public.

Now, however, he regarded the circumstances in which he found himself as without precedent. Still, he did not act precipitously, waiting until 1867 to present his memorial. After stating his grounds for priority, he declared that he had been "robbed of the honor which justly belonged to him," and concluded by praying that Congress would, "as an offset to this foreign appropriation of his rights and in justice to an American inventor, empower him to apply for and take and hold a patent for this his said invention, notwithstanding said imperial award and the aforesaid previous public use. . . ." [18]

Page's memorial was referred to the House Committee on Patents, which heard testimony and issued a seven-page report in March 1867. Therein were some dubious assertions, one being that if Page's claim had been before the French judges "the prize would not have been awarded to Ruhmkorff," another, that Ruhmkorff had imitated the construction of a Page coil. [19] In fact, it is unlikely that he had ever seen a Page coil. He apparently commenced his experiments with high-tension induction totally ignorant of what had already been accomplished by Page, or by Henry, or by Sturgeon in England, Nicholas Callan in Ireland, or anybody else outside France. Indeed, French physicists seem to have been under the unanimous misapprehension that the first experiments with induction coils took place in their country in 1842. [20]

The committee report was quite correct, however, in stating that, aside from an improved mode of winding the secondary and the embodiment of a condenser, there was no essential difference between Ruhmkorff's coils and Page's. A number of authorities attested to this. The roll was noticeably shy on names of men primarily regarded as scientists, only Dr. Charles T. Jackson being of considerable repute. This was the same Jackson whom Page had once rebuked for impugning the "dignity of patents." But Jackson had reason to sympathize with Page now, since it had turned out that his penchant for quarreling publicly over scientific matters had put him in disfavor with the professionalizers also.

Henry, who might have borne strong witness on Page's behalf, refused to be drawn into the affair. Later, George Beardslee, an electrician and inventor who had known Henry since Albany, sent him two very long letters detailing Page's scientific attainments and asking him to state his "views and conclusions." [21] He did not respond. Still, Page's claims were corroborated by testimony from a number of highly reputable inventors and instrument makers. The consensus was summed up by

174

Thomas Hall, who stated that Page's apparatus was "one and the same thing in general form, construction, work, and principle" as Ruhmkorff's, and by Moses Farmer, who added that the difference was "in size only." And, for all the accompanying chauvinistic blather about "a foreigner now unjustly reap[ing] a reward that belongs to Dr. Page," this was a compelling point.[22]

But the Committee on Patents was not subsequently reconvened to report Page's bill out, and so the 39th Congress adjourned without taking action on his behalf. Page was impatient. In mid-1867 he commenced what he conceived as the most powerful possible statement of his position. It also turned out to be his *magnum opus,* a remarkable book titled *History of Induction: The American Claim to the Induction Coil and its Electrostatic Developments.* The book was remarkable because it was the most thorough and knowledgeable treatise yet published on the subject of induction apparatus, and at the same time a shameless case of special pleading: it was written in the third person, and Page's name appeared, on an average, twice on every page. His fundamental contention is quoted at the beginning of this chapter.[23] His own 1838 coil, he wrote, with its divided core, its 3,000-foot secondary circuit, and its automatic, variable-speed interrupter, was a better piece of apparatus than Ruhmkorff's 1851 model. True, it lacked a condenser, but it did embody a novel and effective means of arresting sparks at the break point—Page's invention, not Foucault's, as some believed. Besides, Ruhmkorff's coils had no condensers either until 1853, and that invention was not his but Armand Fizeau's. Finally, Page charged, Ruhmkorff was unable to produce anything nearly as powerful as his own later coils until 1859, when he obtained one built in Boston by Edward S. Ritchie, dissected it, and copied Ritchie's mode of winding the secondary in a series of conical segments.[24]

Page characterized the award made to Ruhmkorff as a blanket insult to the American people, no less than a personal insult to himself and to Ritchie. Evidently, many of the most eminent French scientists neither knew nor cared anything about American science; but, perhaps even worse, in certain instances this myopia seemed deliberate. At least one member of the commission that recommended Ruhmkorff for the Volta Prize, Jamin of L'École Polytechnique, as well as the leading French authority on the history of electrical science, Théodose Du Moncel, *did* know about the connection between Ruhmkorff's imitation of Ritchie's design and the commencement of "his *new*

175

era in coils." By keeping silent, Page charged, these men had "yielded to national prejudice in this matter." [25] He was especially perturbed with Du Moncel, as his marginal annotations in the Patent Office copy of Du Moncel's book on Ruhmkorff's coil eloquently attest.

In February 1868 Page's legislation finally came before the House, with Leonard Myers of Pennsylvania, chairman of the Committee on Patents, carrying the debate. He concentrated on two points: that the purpose of the bill was "to protect the rights of an American inventor against the claims to originality unjustly and mistakenly awarded to a foreigner by the high authority of a foreign power," and that Page was now "in his old age, feeble and in bad health." Though only 56, Page was indeed seriously ill. "Let him," Myers declared, "in declining years, receive the national award which his discovery deserves at our hands, and [let] what has been known as the Ruhmkorff coil become, as it should, the 'Page induction coil.' While we reward merit in this way and make [Page's] name historic we at the same time vindicate our own nationality in the paths of science." [26] The bill passed easily—why would anyone oppose such a well intentioned piece of legislation?

There was a brief debate when it was presented to the Senate a month later, even though it bore the unanimous approval of the patent committees of both houses. Senator Orris Ferry of Connecticut, who spoke in its favor, was not very well versed on the background. Nor did he quite understand what an induction coil was, except that Ruhmkorff's was somehow "a plagiarism from Dr. Page." What he emphasized was the importance of immediate passage, because Page was now feared to be dying. Senator James Grimes of Iowa asked, "Is the patent going to expire when he dies?" When Ferry replied that it was not, Grimes said, "Then I do not see what that has to do with it." [27]

To most of those present, Grimes must have appeared rather dense. The bill was partly a "matter of national pride," but it was also designed to give "a veteran in the science of electricity and magnetism" some small measure of personal satisfaction [28]— seemingly a noble sentiment. In fact, Grimes had made a significant query. But no further debate ensued. The special act was passed without amendment and enrolled the next day. On March 20 it came before President Andrew Johnson. Under other circumstances, Johnson, ever the foe of special privilege, might have balked—20 years before he had led Congressional opposition to raising the examiners' pay, and in 1851 he had been instrumental

176

in killing a supplemental appropriation for Page's locomotive. But he had far more pressing matters on his mind: the Covode Resolution had carried in the House, and his impeachment trial was due to commence shortly. He simply had no time to worry about the propriety of Page's special act and signed automatically.

In mapping his strategy Page had collaborated with Anthony Pollok, one of Washington's most successful patent agents. The two were good friends, having shared the same office building on Seventh Street during the 1850s. Moreover, Page's eldest daughter, Emelyn, had married Pollok's junior partner, Marcellus Bailey, a Civil War hero and the son of a famous abolitionist. On March 26, Bailey delivered Page's petition for a 13-claim patent to the Patent Office. On the 30th the application was approved by Professor Hedrick and the patent ordered to issue by the commissioner. Bearing number 76,654, it took effect on April 14.

Page lived only three weeks longer. Early in 1867 he had begun to suffer from attacks that produced "a strange pressure and disability upon the head, which, though in a measure checked by temporary repose from labor, was nevertheless ready to reassert its power in another form. . . ."[29] In November, just as he finished his *History of Induction,* it settled in his throat and bronchial parts and rendered him unable to speak aloud. Soon, he could no longer continue working, though A. L. Hayes, his assistant, went on signing Page's name to official correspondence, which suggests that he was retained on the Patent Office payroll. For his last two months he was bedridden and suffered greatly. Finally, on the morning of Tuesday, May 5, 1868, he summoned his family to his bedside, silently bid his last to each, and at 1:00 p.m. he died.

The exact nature of Page's fatal illness seems never to have been diagnosed. The suggestion is plausible that it might have been aggravated by "the effect of chemical substances upon the physical man."[30] Moreover, a terrible grief befell him in June 1867—the sudden death of Emelyn, just 22 and married to Marcellus Bailey only three months before. (Later, Bailey married the second-eldest Page daughter, Harriet.) Page knew his classical literature, knew the ingredients of genuine tragedy. As he lay dying he may well have recalled the stories of bright prodigies with flawed characters who ultimately were crushed with sorrow to the grave. He was eulogized by his friend Byron Sunderland as one of the nation's "greatest benefactors," and laid to rest at Oak Hill Cemetery in Georgetown, in a plot belonging to Bailey.[31]

His obituaries were more than just politely laudatory. He almost seemed to have recaptured his scientific standing of time past. One notice stated that he was the "author of many important discoveries in electro-magnetism;" another called him an "eminent physicist, professor, and author;" yet another concluded that:

> In his death science—more especially electrical science—has experienced a severe loss, and it will not be easy to fill his place in the scientific world. He was one of the few men whose lives may be regarded as a public benefit, and whose decease is a loss and misfortune to mankind.[32]

In death people do sometimes retrieve faded glory, and—had this really been the end—the image of "Franklin, Henry, and Page" might have taken popular root. But the story was by no means over. During the next few years Page's name was to become more common currency than ever during his lifetime. Often as not, it was stigmatized. For example, *The Telegrapher,* quoted at the end of the preceding paragraph, spoke about Page many times thereafter, but scarcely ever again approvingly. In the same issue, this weekly, which represented the working people in the industry, ran an item telling how "some excitement [had] been created in telegraph circles" by the claim of Page's heirs that his patent covered virtually "all known forms of telegraphy."[33] This claim had first been aired a few days earlier in Western Union's house organ, which stated that "all automatic closures, repeaters, local circuits, printing machines, &c., are covered by this sweeping patent. . . . Circuit breakers in actual use or manufactured April 15th, are exempt from its operation, but no machinery after that date can be employed without consent of the patentees."[34]

Although the Page patent was *sui generis* and an explanation of its background preceded the printed specifications, it appeared that the intent had not *just* been to "vindicate American science" and give Page "honorable recognition." Indeed, Anthony Pollok was now calling attention to the obvious—that the patent embodied all the rights and privileges of any ordinary patent. Prior to the time it took effect, nobody had publicly mentioned its possible applicability to telegraph apparatus, but it did cover several varieties of circuit breaker, and circuit breakers were indubitably a component of all telegraph lines. Our legislators could scarcely have been more "careless and stupid," the New York *Herald* fumed (in the same editiorial quoted at the begin-

178

ning of this chapter), than to be "hoodwinked into such absurd legislation."[35]

Soon, Pollok appeared in the inner sanctum of Western Union, and offered the Page patent for sale. The price was five hundred thousand dollars. The company would profit by owning rights to the circuit breakers, he suggested, and also to the provision covering the "employment of one electro-magnetic instrument to open and close the circuit of another electro-magnetic instrument"—in short, a relay. This was the substance of claim 14. Claim 14? The act of Congress authorized the commissioner to issue a 13-claim patent, and a 13-claim patent is what the commissioner had ordered to issue on March 30. Nevertheless, there remains to this day in the archival file for U.S. Patent 76,654 a letter from Pollok to the commissioner, over Page's signature, requesting the specifications be amended to embody two additional claims. Although the letter is dated March *31*, these claims were included when the patent issued. It is hard to avoid the conclusion that this maneuver was conceived with malice aforethought, or to disagree with harried litigants who charged that these claims "were interpolated as an attempt to obtain rights and privileges" beyond those authorized by the act of Congress.[36] In the same vein, there were elements to the patent that Page had never described in his experimental researches.

Pollok failed to convince Western Union that what he had was worth a half-million, but he did manage to sell piecemeal assignments to smaller concerns such as the Gold and Stock Telegraph Company. He also made deals with burglar- and fire-alarm companies whose bell-ringing apparatus worked on the same feedback principle as Page's electrotome. In 1871, Western Union decided to offer $25,000 for a half-interest. Pollok accepted. After that, the company actually controlled the patent, although the moiety was left for the time-being with Page's heirs. The reason for this, according to those whom the patent threatened, was so that "in its enforcement the widow and orphan dodge might be played for effect on judges and juries."[37]

Western Union had the patent reissued, and in mid-1872 commenced several infringement suits—one against the New York City Police Department!—the object being to obtain judgements, either by default or collusion, and, on the basis of these judgements, injunctions. While these suits were pending, still others were launched, against two companies once friendly to Page because of his opposition to Morse, the Manhattan Quota-

179

tion Company of Charles T. Chester, and Jay Gould's Atlantic and Pacific Company. Gould directed his employee, Thomas Edison, to devise a technological means of evading the patent—he came up with the chalk-drum "motograph"—while both companies prepared devastating rebuttals. These assaulted the patent on every possible basis, and ultimately destroyed the grounds for legal action against communications companies. Fire-alarm telegraph companies remained vulnerable, though, and were losing lawsuits as late as 1881.[38]

Western Union had meantime tried to milk the patent in all conceivable ways, and in 1876 began suing makers of electrotherapeutic devices. This so infuriated Jerome Kidder, the leading American manufacturer, that he published a merciless personal diatribe against Page, which flatly denied his claim to having invented "any electrical coil whatever," and implied that he was nothing more than a fraud, a thief, and a liar (see plates). Kidder held many electrical patents, including at least one for an induction coil. His applications from 1861 to 1867 had of course been examined by Page, who occasionally appears to have been unduly "illiberal" with Kidder. Once, he rejected a very lengthy application pertaining to a magneto-electric machine, on the grounds that "the extraordinary style of manuscript is very objectionable, rendering the paper entirely too cumbrous for official usages." The writing was perfectly legible, but the words were spaced out about five to a line, and Page insisted that Kidder "condense the manuscript within reasonable limits."[39] Although he passed the application after it was rewritten, Kidder may well have been nursing a grudge over this incident for 13 years.

Kidder's attack was unusual since even the most scathing critics of Pollok and Western Union were usually careful not to suggest that Page himself ever contemplated suing anybody. Still, many one-time partisans of his claims did a complete about-face, deeming Ruhmkorff's Volta Prize "richly deserved," and the Page patent "an outrage on the public."[40] And even his closest friends must have wondered whether Page had been party to a conspiracy with Pollok to cash in on his "honorific" patent. After all, he died virtually penniless, leaving behind a 45 year-old widow with children from six to sixteen. Yet, within just a few years Priscilla had realized nearly $70,000 from the patent, which enabled her to live in high style for the rest of her life and still bequeath each of her five heirs $10,000 when she died in 1899.[41] The question of Page's foreknowledge of what Pollok was about to do is unlikely

180

ever to be resolved. It is worth noting, however, that he did not petition Congress until after it was quite certain he was seriously ill; that nine days before he died he wrote that he had "abused many privileges;"[42] and that soon after Western Union paid over the full amount for the patent, Priscilla and her youngest daughter left for an extended tour of Europe, in company with Mr. and Mrs. Pollok. And, finally, it is questionable that Page could have remained oblivious to the fact that the men who had won control of American science definitely *did* believe that patents were undignified and that issues pertaining to science ought to be settled by *scientists,* not politicians.

The patent expired in 1885, an event meriting front-page mention by the leading electrical trade periodical, even though Western Union had made no attempt to exploit it since Jay Gould took control of the company from Cornelius Vanderbilt and brought suits against the Mutual Union and American Rapid Telegraph companies. These concerns had simply filed the same answer prepared by Gould in the Atlantic and Pacific suit of 1875.[43] The patent's total value to Western Union can only be guessed. Vanderbilt never won a major infringement suit from a competing company, but the patent did serve as a stick with which to beat would-be competitors, especially railroad corporations.

As for Page himself, it was inevitable that the protracted and widely publicized litigation, with all the accompanying charges of bad faith and fraud, would taint his name. It was no doubt in part because the affair of the "notorious Page patent" was only lately concluded that his historiographical fate became so muddled. Peter Parker might recall him as a man of "similar intellect" to Agassiz and Henry. On the other hand, those "quaint collections of sketches of investigators that once passed for history of science and technology"[44] often omitted him altogether. For example, in 1897 George Brown Goode of the Smithsonian listed the up-and-coming scientists of the 1830s as J. W. Draper, W. B. and H. D. Rogers, A. A. Gould, and James D. Dana, while "the leading spirits were Silliman, Hare, Olmsted, Hitchcock, Torrey, De Kay, Henry, and Morse."[45] It seems almost like a calculated slight to tack on to such a list the name of Morse, a man whose pretensions to scientific originality had long since been discounted, while omitting Page, a scientist whom Morse relied on for help nearly as much as he did Gale and Vail.

As for histories written in our own time, Page is usually mentioned in works on electrical technology, and in popular surveys or biographies one occasionally encounters a cryptic reference to "the monopoly of the Page Patent" or the "Page Patent which had been exploited for years in litigation." [46] And a few professional historians of science do notice him—notably Dupree, who recounts the locomotive episode and mentions that the Patent Office employed able men such as Page. But there is virtually nothing of any significance which addresses itself *directly* to Page's career in science or to his role in reforming patent policy. He is absent from the standard biographies of the *Lazzaroni,* and from Dirk Struik's *Yankee Science in the Making,* even though Struik devotes considerable attention to describing the Salem milieu of which Page was a product. Even Carl W. Mitman, the very knowledgeable Smithsonian curator who wrote up Page for the *Dictionary of American Biography,* did not quite know what to do with him. He is cited in the occupational index neither as a scientist nor as an inventor, but as an *experimenter*— tossed into a small mixed bag whose seven other occupants include Robert R. Livingston and Mahlon Loomis.

Now, if historians of American science and its institutional development think of Page first as someone who wasted a lot of money on a quixotic locomotive and perhaps second as someone who schemed to obtain a patent of unsavory repute, then no wonder they have tended to overlook the possibility of his having much significance for their own field. Even if it be conceded that, after all, his locomotive was technically quite an achievement, and that he ought not to be blamed for what was done with his patent long after he was dead, Page still stands guilty of having violated many key precepts of professional decorum, precepts largely formulated by the group led by Henry and Bache who defined American science during the middle third of the 19th century, roughly, Page's Washington years. By involving himself in noxious priority quarrels, by seeking profit from his discoveries, by broadcasting allegations that smacked on anti-intellectualism, and by courting personal political favor in too heavy-handed a manner, Page broke the rules, too many of them. This explains his fate as an outsider in his own time, and perhaps it also helps explain his historiographical fate. Moreover, his career seems to confirm a peculiar and pervasive elitist view of science, a view epitomized in this recent assertion by I. I. Rabi:

> . . . science and technology do not go well together, although they are of the same breed. It is a little bit like the race horse and draft horse being hitched together for practical purposes.

182

In most cases I've seen . . . scientists who have devoted themselves to inventions fail to be scientists after a time.[47]

It is true that Page did "fail to be a scientist after a time," and that he did present quite a different image in the 1850s and 1860s than in the 1830s and 1840s. Indeed, this is precisely why his career *must* be examined in all its separate parts as well as in sum, and from an internal as well as an external perspective. One group of old-fashioned amateurs did *not* overlook Page's science, the proto-internalists whose outstanding representative was Professor Fleming. There were a number of others: even Du Moncel came around, crediting "a ce savant . . . les premières recherches importantes" with induction apparatus.[48] All of them may have had a naive positivistic philosophy. Nearly all seem to have regarded science as something divorced from flesh-and-blood and concrete social and political contexts. Yet, their efforts are valuable precisely *because* of their narrowness, their innocence of extrinsic considerations; in Page's case, it is instructive not only to look at the physics, the politics, and the patents all together, but also to look at each in isolation. This is what Fleming did with the physics. The story of the Page patent probably found its way to University College in Nottingham where Fleming taught, but, if so, did not in the least influence his assessment of Page the electrical scientist. For Fleming could essentially echo William Sturgeon's "very great respect for his high talent as an Experimental Philosopher"—just as if he knew nothing of what happened subsequently.

183

Epilogue

From the Era of Good Feelings
To the Tragic Era

> Begin life as you mean to go through and end it. Make your
> rules and never depart from them for any body.
>
> *Jery Lee Page*
> *to Charles Grafton Page, July 1828*
>
> My life has been very unsatisfactory to me. I have neglected and
> abused many privileges. . . .
>
> *Charles Grafton Page, April 26, 1868*

Charles Page was the embodiment of paradox. He was a man who
could be ahead of his time or left behind. He was both selfish and
generous, prescient and shortsighted, calculating and spontane-
ous, modest and egotistical, transparent and enigmatic. If he was
essentially the same man all his life, he at least *appears* to have
changed greatly—and his needs surely did. Look at him, for
instance, at seven-year intervals from the time he was 21 in 1833.
Then, he had just begun medical school in Boston, and wanted a
career of science; in 1840 he was a country doctor, and probably not
sure what he wanted; in 1847 he was a civil servant concerned about
prestige; in 1854 he was an entrepreneur concerned about money;
in 1861 he was back with the government, and he wanted security;
in 1868 he was seeking a special reward for his contributions to
science—he wanted immortality. And then he died, having used up
his personal allotment of eight times seven years. How ironic that
experimental research he did in the Age of Jackson turned out to
have an immense cash value in the Gilded Age! This was partly
because, as his life drew to a close, a *political* decision was made to
award him a *patent* for a contribution he had made to *physics*.
Whatever may be said about the means, none of that money would
have come to Page's heirs, had he not done science early in his
career, and been regarded as a man who did good science.

Ultimately, nevertheless, Page's biography is tragedy. He felt
best about life when pursuing the Great Creator's secrets as a
youth; the dying man who lamented neglecting and abusing

184

"many privileges" was nothing if not tragic. If, on the other hand, Emerson was right when he wrote "There is properly no history; only biography," Page certainly mirrored some of the salient historical currents of his time. What we can learn from his career suggests that much might be learned from studies of his friends and associates who remain largely in obscurity—men like him in some ways, though in other ways very different—Greenough, or Keller, or Lane, or the Davis brothers. First, since Clio has thought all politicians worthwhile, but only grand heroes in most other realms, our image of what mid-19th-century America was like is decidedly lopsided. To reconstruct in detail the career of an individual such as Keller is perhaps not possible—that remains to be seen. But discoveries can be made about many persons whose biographies could be as crucial to ascertaining the real texture of this period as that of, say, Page's contemporary, Franklin Pierce (1804-1869). It would certainly profit us, for instance, to know as much about the man he chose to be Commissioner of Patents, Charles Mason, as we know about Pierce himself—or as much about Thomas Ewbank as about the Presidents he served under, Zachary Taylor and Millard Fillmore.

As for Page, while in some ways he was certainly an important figure in and of himself, in others his career was significant mainly insofar as it illuminates important themes neglected by most historians. Millions of pages have been written about the years between the "Era of Good Feelings" and the "Tragic Era"— Page's years (and, not entirely by chance, his own life ran just such a course). Between 1812 and the late 1860s the United States underwent a transformation unequaled in magnitude until the transformation of Russia in our own century. Our understanding of certain facets of that transformation is quite thorough, of others it is sketchy at best. Two that merit considerable further study pertain to the philosophy and administration of the American patent system, and the related issue of democracy versus privilege in federal involvement with science and technology.

These are quasi-political matters that involved Page with directness and immediacy. His career is *also* worth examining for the internal substance of his science. Largely because of one well-publicized technological failure, he has often been typecast either as some sort of boondoggler, or, at best, as a shortsighted zealot. Yet, if one looks at his entire career from the beginning, he presents a quite different aspect. Here, definitely, is evidence of the necessity for more carefully defining the categorical pigeonholes to which we assign men of science in 19th-century America. This, and the related matter of reconsidering "the relations of theory and practice," are currently receiving attention by leading scholars, and I expect that their efforts will prove fruitful.

On the other hand, an historian is apt to find it difficult to take the career of *any* individual and analyze its components separately. For here one encounters that venerable philosophical debate about the writing of history—the debate surrounding von Ranke's words, "wie es eigentlich gewesen." What is an historian to do with somebody like Page when he finds certain contemporaries ranking him with the best, others ignoring him? Perhaps this suggests a need to re-examine our conventional wisdom about the professionalization of American science. Perhaps we need to weight matters of "style and tone" differently than Joseph Henry and Alexander Bache did. The qualitative disparities between Page's science and Henry's and Bache's seem to me to be rather slight. But it is possible that external factors must inevitably work to distort historical images of science *qua* science. With Page, the patent matters certainly tend to fuzz up the physics, and the political maneuvering to fuzz up both.

Closely focused internalism may serve as a partial corrective to such problems. But even if the internalist persuasion retains all its present vigor, it should not be surprising if a century from now historians are devoting more attention to Linus Pauling's politics or pronouncements on orange juice than to his molecular biology, and more attention to William Shockley the geneticist than Shockley the physicist. This may in some measure be inevitable; it is even proper, if "the history of science and its cultural influences" are subjects not rightly divorced from each other. Yet, there is much to be said for trying to explain history as did the 18th-century Rationalists—in terms of personal psychology and luck. Moreover, we need sometimes to remind ourselves of the obvious—that in the course of a lifetime people may change enormously. Man, Karl Jaspers writes, "is not what he is simply once and for all, but is a process." Not many of us go through life and end it as we begin it. Perhaps Jery Lee Page was able to; he lived only 25 years. But others do not, and certainly not Charles Page. This says something about his personal psychology, and perhaps a little bit about his personal endowment of luck. That he had the unique career he did is also a reflection of the

186

potentialities and constraints of the world he lived in. Finally, with Page in mind especially, though by no means exclusively, it is worth remembering that historical repute is something which may be strongly affected by seemingly disparate external currents exerting a subtle but powerful inductive influence.

Abbreviations Used in References

AIEE	Transactions of the American Institute of Electrical Engineers
AJS	American Journal of Science
Annals	Annals of Electricity, Magnetism, and Chemistry
APJ	American Polytechnic Journal
ARCP	Annual Report of the Commissioner of Patents
ARJ	American Railroad Journal
ATM	American Telegraph Magazine
CG	Congressional Globe
CGP	Charles Grafton Page
DAB	Dictionary of American Biography
DSB	Dictionary of Scientific Biography
EE	The Electrical Engineer
EW	The Electrical World
JFI	Journal of the Franklin Institute
JHL	Jonathan Homer Lane, "Charles Grafton Page," AJS, 2d ser. 48 (1869): 1–17
JHLP	Jonathan Homer Lane Papers, RG 167, Records of the National Bureau of Standards, National Archives
JHP	Joseph Henry Papers, Smithsonian Institution
JPOS	Journal of the Patent Office Society
JT	Journal of the Telegraph
LC	Library of Congress
MM	Mechanics' Magazine
NI	Washington National Intelligencer
NRC	National Records Center, Suitland, Maryland
PF	Patented Files, RG 241, Records of the U.S. Patent Office, National Records Center, Suitland
Phil Mag	Philosophical Magazine and Journal of Science
Proc AAAS	Proceedings of the American Association for the Advancement of Science
Proc Am Acad	Proceedings of the American Academy of Arts and Sciences
PSWP	Priscilla Sewall Webster Page, Personal Reminiscences (New York, 1886)
RCHS	Records of the Columbia Historical Society
SA	Scientific American

SFBM	Samuel F. B. Morse Papers, Library of Congress
SI	Smithsonian Institution
T&C	*Technology and Culture*
Teleg	*The Telegrapher*
VTC	Vail Telegraph Collection, Smithsonian Institution
WHC	William Hazell Collection, Corte Madera, California
WJR	William J. Rhees Collection, Smithsonian Institution

References

Prologue

1 *A Memorial of Joseph Henry* (Washington, 1880), p. 32.
2 *Teleg* 4 (1868): 311; JHL.
3 *The Historian and History* (New York, 1964), p. 198.
4 John Walton Caughey, *Gold is the Cornerstone* (Berkeley, 1948), p. ix.
5 Review of *Readings in Technology and American Life,* ed. Carroll W. Pursell, Jr., in *T&C* 11 (1970): 104–105.
6 *Philadelphia's Philosopher-Mechanics: A History of the Franklin Institute, 1824–1865* (Baltimore, 1974); *The Emergence of Agricultural Science: Justus Liebig and the Americans, 1840–1880* (New Haven, 1975); *The Formation of the American Scientific Community: The American Association for the Advancement of Science, 1848–60* (Urbana, 1976). I have received an advance copy of Dr. Kohlstedt's book just as my own manuscript goes to press. It is full of provocative ideas, but I have resisted the urge to recast any of my material in light of her findings.
7 Byron Sunderland, *Funeral Address . . . May 7, 1868* (n.p., 1868), p. 5.
8 Carlton Mabee, *The American Leonardo: A Life of Samuel F. B. Morse* (New York, 1943), p. 190.

Chapter One

1 Quoted in JHL, pp. 2–3.
2 Jery Lee Page, Jr., to CGP, [Sept.] 1828, WHC.
3 John J. Greenough to J. H. Lane, Jan. 4, 1869, JHLP.
4 CGP, "Notice of some New Electrical Instruments," *AJS* 26 (1834): 110–112.
5 Sturgeon, "Explanation of the Phenomena, &c.," *Annals* 1 (1836–7): 294; "Remarks on the preceding paper," *Annals* 2 (1838): 143, 145.
6 Sturgeon to Silliman, July 12, 1838, Silliman Family Papers, Yale University Archives, New Haven.
7 "Introductory Address of the Hon. R. J. Walker, of Mississippi, Director of the National Institute," *Proceedings of the April Meeting, 1844* (Washington, 1844), p. 442.
8 "Davis's Manual of Magnetism," *SA,* April 23, 1846, p. 127.
9 Nathan Reingold, ed., *The Papers of Joseph Henry,* Vol. I, *The Albany Years* (Washington, 1972), p. xxv.
10 *The Alternate Current Transformer In Theory and Practice,* Vol. II, *The Utilisation of Induced Currents* (New York and London, 1892), p. 25.
11 Thomas D. Lockwood, "Laminated or Divided Iron and Other Metallic Masses in Electromagnetic Apparatus," *EE* 15 (1893): 5, 27, 57, 82, 108.
12 "Autobiography of Thomas Davenport," unpublished ms. (1851), Vermont Historical Society, Montpelier, p. 2.
13 C. David Gruender, "On Distinguishing Science and Technology," *T&C* 12 (1971): 457.
14 Nathan Reingold, ed., *Science in Nineteenth-Century America: A Documentary History* (New York, 1964), p. 63.
15 The CGP quote at the beginning of this chapter is from an essay in the *APJ* 1 (1853): 4–5.
16 Dirk Struik, *Yankee Science in the Making* (New York, 1962), p. 106.

17 Jery Lee Page, Jr., to CGP, July 18, 182[8?], WHC.
18 PSWP, p. 121.
19 Samuel Eliot Morison, *Three Centuries of Harvard, 1636–1936* (Cambridge, 1936), p. 205.
20 Quoted in JHL, p. 3.
21 *AJS* 31 (1836): 137–141.
22 *Ibid.*, p. 139.
23 Sturgeon, "Explanation of the Phenomena, &c." (note 5 above).
24 CGP, "On the use of the Dynamic Multiplier, with a new accompanying apparatus," *AJS* 32 (1837): 354n.; also, "Galvanism," *ibid.*, p. 197 (from the Salem *Observer*).
25 JHL, p. 5.
26 Auguste De la Rive, *A Treatise on Electricity in Theory and Practice* (London, 1853), I, p. 300; Henry M. Noad, *A Manual of Electricity* (London, 1859), pp. 671–672; A. Graham Bell, "Researches in Telephony," *Proc Am Acad* 12 (1876–7): 1; also, Théodose Du Moncel, *Exposé des Applications De L'Électricité* (Paris, 3d ed. 1873), V, p. 104; A. E. Dolbear, *The Telephone: An Account of the Phenomena of Electricity, Magnetism, and Sound as Involved in its Action* (Boston, 1877), p. 100; Dolbear, "The Telephone—from 1837 to 1882," *New York Review of the Telephone and Telegraph* 1 (May 15, 1882): 102.
27 CGP, "The Production of Galvanic Music," *AJS* 32 (1837): 396–397.
28 CGP, "Experiments in Electro-Magnetism: On the Disturbance of Molecular Forces by Magnetism," *AJS* 33 (1838): 118; "Musical Tones produced by Magnets," *AJS* 48 (1845): 401.
29 Of the half-dozen references to CGP in Henry's laboratory notebooks (JHP) between 1838 and 1840, two concern "Galvanic Music," entries dated April 21, 1838, and April 29, 1840.
30 CGP, "Electro-Mechanics," *APJ* 4 (1854): 305.
31 "Efficiency of Transformers," *EE* 10 (1890): 263.
32 Sturgeon, "Historical Sketch of the rise and progress of Electro-magnetic Engines for propelling machinery," *Annals* 3 (1839): 435.
33 CGP, "On Electro-Magnetism as a Moving Power," *AJS* 35 (1839): 106.
34 *Scientific Researches, Experimental and Theoretical, in Electricity, Magnetism, Galvanism, Electro Magnetism, and Electro-Chemistry* (London, 1852), p. vii.
35 Bernard Finn, *DSB*.
36 Thomas Coulson, *Joseph Henry, His Life and Work* (Princeton, 1950), p. 150.
37 Reingold, *Science in Nineteenth-Century America* (note 14 above).
38 Florian Cajori, *A History of Physics in its Elementary Branches* (New York, 1929), p. 218.
39 Henry to CGP, April 2, 1839, JHP.
40 W. James King, "The Development of Electrical Technology in the 19th Century: 1. The Electrochemical Cell and the Electromagnet," *Contributions from the Museum of History and Technology: Paper 28*, in *United States National Museum Bulletin* 228 (1962): 260.
41 "On a Reciprocating Motion Produced by Magnetic Attraction and Repulsion," *AJS* 20 (1831): 340–343.
42 CGP, "On Electro-Magnetism as a Moving Power," *AJS* 35 (1839): 107.
43 *Ibid.*, p. 106.

191

44 Henry to CGP, Oct. 31, 1838, JHP.
45 CGP to Henry, Nov. 8, 1838, JHP.
46 *AJS* 36 (1839): 143.
47 CGP to Henry, April 11, 1868, JHP.
48 Pierre Duhem, *The Aim and Structure of Physical Theory* (New York, reprint 1962), p. 66.
49 Coulson (note 36 above), pp. 54, 144.
50 CGP, *History of Induction: The American Claim to the Induction Coil and Its Electrostatic Developments* (Washington, 1867), p. 98.
51 CGP, "On a new compound electro-magnet, for the production of the magnetic electrical spark, and also for attractive force," *AJS* 34 (1838): 168.
52 CGP, "Researches in Magnetic Electricity and new Magnetic Electrical Instruments: 1. Compound Electro-Magnets for the Magnetic Electrical spark, shock, and decomposition," *AJS* 34 (1838): 365, 366.
53 *Ibid.*, p. 367.
54 "On the theory of Magnetic Electricity," *Annals* 1 (1837): 265.
55 George H. Daniels, *American Science in the Age of Jackson* (New York, 1968), p. 193.
56 *The Rise of American Civilization* (New York, rev. ed. 1940), pp. 741–742.
57 Fleming (note 10 above), pp. 24–25.
58 CGP, "New Magnetic Electrical Machine, or Magneto-Electric Multiplier, convertible into an Electro-Magnetic Engine," *AJS* 34 (1838): 372.
59 CGP, "Magneto-Electric and Electro-Magnetic Apparatus and Experiments," *AJS* 35 (1839): 262.
60 *Ibid.*, pp. 264–265.
61 *Engines of Democracy: Inventions and Society in Mature America* (New York, 1940), p. 191.
62 CGP, "New Magnetic Electrical Machine of great power, with two parallel horse-shoe magnets, and two straight rotating armatures, affording each, in an entire revolution, a constant current in the same direction," *AJS* 34 (1838): 163–167.
63 CGP, "Magneto-Electric and Electro-Magnetic Apparatus and Experiments" (note 59 above), p. 252.
64 CGP, "Magneto-Electric and Electro-Magnetic Apparatus and Experiments: Double Helix for Inducing Magnetism" (note 59 above) p. 261.
65 CGP, "Description of a remarkable echo in Fairfax Co., Virginia," *AJS* 36 (1839): 174–175.
66 CGP, "Magneto-Electric and Electro-Magnetic Apparatus and Experiments: Compound Electro-Magnet and Electrotome for Shocks, Sparks, &c" (note 59 above), p. 256.
67 H. S. Osborne, "Joseph Henry—Pioneer in Electrical Science," *Electrical Engineering* 61 (1942): 553.
68 A. E. Kennelly, "The Work of Joseph Henry In Relation to Applied Science and Engineering," *Science* 76 (1932): 1.
69 Mitchell Wilson, "Joseph Henry," *SA*, July 1954, p. 76.
70 JHL, p. 3.
71 *Exposé des Applications de L'Électricité* (Paris, 3d ed. 1873), I, p. xii.
72 Arthur P. Molella and Nathan Reingold, "Theorists and Ingenious Mechanics: Joseph Henry Defines Science," *Science Studies* 3 (1973): 349.

192

Chapter Two

1 Brooke Hindle, *Technology in Early America* (Chapel Hill, 1966), pp. 4–5; Eugene Ferguson, *Bibliography of the History of Technology* (Cambridge and London, 1968), pp. vii–viii.

2 Molella and Reingold (note 72, Ch. I).

3 Franklin L. Pope, "The Inventors of the Electric Motor . . . With Special Reference to the Work of Thomas Davenport," *EE* 11 (1891): 2; also, Pope, "The Inventions of Thomas Davenport," *AIEE* 8 (1891): 93–97; Dorman B. E. Kent, "Address at the 125th Anniversary of the Birth of Thomas Davenport," *Proceedings of the Vermont Historical Society for the Years 1926–1927–1928* (Montpelier, 1929), pp. 207–232.

4 CGP, "Electro Magnetism," *AJS* 36 (1839): 352.

5 CGP to Davenport, April 28, 1838, in Pope, "The Inventors of the Electric Motor" (note 3 above), p. 71.

6 Davenport to CGP, Nov. 2, 1838, *ibid.*

7 "Autobiography of Thomas Davenport" (note 12, Ch. I), p. 5.

8 CGP to Henry, Nov. 8, 1838, JHP.

9 Samuel Eliot Morison, *The Maritime History of Massachusetts 1783–1860* (Boston, 1921), p. 217.

10 *Science in the Federal Government: A History of Policies and Activities to 1940* (New York, 1957), p. 64.

11 PSWP, p. 80.

12 Henry to Harriet Henry, May 3, 1847, JHP, quoted in Wilcomb E. Washburn, "The Influence of the Smithsonian Institution on Intellectual Life in Mid-Nineteenth-Century Washington," *RCHS, 1963–1965* (1966): 100, 102.

13 Bache to Henry, Dec. 4, 1846, quoted in *ibid.*, p. 98.

14 F. W. Putnam, "Henry Wheatland," *Proc Am Acad*, ns 23 (1895–6): 364.

15 *Ibid.*

16 "Entomological Cabinet," *AJS* 39 (1840): 211.

17 R. A. Tilghman to Henry, Aug. 19, 1847, JHP.

18 "Anniversary Address of the President of the Philosophical Society of Washington" (Nov. 18, 1871), *Bulletin of the Philosophical Society of Washington* (Washington, 1874), in *Smithsonian Miscellaneous Collections* 20 (1881): ix.

19 "Obituary: Professor Charles Grafton Page," *Teleg* 4 (1868): 319.

20 Reingold, "Lane, Jonathan Homer," *DSB*.

21 Reingold, "Alexander Dallas Bache: Science and Technology in the American Idiom," *T&C* 11 (1970): 166.

Chapter Three

1 "Report: The select committee appointed to take into consideration the state and condition of the Patent Office . . . ," *S. Doc. No. 338*, 24 Cong., 1 sess., April 28, 1836, reprinted as "1836 Senate Committee Report," *JPOS* 18 (1936): 84.

2 William I. Wyman, "Dr. William Thornton and the Patent Office to 1836," *JPOS* 18 (1936): 84.

3 Wyman, "The Patent Act of 1836," *JPOS* 1 (1919): 210.

4 William Elliot to John D. Craig, Jan. 16, 1830, "A communication from the

Secretary of State in relation to the Patent Office," *H. Doc. No. 38*, 21 Cong., 1 sess., Jan. 27, 1830, p. 4.

5   Thaddeus Hyatt, "Charles M. Keller and the American Patent Office," *SA*, May 21, 1859, p. 310; Levin H. Campbell, *The Patent System of the United States* (Washington, 1891), pp. 38-39.

6   "1836 Senate Committee Report" (note 1 above), p. 857.

7   "An Act to promote the progress of useful arts, and to repeal all acts and parts of acts heretofore made for that purpose," 5 *U.S. Statutes at Large* 117.

8   Nathan Reingold, "U.S. Patent Office Records as Sources for the History of Invention and Technological Property," *T&C* 1 (1960): 161.

9   Quoted in *An Account of the Destruction by Fire of the North and West Halls of the Model Room in the United States Patent Office Building ... Together with a History of the Patent Office From 1790 to 1877* (Washington, 1877), p. 13.

10 PF 136, 765, 1029, and 1088.

11 E.g., PF 348, 613, 1023.

12 Harvey W. Mortimer, "Patents a Century Ago," *JPOS* 46 (1964): 666-670.

13 Inventory-Nomination Form, National Register of Historical Places, Archives of the National Survey of Historic Sites and Buildings, National Park Service, Washington, D.C.; also, Wyman, "The Patent Office Building," *JPOS* 1 (1919): 255-257; "Memento Mori [Elliot obituary]," *SA*, Nov. 18, 1854, p. 77; Robert W. Fenwick, "The Old and the New Patent Office," *Proceedings and Addresses: Celebration of the Beginning of the Second Century of the American Patent System at Washington, D.C.* (Washington, 1892), pp. 454-471.

14 Edmund Burke, *ARCP* 1848, p. 5.

15 Application, Dec. 11, 1841; Thomas P. Jones to Ellsworth, Dec. 28, 1841, PF 2534.

16 Donovan to Ellsworth, Dec. 18, 1841, Keller to Ellsworth, Dec. 24, 1841, *ibid.*

17 Bache to Francis Markoe, July 21, 1841, National Institute Collection, SI, quoted in Sally Kohlstedt, "A Step Toward Scientific Self-Identity in the United States: The Failure of the National Institute, 1844," *Isis* 62 (1971): 354.

18 PF 2541.

19 Morgan Sherwood, "Patent Nonsense in the History of Technology," "Program Summaries," *T&C* 13 (1972): 449-450.

20 CGP to Ellsworth, Jan. 31, 1844, *ARCP* 1843, pp. 310, 332.

21 *Ibid.*, p. 333.

22 *Ibid.* The quote from Robert Walker preceding CGP's is from his address to the April 1844 meeting of the National Institute (note 7, Ch. I), p. 446.

23 Ellsworth, *ARCP* 1845, p. 4.

24 *Ibid.*

Chapter Four

1   Ellsworth, *ARCP* 1844, p. 5.

2   CGP, "The Patent Office," *APJ* 1 (1853): 380.

3   W. P. N. Fitzgerald to Edmund Burke, *ARCP* 1845, p. 45.

4   Ellsworth, *ARCP* 1844, pp. 4-5.

5   CGP, "Notice of a Spiral Magnet, by which Secondary Currents may be demonstrated in the body of the Magnet," *JFI*, 3d ser. 3 (1842): 166-167.

6 CGP, "Description of a new plate, or quantity, Helix, for Electro Magnetic Apparatus," *ibid.*, pp. 167–168.

7 *Abstract of the Proceedings of the Fifth Session of the Association of American Geologists and Naturalists* (Washington, 1844), p. 89.

8 Kohlstedt (note 17, Ch. III), p. 360.

9 PSWP, pp. 100, 101.

10 *Ibid.*, p. 101.

11 *Ibid.*, p. 106.

12 Mrs. E. F. Ellet, *The Queens of American Society* (Philadelphia, 1867), p. 375.

13 PSWP, p. 91.

14 Webster to P. S. W. Page, Aug. 1, 1844, in *ibid.*, p. 102.

15 CGP, "The Patent Law," *APJ* 2 (1853): 399.

16 CGP, "Career of Science" (note 15, Ch. I), p. 5. This is also the source of the quote at the beginning of the chapter.

17 PSWP, p. 110.

18 John W. Caughey, "Herbert Eugene Bolton," *American West* 1 (Winter 1964): 56.

19 CGP, "On the probable Conduction of Galvanic Electricity through Moist Air," *AJS*, 2d ser. 2 (1846): 205–206; also, "Electric Conduction," *ibid.*, pp. 406–407.

20 CGP, "Law of Electro-Magnetic Induction," *AJS*, 2d ser. 2 (1846): 202–204.

21 George Iles, *Leading American Inventors* (New York, 1912), p. 165; Franklin L. Pope, "The American Inventors of the Telegraph," *The Century*, April 1888, p. 943; Mabee (note 8, Prologue), pp. 291, 299, 413; Philip Dorf, *The Builder: A Biography of Ezra Cornell* (New York, 1952), p. 85.

22 W. James King, "The Development of Electrical Technology in the 19th Century: 3. The Early Arc Light and Generator" (note 40, Ch. I), pp. 345–350; Percy Dunsheath, *A History of Electrical Engineering* (London, 1962), p. 107; Edouard Hospitalier and Julius Maier, *The Modern Applications of Electricity* (London, 1883), I, pp. 56–57; Silvanus P. Thompson, *Dynamo-Electric Machinery* (New York and London, 7th ed. 1904), I, pp. 10–11, 15; "The Magneto-Electric Engine," *SA*, Nov. 18, 1856, p. 69; Charles E. Buell, "Converting Mechanical Power into Electricity," *Review of the Telegraph and Telephone* 1 (1883): 369–370.

23 "Copy of voucher No. 709 . . . ," June 20, 1844; Morse to Vail, July 3, 1844; Vail to Morse, July 4, 1844, Vol. 18, SFBM; CGP to Vail, July 5, 1844, Box 1, VTC.

24 "Description of some experiments made by Mr. Vail [1843–44]," p. 29; also, pp. 3, 4, 5, 27, 28, 30, 40, Box 5, VTC.

25 Harold Sharlin, *The Making of the Electrical Age* (London, 1963), p. 139.

26 CGP, "Improvements in the magneto-electric machine, and application of this instrument to operate the magnetic telegraph," *ARCP* 1844, pp. 440–441, reprinted in part in *AJS* 48 (1845): 393–394, and in full in *The American Journal of Improvements in the Useful Arts and Mirror of the Patent Office* 1 (1846): 58.

27 Vail, "Telegraph Jrnl. Nov. 1844–Jan 1845," Dec. 25, 1844, Box 6, VTC.

28 CGP, "Improvements in the magneto-electric machine" (note 26 above); Vail, "Dr. Page's Magneto Electric Machine," *The American Electro Magnetic Telegraph* (Philadelphia, 1845), pp. 145–149; "Description of some Experiments made by Mr. Vail," unp., Box 5, VTC.

29 "Galvanism," *SA*, Jan. 8, 1846, p. 66.
30 "Appendix to Section on Magneto-Electric Machines," *History of Induction* (note 50, Ch. I), p. 125.
31 Henry to CGP, May 13, 1852, JHP.
32 "Copy of the Patent papers of Morse's Electro Magnetic Telegraph," and "Articles of Agreement and Association constituting Magnetic Telegraph Company and providing for the government thereof," in bound volume entitled "Copies of contracts of correspondence with Prof. Jackson, Sir John Campbell & others," pp. 40–43, 45–52, Box 7, VTC.
33 CGP to Morse, July 24 and 28, 1845, Vol. 20, SFBM.
34 CGP to Morse, Feb. 10, 1846, Vol. 21, SFBM.
35 "Samuel F. B. Morse & others *vs* Henry O'Reilly & others, Affidavit of Charles G. Page of Washington, D.C., one of the Chief Examiners in the Patent Office of the United States [Aug. 7, 1848]," and "Reply of Charles G. Page to the interrogatories hereto prefixed [Aug. 12, 1848]," deposition in bound volume, "Copies of contracts . . . ," Box 7, VTC.
36 Louisville *Courier*, Feb. 9, 1848; CGP to Amos Kendall, Feb. 22, 1848, Vol. 24, SFBM; CGP to Loomis, June 12, 1849, Loomis Papers, Beinecke Library, Yale University; E. Fitch Smith to Morse, Nov. 28, 1849, and Gale to Morse, Nov. 27, 1849, Box 27, SFBM.
37 Elmer Louis Kayser, *The George Washington University, 1821–1966* (Washington, 1966), p. 11.
38 Quoted in Charles Moore, ed., *Joint Select Committee to Investigate the Charities and Reformatory Institutions in the District of Columbia. Part III.—Historical Sketches . . .* (Washington, 1898), p. 5.
39 *Anniversary Oration Delivered Before the Medical Society of the District of Columbia September 26, 1866* (Washington, 1869), p. 56.
40 CGP to Henry, Oct. 3, 1849, JHP.
41 CGP to Henry, Dec. 4, 1846, JHP.
42 CGP to Henry, July 6, 1847, JHP.
43 CGP to Henry, July 7, 1847, JHP.
44 Henry to CGP, July 8, 1847, JHP.
45 "Revolution of a Magnet on its own axis without the use of Mercurial Conductors and also without Visible support," *AJS*, ns 3 (1847): 252–254.
46 CGP to Henry, Aug. 14, 1847, JHP.
47 CGP to Henry, April 25, 1848, JHP.
48 CGP to Henry, May [5?], 1848, JHP.
49 CGP to Henry, Dec. 11, 1846, JHP.
50 Henry to CGP, Dec. 29, 1846 (draft), JHP.
51 Coulson (note 36, Ch. I), p. 184.
52 CGP to Henry, May 25, 1847, JHP.
53 Lindsly to Henry, May 28, 1847, JHP.
54 Lindsly to A. Barnes, May 29, 1847, Archives General 1847: Faculty Positions, Archives of the University of Pennsylvania.
55 Tho. Miller, J. Riley, W. P. Johnston, Jno. Fredk. May, J. M. Thomas, and Grafton Tyler to University of Pennsylvania, May 27, 1847, *ibid.*
56 Choate to George Emlings, June 2, 1847, *ibid.*
57 CGP to Henry, July 6, 1847, JHP.
58 CGP to Henry, Sept. 7, 1847, JHP.
59 CGP to Hare, Feb. 17, 1848, Hare Papers, University of Pennsylvania.

60 CGP, "Axial Galvanometer and Double Axial Reciprocating Engine," *AJS* 49 (1845): 139.

61 "Memorial of Charles G. Page praying an investigation of a mode discovered by him of applying electro-magnetic power to purposes of navigation and locomotion," *S. Mis. Doc. No. 59*, 30 Cong., 2 sess., Feb. 20, 1849.

62 CGP to Henry, Sept. 14, 1848, JHP.

Chapter Five

1 *CG*, Feb. 20, 1849, pp. 559-560.

2 *Ibid.*, p. 560.

3 *Electricity vs. Steam: Part of Prof. Page's Lecture on Electro-Magnetic Power* (Washington, 1849), p. 2.

4 *Ibid.*, p. 3.

5 *Ibid.*, p. 4.

6 "Report: The Select Committee of the Senate, to which was referred the memorial of Professor Page," *Rep. Com. 325*, 30 Cong., 2 sess., Feb. 28, 1849.

7 *CG*, March 2, 1849, p. 654.

8 *CG*, Aug. 9, 1850, p. 1554.

9 "Extracts From a Speech of Mr. Benton, Of Missouri . . . On the Introduction of a Bill to provide for the location and construction of a Central National Road . . . ," appended to *Electricity vs. Steam* (note 3 above), p. 12.

10 The quote at the beginning of this chapter from Fleischmann is in his *Erwerbszweige, Fabrikwesen und Handel der Vereinigten Staaten von Nordamerica* (Stuttgart, 1852), trans. by E. Vilim as *Trade, Manufacture, and Commerce in the United States of America* (Jerusalem, 1970), p. 101.

11 Henry Nash Smith, *Virgin Land: The American West as Symbol and Myth* (New York, reprint 1970), p. 22.

12 "Extracts From a Speech of Mr. Benton" (note 9 above), p. 15.

13 *Electricity vs. Steam* (note 3 above), p. 1.

14 CGP to William Ballard Preston, Oct. 2, 1849, *H. Ex. Doc. 5*, 31 Cong., 1 sess., p. 445.

15 "Electro Magnetism as a Motive Power," *SA*, July 13, 1850, p. 339.

16 Davenport to *Brandon* [Vermont] *Post*, Sept. 26, 1850, in Pope, "The Inventors of the Electric Motor" (note 3, Ch. II), pp. 95-96.

17 "Electro Magnetism Triumphant Over Steam," *SA*, Oct. 12, 1850, p. 32.

18 "Electro Magnetic Engine—Letter from Prof. Page," *SA*, Oct. 19, 1850, p. 36.

19 *CG*, Aug. 9, 1850, p. 1554.

20 CGP to Lane, Aug. 10, 1850, JHLP.

21 "Report from the Secretary of the Navy Transmitting a Copy of the report of Professor Charles G. Page . . . ," *S. Ex. Doc. No. 61*, 31 Cong., 1 sess., Aug. 30, 1850, pp. 213-216; reprinted in *JFI*, 3d ser. 20 (1850): 267-271, and *Phil Mag*, 4th ser. 1 (1851): 161-167.

22 "Professor Page's Electro-magnetic power," *NI*, Aug. 29, 1850, appended to "Report from the Secretary of the Navy" (note 21 above), pp. 217-218.

23 "Report from the Secretary of the Navy" (note 21 above), p. 4.

24 *CG*, Sept. 23, 1850, pp. 1925-1926.

25 Dupree (note 10, Ch. II), p. 78.

26 *CG*, March 1, 1851, p. 762.

27 "Electro-Magnetic Engine—A New Safeguard Wanted," *SA*, March 15, 1851, p. 204.

28 "The First Locomotive That Ever Made a Successful Trip With Galvanic Power," *APJ* 4 (1854): 260.

29 "Electro-Magnetic Locomotive *versus* Steam Locomotive," *NI*, April 3, 1851.

30 Greenough (note 28 above), p. 259.

31 CGP, "Electro-Mechanics," *APJ* 1 (1853): 305–307, 369–370.

32 *NI*, April 30, 1851; the first and third quotations at the beginning of this chapter are from "Page's Electro Magnetic Engine," *ARJ*, 2d ser. 7 (1851): 698, and "Attempted Application of Electro-Magnetism as a Motive-Power," *ATM* 1 (1853): 267.

33 "Some Early Experiences with Electric Motors," *EW* 7 (1886): 234.

34 CGP, "Electro-Mechanics," *APJ* 4 (1854): 305.

35 William Chauncy Langdon to Lane, Aug. 7, 1852, JHLP.

36 "Electro-Magnetism as a Motive Power," *SA*, Nov. 8, 1851, p. 61, and Nov. 15, 1851, pp. 65, 68; reprinted as "Description of Professor Page's Electro-Magnetic Engine," *MM* 56 (1852): 21–25.

37 Greenough, "Prof. Page's Electric Engine," *SA*, Aug. 9, 1854, p. 394.

38 H. Stafford Hatfield, *The Inventor and His World* (New York, 1933), pp. 72–73.

39 CGP, "Electro-Mechanics" (note 34 above).

40 Abbott Payson Usher, *A History of Mechanical Inventions* (Cambridge, Mass., rev. ed. 1954), p. 74.

41 See Robert C. Post, "On the Application of Electro-Magnetism as a Motive Power: Robert Davidson's *Galvani* of 1842," *Railroad History*, No. 130 (1974): 5–22.

42 J. J. Ampère, *Promenade en Amérique* (Paris, 1855), I, p. 357.

43 *AJS*, 2d ser. 11 (1851): 86–89.

44 Faraday, "On the Conservation of Force," *Proceedings of the Royal Institution* 2 (1857), in *Experimental Researches in Chemistry and Physics* (London, 1859), p. 458.

45 E.g., Byron Sunderland, "Washington As I First Knew It," *RCHS* 5 (1902): 202; Edwin J. Houston, *Electricity in Everyday Life* (New York, 1905), II, p. 402; Park Benjamin, ed., *Modern Mechanism . . . Being a Supplement to Appleton's Cyclopedia of Applied Mechanics* (New York, 1895), p. 535; T. C. Martin, "Electric Cars and Trains," in Waldemar Kaempffert, ed., *A Popular History of American Invention* (New York, 1924), II, p. 112.

46 CGP to Henry, April 13, 1851, JHP.

47 Page's comment regarding Joule at the beginning of this chapter is from "Electro-Mechanics" (note 34 above).

48 "The Improvement of the Mechanical Arts: Closing Address at the Exhibition of the Metropolitan Mechanics' Institute of Washington," in *Scientific Writings of Joseph Henry* (Washington, 1886), I, p. 317.

49 Lane, diary entry for June 10, 1848, JHLP.

Chapter Six

1 Charles F. Adams, ed., *Memoirs of John Quincy Adams* (Philadelphia, 1876), XII, pp. 188–189; also, William I. Wyman, "Henry L. Ellsworth, The First Commissioner of Patents," *JPOS* 1 (1919): 524–529, and Claribel R. Barnett in *DAB*.

2 Burke, *ARCP* 1845, p. 4. The quotation at the beginning of this chapter is also from this report, p. 5.

3 Leonard D. White, *The Jacksonians: A Study in Administrative History, 1829-1861* (New York, 1954), p. 376.

4 "The Delay at the Patent Office," *The American Journal of Improvements in the Useful Arts and Mirror of the Patent Office* 1 (1846): 44.

5 Burke, *ARCP* 1846, p. 4.

6 Burke to H. H. Sylvester, July 16, 1846, "Report: The Committee on Patents, to whom was referred the petition of Thomas G. Clinton . . . ," *H. R. Report No. 839,* 30 Cong., 1 sess., Aug. 10, 1848, p. 203.

7 CGP to Burke, Jan. 4, 1847, in *ARCP* 1846, p. 15.

8 Frank Luther Mott, *A History of American Magazines 1850-1865* (Cambridge, Mass., 1938), p. 324.

9 "The Patent Office," *SA,* Oct. 2, 1847, p. 13.

10 "The United States Patent Office," *SA,* May 8, 1847, p. 261.

11 *Ibid.*

12 "Report of the Patent Office," *SA,* June 28, 1848, p. 317.

13 "Report of the Commissioner of Patents," *SA,* April 22, 1848, p. 245.

14 "Report of the Patent Office" (note 12 above).

15 "What to do with part of the Smithson Bequest," *SA,* Jan. 1, 1848, p. 117.

16 *Ibid.*

17 Reingold, *Science in Nineteenth-Century America* (note 14, Ch. I), p. 153.

18 Dupree (note 10, Ch. II), p. 81.

19 "The Improvement of the Mechanical Arts" (note 48, Ch. V), p. 306.

20 The debates on this bill are reported in the *CG,* 30 Cong., 1 sess., Dec. 29, 1847 through May 18, 1848. This narrative, however, is derived from "Debate on a Bill to Increase Force and Salaries in the Patent Office," *JPOS* 1 (1919): 588-596, which combines all significant material from the *Globe* in one concise source.

21 "Congress and Inventors," *SA,* April 29, 1848, p. 253.

22 "Debate" (note 20 above), May 17, 1848, p. 595.

23 "Congress and Inventors" (note 21 above).

24 "Report: The Committee on Patents to whom was referred the petition of Thomas G. Clinton" (note 6 above), p. 112.

25 N. J. Brumbaugh, "Thomas Ewbank, Commissioner of Patents 184[9] to 1852," *JPOS* 2 (1919): 3[-11]; also, C. W. Mitman in *DAB.*

26 "The New Commissioner of Patents," *SA,* May 19, 1849, p. 277.

27 Mitman, *DAB.*

28 CGP to the Trustees of Mississippi University, June 13, 1848, JHLP. Lane's paper was "On the Law of Electric Conduction in Metals," *AJS,* 2d ser. 1 (1846): 230-241.

29 Lane Diary, July [?], 1848, JHLP.

30 JHL, p. 3.

31 CGP to Bache, July 9, 1852, JHLP.

32 Cleveland Abbe, "Biographical Memoir of Jonathan Homer Lane, 1819-1880," National Academy of Sciences *Biographical Memoirs* 3 (1895): 256.

33 John C. Calhoun, in *CG,* March 3, 1849, p. 693.

34 Leonard D. White, *The Republican Era: A Study in Administrative History, 1869-1901* (New York, 1958), p. 226.

35 "Encroachments on the Patent Office.—The Remedy," *SA,* Sept. 22, 1855, p. 13.

36 "Business at the Patent Office," *SA*, April 21, 1849, p. 245.
37 R. V. DeWitt, "Ancient Work on Mechanics," and editors' reply, *SA*, June 17, 1848, p. 309.
38 Maher, "Prize Essay . . . on the Patent Laws, With Suggestions of Alterations and Additions For Their Improvement," *SA*, April 28, 1849, p. 256.
39 *Ibid.*, May 5, 1849, p. 264.
40 *Ibid.*
41 Junius, "Patent Laws.—Subjects of Patents," *SA*, June 16, 1849, p. 312.
42 *Ibid.*, June 30, 1849, p. 328.
43 Junius, "Patent Laws and Business," *SA*, July 7, 1849, p. 336; July 21, 1849, p. 352.
44 "The Patent Laws," *SA*, July 28, 1849, p. 357.
45 "The New Commissioner of Patents," *SA*, May 19, 1849, p. 277.
46 Lane Diary, June 26, 1848, JHLP.
47 Peale to John F. Frazer, April 21 and 13, 1852, John Fries Frazer Papers, American Philosophical Society.
48 Gale to S. F. B. Morse, Aug. 16, 1852, Vol. 31, SFBM.
49 CGP to Bache, July 9, 1852, JHLP.
50 "Patent Office Report," *SA*, Jan. 26, 1850, p. 149.
51 *Ibid.*
52 A concise summary of the House debate of March 12, 1850, is contained in "Printing of the Patent Office Report," *SA*, March 23, 1850, p. 210.
53 "Reform of the Patent Laws," *SA*, April 13, 1850, p. 237.
54 "The Patent Office, and Reform of the Patent Laws," *SA*, June 15, 1850, p. 307; June 22, 1850, p. 317.
55 Junius, "Reform of the Patent Laws," *SA*, Oct. 12, 1850, p. 29; "Powers of the Patent Office," *SA*, July 27, 1850, p. 357.
56 "Important from Washington.—Another New Patent Bill before Congress," *SA*, Jan. 3, 1857, p. 133.
57 Quoted in "Commissioner of Patents," *SA*, Oct. 26, 1850, p. 45.
58 "Commissioner of Patents' Report," *SA*, Nov. 23, 1850, p. 77.
59 Junius, "Decisions of the Patent Office," *Ibid.*, p. 76.
60 Daclede, "Patent Office Reform," *SA*, Dec. 28, 1850, p. 118. This is also the source of the quote at the beginning of the chapter.
61 *Ibid.*
62 E.g., CGP to Burke, Jan. [?], 1846, *ARCP*, 1845, p. 44.
63 CGP, "Rules of the Patent Office," *APJ* 1 (1853): 270; "Our Journal," *APJ* 1 (1853): 3.
64 Henry, "The Improvement of the Mechanical Arts" (note 48, Ch. V), p. 309.
65 *Ibid.*, p. 319.
66 "The Smithsonian Institute," *SA*, March 11, 1854, p. 205.
67 Quoted in "The Smithsonian Institute Again," *SA*, Oct. 7, 1854, p. 13.
68 Quoted in "The Smithsonian Institute," *SA*, Jan. 27, 1855, p. 157.
69 *Ibid.*
70 "The Smithsonian Institute," *SA*, Dec. 26, 1846, p. 109; "The Smithsonian Institute" (note 66 above).
71 Kohlstedt (note 17, Ch. III), p. 361; "The Scientific Association," reply to letter from Wm. D. Arnold, *SA*, Sept. 17, 1859, p. 187.
72 CGP, *Psychomancy. Spirit-Rappings and Table Tippings Exposed* (New York, 1853), pp. 15, 19, 23, 27.

73 Henry to Bache, Aug. 9, 1839, in Reingold, *Science in Nineteenth-Century America* (note 14, Ch. I); CGP, *Psychomancy* (note 72 above), p. 21.
74 Lillian B. Miller, *The Lazzaroni: Science and Scientists in Mid-Nineteenth Century America* (Washington, 1972), p. 4.
75 CGP, "Dignity of Patents," *APJ* 1 (1853): 28.

Chapter Seven

1 "Design to Convert the Patent Office from its Legitimate Use," *SA*, Jan. 25, 1851, p. 149.
2 "History and Description of the U.S. Patent Office Building," *SA*, Feb. 1, 1851, p. 157.
3 "Abuses in the Patent Office, illustrated by Ex-Commissioner Burke," *ATM* 1 (1851): 12.
4 "Patent Office Report for 1850.—No. 3," *SA*, Oct. 4, 1851, p. 21.
5 "Patent Office Report for 1850.—No. 4," *SA*, Oct. 25, 1851, p. 29; "Patent Office Report for 1850.—No. 6," *SA*, Oct. 25, 1851, p. 45.
6 "Dr. Jackson's Address Before the American Institute," *SA*, Nov. 1, 1851, p. 51; also, Betty Mac Quitty, *Victory Over Pain: Morton's Discovery of Anaesthesia* (New York, 1971), p. 132.
7 "Patent Office Report for 1850.—No. 3" (note 4 above).
8 *New York Times,* April 26 and 29, 1852; "The New York Times and the Patent Laws," *SA*, May 9, 1852, p. 269.
9 Gale to Morse, Aug. 16, 1852, Vol. 31, SFBM.
10 "Smithsonian Legacy: Memorial of Charles Lewis Fleischmann . . . Jan. 10, 1839," *H. R. Doc. No. 70,* 25 Cong., 3 sess.
11 Greenough, "Patent Office Report for 1851," *APJ* 1 (1853): 178–179; Greenough also published a series on "The Progress of Legislation Upon Exclusive Privileges," *APJ* 1 (1853): 29–35, 173–174; 3 (1854): 81–84, 145–151.
12 CGP, "Dignity of Patents" (note 75, Ch. 6).
13 *Ibid.,* p. 29.
14 Gale to Morse, Feb. 9, 1852, SFBM.
15 Reingold, "Two Views of Maury . . . and a Third," *Isis* 55 (1964): 372.
16 See Rossiter (note 6, Prologue), p. 81.

Chapter Eight

1 *APJ* 1 (1853): 5.
2 CGP, "On a New Electro Magnetic Apparatus for Equalizing Motion for Telegraphic and other Purposes," *APJ* 1 (1853): 83; "On a New Thermo-Galvanometer," *APJ* 2 (1853): 84; "Vibrations of Trevelyan's Bars by the Galvanic Current," *APJ* 2 (1853): 315–317.
3 CGP, "Practical Results from the Discovery and Study of Polarized Light," *APJ* 2 (1853): 393.
4 *Ibid.,* p. 394.
5 Reingold, "Definitions and Speculations: The Professionalization of Science in America in the Nineteenth Century," in *The Pursuit of Knowledge in the Early American Republic,* eds. Alexandra Oleson and Sandborn C. Brown (Baltimore and London, 1976), pp. 33–69.
6 CGP, "Important Discovery in Grafting the Peach Tree," *APJ* 1 (1853): 220
7 CGP, "The Petunia," *APJ* 3 (1854): 269.

8   CGP, "Innovations," *APJ* 2 (1853): 240.

9   *APJ* 1 (1853): 25.

10 *Ibid.*, p. 26.

11 CGP, "The Unwritten Rules of the Patent Office," *APJ* 1 (1853): 27.

12 "Report: The Committee on Patents to whom was referred the petition of Thomas G. Clinton" (note 6, Ch. VI), p. 213.

13 CGP, "Some of the Written Rules of the Patent Office," *APJ* 1 (1853): 119.

14 "Information to Persons Having Business to Transact at the United States Patent Office," *S. Ex. Doc. 118*, 32 Cong., 1 sess., p. 516; CGP, "Some of the Written Rules of the Patent Office" (note 13 above), p. 120.

15 CGP, "Rules of the Patent Office," *APJ* 1 (1853): 174.

16 *Ibid.*, p. 175.

17 *Ibid.*

18 *Ibid.*

19 *Ibid.*, p. 176.

20 CGP, "Rules of the Patent Office.—No. 4," *APJ* 1 (1853): 270-271.

21 CGP, "The Patent Office.—No. V," *APJ* 1 (1853): 327.

22 *Ibid.*, pp. 327-328; "The Patent Office," *APJ* 1 (1853): 380-381.

23 *Ibid.*, p. 382; "The Patent Law," *APJ* 2 (1853): 398.

24 "American Contributions to Chemistry," *The American Chemist* 5 (1874-5): 88.

25 CGP, "The Patent Law" (note 23 above), p. 399.

26 *Ibid.*, pp. 399-400.

27 *Ibid.*, p. 400.

28 C. R. Tomkins, *A History of the Planing Mill* (New York, 1889), pp. 31-32.

29 *New York Industrial Exhibition. Special Report of Mr. Joseph Whitworth* (London, 1854), reprinted in Nathan Rosenberg, ed., *The American System of Manufactures* (Edinburgh, 1969), p. 385.

30 N. J. Brumbaugh, "Charles Mason. Commissioner of Patents, 1853-1857," *JPOS* 2 (1919): 122-126; George W. Cullom, *Biographical Register of the Officers and Graduates of the U.S. Military Academy* (New York, 1868), I, p. 22.

31 "Resignation of the U.S. Commissioner of Patents," *SA*, July 14, 1855, p. 357.

32 Quoted in *ibid.*

33 "The Patent Office once more—Defence of the Secretary of the Interior," *SA*, Nov. 3, 1855, p. 58; "Alarming Encroachments on the Patent Office," *SA*, Sept. 8, 1855, p. 411; "More Encroachments on the Patent Office," *SA*, Oct. 20, 1855, p. 45.

34 Mason's Diary, Oct. 14, 1855, Manuscripts Division, LC, quoted in Leila Sellers, "Commissioner Charles Mason and Clara Barton," *JPOS* 22 (1940): 819.

35 Quoted in *SA*, Nov. 14, 1857, p. 78.

36 "The New Commissioner of Patents," *SA*, Sept. 19, 1857, p. 13; "Patent Office Management.—Liberality of Examiners . . . ," *SA*, Oct. 17, 1857, p. 45; "The Commissioner of Patents and the Patent Office," *SA*, Sept. 12, 1857, p. 5.

37 "State of Affairs at the Patent Office," *SA*, Dec. 26, 1857, p. 125.

38 Lane to Davis, Oct. 26, 1858, JHLP.

39 E.g., "Death of Dr. Gale," *EW* 2 (1883): 141; Reingold's *DSB* essay on Lane.

40 "Dr. Everett, of the U.S. Patent Office," *The Inventor* 2 (1857): 331.

41 "The Patent Office and its Management," *SA*, April 9, 1859, p. 253.
42 For biography of Holt see E. D. Sewall, "Joseph Holt, Sixth Commissioner of Patents," *JPOS* 2 (1919): 171–185, and Mary Bernard Allen in *DAB*.
43 "Trouble at the Patent Office—Revising Board Appointed," *SA*, Nov. 3, 1860, p. 299; cf. "Philip Francis Thomas," *JPOS* 2 (1920): 275–282.
44 "New Order of Things at the Patent Office," *SA*, Nov. 10, 1860, p. 313; "The Patent Office and Its Administration," *SA*, Nov. 24, 1860, p. 345; "An Effort to Defend the New Movement at the Patent Office," *SA*, Dec. 1, 1860, p. 361; "Patent Laws and the Patent Office," *SA*, Dec. 15, 1860, p. 394.
45 "The Future of Patents," *SA*, Feb. 9, 1861, p. 83 (from the *NI*).
46 PF 17,808, 26,517, 26,518, 30,688, 31,901.

Chapter Nine

1 "Who Ought to be the Commissioner of Patents?" *SA*, Feb. 16, 1861, p. 105; cf. F. W. Dahn, "David P. Holloway," *JPOS* 2 (1920): 326–332.
2 CGP to Lane, May 6, 1862, JHLP.
3 PSWP, p. 112; JHL, p. 17.
4 CGP to Kendall, Feb. 22, 1848, SFBM.
5 CGP, "Invention of the Magnetic Telegraph," n.p., March 26, 1860. In the 1870s this was published in France by Théodose Du Moncel.
6 Kendall to CGP, April 2, 1860, SFBM.
7 CGP to Kendall, April 4, 1860, *ibid.* Page later published a more detailed version of his flyer, "History of the Magnetic Telegraph: The Receiving Magnet," *Teleg* 3 (1866): 15–16; cf. "A Chapter in the Early History of the Telegraph," *Teleg* 4 (1867): 105.
8 Kendall to CGP, April 5, 1860, SFBM.
9 CGP to Kendall, April 7, 1860, *ibid.*
10 Kendall to Morse, April 9, 1860, *ibid.*
11 Morse to CGP, April [?], 1860 (draft), *ibid.*
12 "Prix Napoléon III pour L'électricité," *Les Mondes* (1863): 337 (from *Le Moniteur Universel*); also, "Galvanism as an Industrial Agent," *The Inventor* 2 (1857): 290; J. B. A. Dumas, "Application de L'Électricité. Rapport à L'Empereur," *L'Invention* 19 (1864): 321–334; J. Nicklès, "Prize for applications of the Electric Pile," *AJS*, 2d ser. 39 (1865): 79–81.
13 "H. D. Ruhmkorff," *La Nature* 6 (1878): 97.
14 Footnote to the report by Nicklès, Silliman's European correspondent, *AJS* 15 (1853): 114.
15 S.H.W., "Professor Page the Inventor of the Ruhmkorff Coil," *SA*, Jan. 28, 1865, p. 69; also, "The Ruhmkorff Coil," *ibid.*, p. 6.
16 "Ruhmkorff's Induction Coil," *American Artisan* 1 (Nov. 2, 1864): 202.
17 "An Examination of the Page Patent, as Affecting Telegraphic Interests," *Teleg* 7 (1871): 209.
18 *Memorial to the Congress of the United States by Charles G. Page on His Invention of the Induction Coil and Automatic Circuit Breaker* (Washington, 1867). A copy of this is included in *Decisions of the Commissioner of Patents for the Year 1880* (Washington, 1881), pp. 352–353.
19 "Charles Grafton Page [To Accompany H. R. No. 102]: Report Prepared by the Committee on Patents," *H. Mis. Doc. 30*, 40 Cong., 1 sess., pp. 2, 5.
20 E.g., Antoine César et Edmond Becquerel, *Traité D'Électricité et de Magnétisme*, Tome Troisième, *Magnétisme et Electro-Magnétisme* (Paris, 1856), p. 241; see also Emil Kosack, *Heinrich Daniel Rühmkorff, ein Deutcher*

Erfinder. Ein Lebensbild zu seinem 100. Geburtstage (Leipzig and Hannover, 1903), p. 14.

21 Beardslee to Henry, June 18, 1868, June 20, 1868, WJR.

22 "Report Prepared by the Committee on Patents" (note 19 above), p. 6.

23 CGP, *History of Induction* (note 50, Ch. I), p. 116.

24 *Ibid.*, pp. 45–47, 104–107; also, William B. Rogers, "Ruhmkorf's [*sic*] Apparatus constructed by E. S. Ritchie of Boston," *AJS*, 2d ser. (1857): 451–452; Rogers, "Notice of a Powerful Induction Coil constructed by E. S. Ritchie of Boston, U. S.," *Edinburgh New Philosophical Journal* 6 (1857): 189–190.

25 CGP, *History of Induction* (note 50, Ch. I), p. 119; "Statements by Prof. Mac Culloch," in E. S. Ritchie, "On Electrical Machines," *JFI* 43 (1862): 58–60; A. E. Dolbear, "Edward Samuel Ritchie," *Proc Am Acad* 23 (1895–1896): 359–360.

26 *CG*, Feb. 11, 1868, pp. 1178–1179.

27 *Ibid.*, March 17, 1868, p. 2026.

28 "Report Prepared by the Committee on Patents" (note 19 above), p. 7.

29 Sunderland (note 7, Prologue), p. 7.

30 *Ibid.*

31 *Ibid.*, p. 5; Archives of the Vital Records Section of the Bureau of Vital Statistics, Washington, D.C., and of Oak Hill Cemetery.

32 *American Artisan* 6 (1868): 280; *The American Annual Cyclopedia and Register of Important Events for the Year 1868* (New York, 1871), VIII, p. 607; *Teleg* 4 (1868): 319.

33 "The Induction Coil Patent of Prof. Charles G. Page," *Teleg* 4 (1868): 320.

34 "Death and a Fortune—A Sweeping Patent. Obituary," *JT* 1 (May 15, 1868): 4.

35 Quoted in "A New Telegraph Patent for Old Inventions," *SA*, June 13, 1868, pp. 377–378.

36 "The Page Patent Litigation.—Answer of the Manhattan Quotation Company," *Teleg* (1874): 49.

37 "The Page Patent.—The Attempts to Enforce it to be Resisted," *Teleg* 8 (1872): 468; also, "An Examination of the Page Patent, as Affecting Telegraph Interests," *Teleg* 7 (1871): 209.

38 "Priscilla W. Page, as Administratrix, &c., and the Western Union Telegraph Company *vs.* The Holmes Burglar Alarm Telegraph Company," Circuit Court, S. D. New York, Feb. 17 and May 6, 1880: 17 *Blatchford* 484; 1 *Fed. Reporter* 304; 2 *Fed. Reporter* 330. "Gamewell Fire-Alarm Telegraph Co. *vs.* City of Chillicothe," Circuit Court, S. D. Ohio, May 1881: 7 *Fed. Reporter* 351.

39 CGP to Kidder, Dec. 16, 1863, PF 41,927.

40 "The Western Union Telegraph Company and the Ruhmkorff Coil," *Teleg* 12 (1876): 152; "The Page Patent Litigation," *Teleg* 10 (1874): 29.

41 "Inventory of goods, chattels, and personal estate of Charles Grafton Page," May 13, 1868; "Estate of Chas. Grafton Page, First and Final account of administrators . . . ," Dec. 4, 1900, RG 21, Wills and Estate Records of Residents of the District of Columbia, NRC.

42 Statement dated April 26, 1868, WHC.

43 "The Page Patent," *The Electrical Review* 6 (April 4, 1885): 1.

44 Reingold, "Alexander Dallas Bache" (note 21, Ch. II), p. 163.

45 "The Beginnings of American Science. The Third Century," *A Memorial of George Brown Goode Together With a Selection of his Papers on Museums*

and on the *History of Science in America (Annual Report of the Smithson-*
ian Institution . . . 1897. Report of the United States National Museum.
Part II [Washington, 1901]), p. 452.

46   Mitchell Wilson, *American Science and Invention: A Pictorial History* (New
York, 1954), p. 288; Julius Grodinsky, *Jay Gould: His Business Career,*
1867-1892 (Philadelphia, 1970), p. 451.

47   "The Interaction of Science and Technology," in *The Impact of Science on*
Technology, eds. Aaron W. Warner, *et al.* (New York and London, 1965),
p. 10.

48   Du Moncel, *Exposé des Applications de L'Électricité,* II, p. 238; also, George
B. Prescott, *Electricity and the Electric Telegraph* (New York, 1888), I,
p. 131; F. Uppenborn, *History of the Transformer* (London and New York,
1889), pp. 609; Frederick Bedell, *The Principles of the Transformer*
(London and New York, 1896), pp. 290-292; Cajori, *A History of Physics in*
its Elementary Branches (note 38, Ch. I), pp. 250-251; H. Armagnat, *La*
Bobine D'Induction (Paris, 1905), pp. 10-12 (trans. & ed. by Otis Allen
Kenyon, *The Theory, Design and Construction of Induction Coils* [New
York, 1909], p. 8); E. Taylor-Jones, *The Theory of the Induction Coil*
(London, 1921), pp. 1-2; George Shiers, "The Induction Coil," *SA,* May
1971, pp. 80-87.

. Sources

As a belated convert to brevity with regard to "scholarly apparatus," I prefer to limit myself here to noting manuscript reposito-
ries with pertinent documents and to listing Page's articles, books,
published correspondence, government reports, and patents.
Nearly all the secondary sources that I found directly relevant
are cited in the notes; to list those indirectly relevant would be
literally irrelevant, because such a list would include much of
everything I have ever read. (Anybody interested in a secondary
bibliography can find one in this book's prior incarnation as a
doctoral dissertation, University Microfilms #74-11,561.) Here,
first, the archives:

American Philosophical Society, Philadelphia: John F. Frazer
Papers.
Bureau of Vital Statistics, Washington, D.C.: Vital Records Sec-
tion.
Essex Institute, Salem, Massachusetts: Archives, James Duncan
Phillips Library.
Fairfax County Courthouse, Fairfax, Virginia: Land Records.
Franklin Institute, Philadelphia: O. W. Gibbs Papers.
George Washington University, Washington, D.C.: Archives of
the University Historian.
Harvard College Library Archives, Cambridge.
Joseph W. Hazell Collection (private), Corte Madera, California:
Page Family Papers.
Historical Society of Pennsylvania, Philadelphia: Titian R. Peale
Papers.
Library of Congress, Washington, D.C.: Alexander Dallas Bache
Papers, Matthew Fontaine Maury Papers, Samuel F. B. Morse
Papers.
National Archives, Washington, D.C.: Record Group 45—Old
Military Records Division, Miscellaneous Letters Received by
the Secretary of the Navy, 1801–1884; Record Group 167—
Records of the National Bureau of Standards, J. H. Lane
Papers.
National Records Center, Suitland, Maryland: Record Group
21—Wills and Estate Records of Residents of the District of
Columbia; Record Group 241—Records of the United States
Patent Office, Patented Files.

206

Renssalaer Polytechnic Institute, Troy, New York: Eben N. Horsford Papers.

Smithsonian Institution Archives, Washington, D.C.: Alexander Dallas Bache Collection, Spencer F. Baird Papers, Joseph Henry Papers, William J. Rhees Collection, Vail Telegraph Collection.

Smithsonian Institution, National Museum of History and Technology: Archives of the Division of Electricity.

University of California, Los Angeles, Department of Special Collections: Moses G. Farmer Papers.

University of Pennsylvania: Archives General 1847: Faculty Positions; Robert Hare Papers.

Vermont Historical Society Archives, Montpelier.

Yale University Archives: Silliman Family Papers; Beinecke Rare Book and Manuscript Library: Elias Loomis Papers.

These collections include all the Page manuscript material that I know of, though I would not be surprised if there were others, perhaps quite a number of them. I would be even less surprised to find that the following list of publications is incomplete, but it is at least suggestive of the substance of Page's career in its major facets:

"Notice of some New Electrical Instruments." *AJS* 26 (1834): 110–112.

"Movements on the Surface of Water produced by the Vibration of Glass." *AJS* 30 (1836): 192.

"Method of increasing shocks, and experiments, with Prof. Henry's apparatus for obtaining sparks and shocks from the Calorimotor." *AJS* 31 (1836): 137–141. Reprinted in *Annals* 1 (1837): 290–295, along with Sturgeon's "Explanation of the Phenomena, &c."

"Galvanism." *AJS* 32 (1837): 197–198. From the Salem *Observer*.

"On the use of the Dynamic Multiplier, with a new accompanying apparatus." *AJS* 32 (1837): 354–360.

"The Production of Galvanic Music." *AJS* 32 (1837): 396–397.

"Experiments in Electro-Magnetism." *AJS* 33 (1838): 118–120. Reprinted in *Annals* 2 (1838): 214–218. In Jan. 1845, the *London Electrical Magazine* claimed that the production of musical tones in magnets and iron bars was a European discovery of 1842. In response, Page inserted a note in the *AJS* 48 (1845): 401, calling attention to the fact that he had described that phenomenon in both this paper and the preceding one.

"Electro-Magnetic Apparatus and Experiments." *AJS* 33 (1838): 190-192. Reprinted in part in *Annals* 2 (1838): 142-145, along with Sturgeon's remarks.

"Rotary Multiplier, or Astatic Galvanometer." *AJS* 33 (1838): 376-379. Reprinted, along with remainder of the above paper and a note by Sturgeon, in *Annals* 2 (1838): 286-290.

"New Magnetic Electrical Machine of great power; with two parallel horse-shoe magnets, and two straight rotating armatures, affording each, in an entire revolution, a constant current in the same direction." *AJS* 34 (1838): 163-169. Reprinted in *Annals* 3 (1839): 389-393.

"Researches in Magnetic Electricity and new Magnetic Electrical Instruments: 1. Compound Electro-Magnets for the Magnetic Electrical spark, shock, and decomposition. 2. New Magnetic Electrical Machine, or Magneto-Electric Multiplier, convertible into an Electro-Magnetic Engine." *AJS* 34 (1838): 364-373. Reprinted in *Annals* 3 (1839): 478-486.

"On Electro-Magnetism as a Moving Power." *AJS* 35 (1839): 106-111. Reprinted in *Annals* 3 (1839): 554-559.

"Magnetic Electrepeter and Electrotome, to be used with flat spirals." *AJS* 35 (1839): 112-113. Reprinted in *Annals* 3 (1839): 559-560.

"Magneto-Electric and Electro Magnetic Apparatus and Experiments." *AJS* 35 (1839): 252-268.

"Galvanic Batteries—On the Benefit of Fresh Immersion." *AJS* 36 (1839): 137-140.

"Description of a remarkable echo in Fairfax Co., Virginia." *AJS* 36 (1839): 174-175.

"Application of the Galvanoscope to detect the Failure of Water in Steam Boilers." *AJS* 36 (1839): 141-143.

"Electro Magnetism." *AJS* 36 (1839): 350-353.

"Observations on Electricity." *AJS* 36 (1839): 353-354.

"Magneto-Electric Multiplier." *AJS* 37 (1839): 275-276.

"Notice of a Spiral Magnet, by which Secondary Currents may be demonstrated in the Body of a Magnet." *JFI*, 3d ser. 3 (1842): 166-167.

"Description of a New Plate, or Quantity, Helix, for Electro Magnetic Apparatus." *JFI*, 3d ser. 3 (1842): 167-168.

"Report of the First Examiner on the Arts." *ARCP* 1843, pp. 310-333.

"Report of Charles G. Page, Examiner &c." *ARCP* 1844, pp. 508-518.

"Improvement in the magneto-electric machine, and application of this instrument to operate the magnetic telegraph." *ARCP* 1844, pp. 440-441. Among the several periodicals to reprint this was the *AJS* 48 (1845): 392-393.

"New Electro-Magnetic Engine." *AJS* 49 (1845): 131-135.

"Axial Galvanometer, and Double Axial Reciprocating Engine." *AJS* 49 (1845): 136-142.

"Report of Charles G. Page, Examiner &c." *ARCP* 1845, pp. 25-44.

"Remarkable Paraselene witnessed on the night of 19th April, 1845." *AJS*, 2d ser. 1 (1846): 136.

"Axial Galvanometer." *AJS*, 2d ser. 1 (1846): 242-244.

"Law of Electro-Magnetic Induction." *AJS*, 2d ser. 2 (1846): 202-204.

"On the Probable Conduction of Galvanic Electricity Through Moist Air." *AJS*, 2d ser. 2 (1846): 204-209.

"Electric Conduction." *AJS*, 2d ser. 2 (1846): 406-407.

"To the Hon. Edmund Burke, Commissioner of Patents." *ARCP* 1846, pp. 15-40.

"Revolution of a Magnet on its own Axis without the use of Mercurial Conductors, and Also without Visible Support." *AJS*, 2d ser. 3 (1847): 252-254.

"The Electro-Telegraph." New York *Journal of Commerce*, July 16, 1847. From *NI*.

"Singular Property of Caoutchouc, illustrating the value of Latent Heat in giving Elasticity to solid bodies, and the distant functions in this respect of latent and free or sensible heat." *AJS*, 2d ser. 3 (1847): 341-342.

"To the Hon. Edmund Burke, Commissioner of Patents." *ARCP* 1847, pp. 19-49.

"Report of Charles G. Page, Examiner of Patents." *ARCP* 1848, pp. 20-30.

"Memorial of Charles G. Page praying an investigation of a mode discovered by him of applying electro-magnetic power to purposes of navigation and locomotion." *S. Mis. Doc. 59*, 30 Cong., 2 sess. Washington: Tippin and Streeper, 1849.

Electricity vs. Steam . . . Part of Prof. Page's Lecture on Electro-Magnetic Power, Delivered in Washington, February 21, 1849, before the Special Committee from the Senate of the United States. Washington: J. T. Towers, Printer, 1849. Also included are Page's memorial to Congress, the report of the special committee to which his memorial was referred, and extracts from Thomas Hart Benton's speech of February 7, 1849, on the introduction of a bill to provide for a Central National Road.

"Polarization of Galvanic Light." *AJS*, 2d ser. 7 (1849): 375. Page published this experiment believing it to be original, then later discovered that the credit belonged to Arago and acknowledged this in the *AJS*, 2d ser. 8 (1849): 146.

Page to William Ballard Preston, Secretary of the Navy, Oct. 2, 1849. *H. Ex. Doc. 5*, 31 Cong., 1 sess. (Washington: Printed for the House of Reps., 1849): 445.

"Examiners' and Machinists' Reports." *ARCP* 1849, Pt. I, pp. 403–419.

"Vibrations of Trevelyan's bars by the Galvanic Current." *AJS*, 2d ser. 9 (1850): 105–108. Page published virtually this same article in the *APJ* 2 (1853): 315–317.

"On Electro-magnetism as a Moving Power." *AJS*, 2d ser. 10 (1850): 343–345, 473–476.

"On Electro-Magnetism as a Motive Force." *Proc AAAS*, Third Meeting, Charleston, March 1850 (Charleston: Walker and James, 1850): 17–18 (abstract). Reports of Page's demonstrations also appeared in the *JFI*, 3d ser. 20 (1850): 267–271; and *SA* 6 (Sept. 21, 1850): 2.

"Singular Property and Extraordinary Size and Length of the Secondary Spark." *AJS*, 2d ser. 10 (1850): 349.

"Report from the Secretary of the Navy Transmitting a Copy of the report of Professor Charles G. Page, on electro-magnetic power as a mechanical agent for the purposes of navigation and locomotion" (Washington: Wm. Belt, 1850): 1–5. *S. Ex. Doc. 61*, 31 Cong., 1 sess. Page to William A. Graham, Aug. 30, 1850. Appended is a report from the *NI*, Aug. 29, 1850, with comments on Page's work by Benjamin Silliman, Sr., Walter R. Johnson, Joseph Henry, and Benjamin Peirce. Page's report was reprinted in the *JFI*, 3d ser. 20 (1850): 267–271, and the *Phil Mag*, 4th ser. 1 (1851): 161–167, in the latter along with an article from the *NI*, Sept. 11, 1850. It also appeared, under a different cover-letter dated Nov. 12, 1850, as *S. Ex. Doc. 7* of the 31 Cong., 2 sess.

"Electro Magnetic Engine—Letter from Prof. Page." *SA* 6 (Oct. 19, 1850): 36.

"Examiners' and Machinists' Reports." *ARCP* 1850, Pt. I, pp. 304–308.

"On the time required to raise the Galvanic Current to its

maximum in Coiled Conductors, and its importance in Electro-Mechanics." *AJS*, 2d ser. 11 (1851): 86-89.

"Electro-Magnetic Experiments." *SA* 6 (March 29, 1851): 222.

"Electro-Magnetic Locomotive." *AJS*, 2d ser. 11 (1851): 139-141. From *NI*, May 3, 1851.

"A new figure in Mica and other Phenomena of Polarized Light." *AJS*, 2d ser. 11 (1851): 89-91. An excerpt from this paper was printed in the *Phil Mag*, 4th ser. 1 (1851): 262-263.

"On the direction of the Spark from Secondary Currents under the influence of Helices or Magnets." *AJS*, 2d ser. 11 (1851): 191-192.

"On the Conduction and Distribution of the Galvanic Current in Liquids." *AJS*, 2d ser. 11 (1851): 192-193.

"On Telegraphs, and on Gutta Percha as a means of insulation." *AJS*, 2d ser. 11 (1851): 287-290.

Page to William A. Graham, Secretary of the Navy, Nov. 28, 1851. *Report of the Secretary of the Navy* (Washington: A. Boyd Hamilton, 1852): 64-67. *H. Ex. Doc. 1*, 32 Cong., 1 sess.

"The Economical Constant Battery." *AJS*, 2d ser. 13 (1852): 257-260.

"Our Journal." *APJ* 1 (1853): 3-4.

"Career of Science." *APJ* 1 (1853): 4-5.

"Electro-Mechanics." *APJ* 1 (1853): 5-12, 81-82, 161-163, 225-227, 305-307, 369-370; 4 (1854): 305-306.

"On the Vital Properties of Electricity." *APJ* 1 (1853): 13-16.

"The Magne-Crystallic Theory." *APJ* 1 (1853): 16.

"On a New Rheostat." *APJ* 1 (1853): 16-17.

"The Patent Office." *APJ* 1 (1853): 25-27, 327-328, 380-382; 2 (1853): 79.

"Dignity of Patents." *APJ* 1 (1853): 27-29.

"On a New Electro Magnetic Apparatus for Equalizing Motion for Telegraphic and Other Purposes." *APJ* 1 (1853): 83.

"On a New Thermo-Galvanometer." *APJ* 1 (1853): 84.

"Some of the Written Rules of the Patent Office." *APJ* 1 (1853): 119-120.

"Rules of the Patent Office." *APJ* 1 (1853): 174-176, 269-271.

"Important Discovery in Grafting the Peach-Tree." *APJ* 1 (1853): 220-221.

"Patent Office Report." *APJ* 1 (1853): 327.

"On a New Voltameter." *APJ* 2 (1853): 15.

"Decisions of Assistant Judge of the Circuit Court of the District of Columbia In Matters of Appeal from the Decision of the Commissioner of Patents." *APJ* 2 (1853): 22.

"Book Notices. The Working Farmer." *APJ* 2 (1853): 160.

"Innovations." *APJ* 2 (1853): 240.

"Practical Results From the Discovery and Study of Polarized Light." *APJ* 2 (1853): 393–394.

"The Patent Law." *APJ* 2 (1853): 397–400.

Psychomancy: Spirit Rappings and Table Tippings Exposed. New York: D. Appleton and Company, 1853.

"Improvement in Electro-Magnetic Engines," Pat. 10,480, *ARCP* 1854, Pt. 1, pp. 223–224 (abstract).

"Successful and Easy Mode of Preventing the Ravages of the Peach Insect." *APJ* 3 (1854): 6.

"Artificial Fecundation of Flowers." *APJ* (1854): 95–98.

"A Meteorological Phenomenon." *APJ* (1854): 217–219.

"The Petunia." *APJ* 3 (1854): 269–272.

"Professor C. G. Page's Patent Electro-Axial Engine." *APJ* 3 (1854): 273–277. Includes a postscript by John J. Greenough.

"Wood Gas." *SA* 9 (Oct. 28, 1854): 50.

"Improvement in Locking Cylindrical Door Bolts," Pat. 17,808, *ARCP* 1857, Pt. 1, p. 436 (abstract).

"Combined Umbrella and Head Rest," Pat. 20,507, *ARCP* 1858, Pt. II, p. 224 (abstract).

"Improvement in Pipe Couplings," Pat. 26,517 (with Ralph J. Falconer), "Improvement in Door Bolts," Pat. 26,518, *ARCP* 1859, Pt. I, p. 743 (abstract).

"Invention of the Magnetic Telegraph." n.p., March 26, 1860. Two copies of this are in SFBM, one briefly annotated by Morse. Théodose Du Moncel, *Exposé des Applications de L'Électricité*, III, *Télégraphie Electrique* (3d ed., Paris: Librairie Scientifique, Industrielle et Agrigole, 1874): 87–89, translates it in full.

"Improvement in Aural Instruments," Pat. 30,688, *ARCP* 1860, Pt. I, p. 751 (abstract).

"The Future of Patents." *SA*, ns 4 (Feb. 9, 1861): 83. From *NI*.

"Improved Refrigerator," Pat. 31,901, *ARCP* 1861, Pt. I, p. 263 (abstract).

"Gun Cotton." *SA*, ns 14 (Jan. 7, 1866): 21.

"History of the Magnetic Telegraph: The Receiving Magnet." *Teleg* 3 (Sept. 15, 1866): 15–16.

"Interesting Acoustic Phenomenon." *SA*, ns 15 (Sept. 22, 1866): 197.

Memorial to the Congress of the United States by Charles G. Page on his Invention of the Induction Coil and Automatic Circuit Breaker. Washington: Polkinhorn & Son, 1867. A copy of this is included in *Decisions of the Commissioner of Patents for the Year 1880* (Washington: G.P.O., 1881): 352–353.

American Claim to the Induction Coil. Washington, 1867. Prospectus for *History of Induction,* below.

History of Induction: The American Claim to the Induction Coil and its Electrostatic Developments. In Three Parts. I. Induction and Induction Apparatus. II. Contact or Circuit Breakers. III. Electrostatic Properties of Induction Coils and Magneto-Electric Machines. Washington: Intelligencer Printing House, 1867.

"Induction Coil Apparatus and Circuit Breaker," Pat. 76,654, *ARCP* 1868, Pt. I, p. 807 (abstract).

"Electro Magnetism as a Motive Power." *SA,* ns 18 (May 16, 1868): 308.

"To the Building Committee of the Smithsonian Institution, on the action of frost upon certain materials for building." *Journal and Reports of the Building Committee of the Smithsonian Institution, From 1847 to 1868. (Smithsonian Miscellaneous Collections,* Vol. 18.) Washington: Published by the Smithsonian Institution, 1880. Page's report, pp. 600–601, is dated March 5, 1847.

213

1. Jere Lee Page

2. Lucy Lang Page

3. Charles Grafton Page

4. Priscilla Sewall Webster Page

(Courtesy of Mrs. Joseph W. Hazell)

5. *Washington City as it looked when Page first saw it, 1838 (Library of Congress)*

INVENTIONS

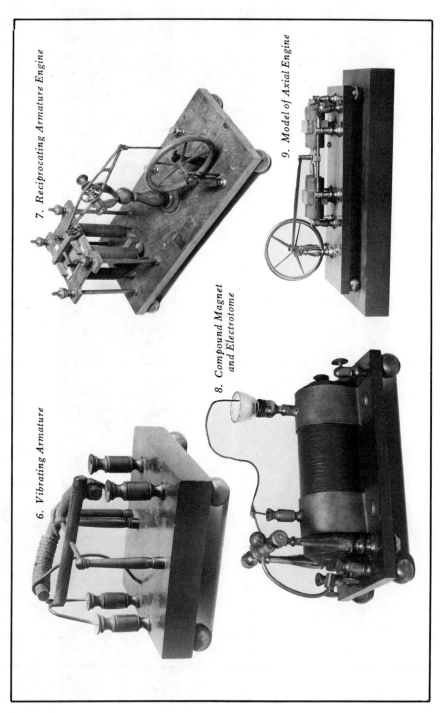

7. *Reciprocating Armature Engine*

9. *Model of Axial Engine*

6. *Vibrating Armature*

8. *Compound Magnet and Electrotome*

(*Smithsonian Institution*)

10. *South facade of the Patent Office, 1846 (Library of Congress)*

11. *Grafton Cottage, in the district now known as Brightwood, about 1855*

(Courtesy of Mrs. Joseph W. Hazell)

12. *Daniel Davis, Jr.*

13. *Samuel F. B. Morse*

14. *Alfred Vail*

15. *Joseph Henry*

16. Daniel Webster

17. Rufus Choate

18. Thomas Hart Benton

(Library of Congress)

19. *Henry L. Ellsworth*

20. *Edmund Burke*

21. *Thomas Ewbank*

22. *Charles Mason*

(Smithsonian Institution)

Toledo May 24th 1854,

Sir

As assignee of Jas S Rowley I fully concur in the power of attorney given by him to Messrs Page, Greenough & Fleischmann to its full extent, in his case now pending for an alleged improvement in carriages.

R H Gibson

Hon Chas Mason
Comr of Patents

23. *Page as entrepreneur (National Archives)*

UNITED STATES PATENT OFFICE.

CHAS. G. PAGE, OF WASHINGTON, DISTRICT OF COLUMBIA.

COMBINED UMBRELLA AND HEAD-REST.

Specification of Letters Patent No. 20,507, dated June 8, 1858.

To all whom it may concern:

Be it known that I, CHARLES G. PAGE, of Washington, District of Columbia, have invented an Improvement in Portable Head-Rests for Travelers, and that the following is a full, clear, and exact description of the principle or character which distinguishes it from all other things before known and of the usual manner of making, modifying, and using the same, reference being had to the accompanying drawings, of which—

Figures 1, 2, 3, 4, 5 and 7 represent various forms of head rest; Fig. 6, one of the rests adapted to the umbrella so as to form the handle of the umbrella and Fig. 8 one of the rests ready for use.

My invention consists in so combining a head rest with an umbrella as to furnish a convenient and comfortable resting place for the head, thereby enabling persons to sleep when traveling in railroad cars or elsewhere; while the combination does not encumber the umbrella or interfere with its ordinary uses. A variety of devices have been essayed hitherto, for portable head rests for travelers, but the practical objection to a head rest is the trouble of carrying an extra article of luggage or baggage. As travelers generally carry umbrellas, this peculiar combination removes such practical objection.

Another objection to an independent or a special head rest is the expense of the article, which is of occasional use, only, whereas if the head be an integral part of an umbrella as according to Figs. 1, 2, 3, 4 and 6, or if it be affixed to the umbrella in any such way that when in use the umbrella forms an integral part of the head rest, as according to Figs. 5, 7 and 8, the expense of such head rest will be very small.

One of the advantages of this peculiar combination of a head rest and umbrella is derived from the umbrella covering itself which makes a part of the comfort of the support for the head and back when leaning against it.

Fig. 7 represents a head rest *a* attached to an umbrella ready for use. The rest is a thin strip of metal (or other convenient material) and is fastened to the umbrella by bands *b* or clasps tied by strings or secured in other well known ways. When the rest is not needed for use it may be tied anywhere upon the inside of the umbrella so as always to be in readiness when required.

For the purpose of rendering the rest compact so as not to inconvenience the umbrella, it may be made in two or more parts hinged together so as to fold up, or it may be shortened by other well known devices for rendering such articles portable.

In using the head rest, the umbrella is placed behind the back and against the back of the seat and the pressure of the body will keep it in place while the head is supported by the rest.

Another mode of applying my invention is shown in Fig. 2, in which *c* is the handle of the umbrella and *d* the rod or stem to which it is usually attached by the screw *e*. The handle *c* has one of its faces curved to adapt it to the purpose of a head rest, and when required for use as a head rest, it is unscrewed from the rod and the screw inserted into the hole *h* which is provided with a metallic nut let into the handle for the purpose of strength.

Another mode of applying my invention is shown in Figs. 1, 2, 3, 4, 6 and 8, in which the handle is attached to the rod as in Fig. 2 and has also one of its faces curved to adapt it to the back of the head. In this handle are two oblong openings *i*, *i* through which the ends of the umbrella bows *k*, *k*, are to pass when it is to be used for a head rest. In most instances the rest or handle will be too high for a person's head, and the head will then rest easily in the space *m*, *m*, between the separated bows. The rest or handle in this case serves as a yoke to divide and hold apart the bows, as clearly shown in Fig. 8, and the covering of the umbrella makes a soft cushion for the head.

Instead of perforating the handle, the yoke may be made by an additional strip or guard piece *n*, *n*, Fig. 4 or by means of strings or chains *p*, *p*, Fig. 3. Instead of connecting the yoke with the handle it may be made separate and the handle made in the ordinary way.

Fig. 5 exhibits a separate yoke made of a strip of metal or other suitable material, which when out of use is to be tied or otherwise fastened within the umbrella so as not to be an encumbrance.

What I claim as my invention is—

Combining a head rest with an umbrella as herein set forth.

CHAS. G. PAGE.

Witnesses:
THOS. E. SLOYD,
R. G. CAMPBELL.

24. Another side of Page the inventor (National Archives)

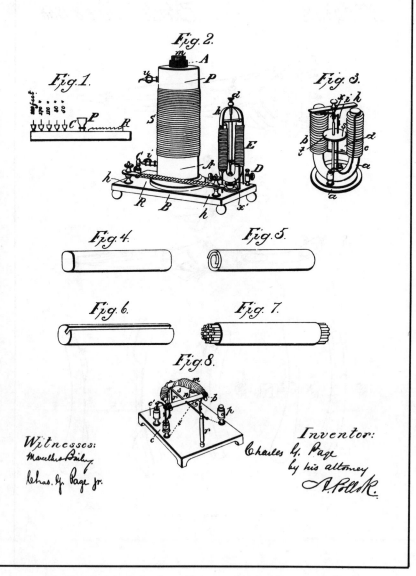

C. G. PAGE.

Induction Coil Apparatus and Circuit Breaker.

No. 76,654. Patented Apr. 14, 1868.

Fig. 1.

Fig. 2.

Fig. 3.

Fig. 4.

Fig. 5.

Fig. 6.

Fig. 7.

Fig. 8.

Witnesses:
Marcellus Bailey
Chas. G. Page Jr.

Inventor:
Charles G. Page
by his attorney
A. Pollok.

25. *Drawings for induction coil patent of 1868 (National Archives)*

2 Sheets—Sheet 2

C. G. PAGE.

Induction Coil Apparatus and Circuit Breaker.

No. 76,654.   Patented Apr. 14, 1868.

26. *Drawings for induction coil patent of 1868 (National Archives)*

THE ANSWER

To the False Memorial by Charles G. Page to Congress, in his attempts to appropriate Dr. Jerome Kidder's Improvements in Electrical Apparatus.

PAGE

THE INVENTOR OF THE

RUHMKORFF COIL,

NOR OF ANY

Electrical Coil Whatever,

NOR OF ANY

MECHANICAL DEVICE NOW USED

IN THE

Manufacture of Electrical Apparatus.

~~~~~~~~~~

By JEROME KIDDER, M. D.,

Inventor of Improved Electro-Medical Apparatus, producing Physiologically Different Qualities of Electricity.

NEW YORK:
NELSON ROW, STEAM BOOK AND JOB PRINTER,
No. 44 West Broadway.

1876.

27. *Title page from Jerome Kidder's attack, 1876 (Smithsonian Institution)*

INDEX

Abolitionism, 38, 177

Acoustics, 18-19, 31, 35, 103; CGP patents hearing aid, 160

Adams, John Quincy, 45; on Henry Ellsworth, 108

Agassiz, Louis, 1, 5, 132, 142, 143, 170, 181

Albany Academy, 9

Albany *Knickerbocker*, attacks Henry, 130

Alexander, C. M., 160

American Academy of Arts and Sciences, contrasted to Smithsonian by *Scientific American*, 130

American Artisan, 139

American Association for the Advancement of Science (AAAS), 62, 105; CGP describes experiments to members, 92; and *Scientific American*, 107, 131

American Journal of Science, The, 1, 2, 9, 15, 25, 44, 76, 106, 139

American Polytechnic Journal, 139, 143, 146, 153

American Railroad Journal, 100; on CGP's locomotive, 84

American Rapid Telegraph Co., sued by Western Union, 181

American Telegraph Magazine, on CGP's locomotive, 84

Amherst College, CGP's elder brother advises him to attend, 14

Ampère, André-Marie, 17, 66, 75, 80

Ampère, J. J., interest in CGP's locomotive, 103

Annals of Electricity, Magnetism, and Chemistry (Sturgeon's), 10, 15, 16

Antisell, Thomas, 51, 162; background, 155

Arago, Dominique, 13, 77

Ashburton, Lord, 64

Association of American Geologists and Naturalists, 62. *See also* American Association for the Advancement of Science

Atlantic and Pacific Co., sued by Western Union, 180, 181

Autotransformer. *See* Dynamic Multiplier

Axial engine. *See* Electric motors

Bache, Alexander Dallas, 3, 11, 31, 117, 123, 131, 164, 172, 182, 186; diversity of pursuits, 47; laments scarcity of jobs with time for research, 55; salary, 61; relinquishes time before AAAS to CGP, 92, 105; CGP asks to investigate economics of his motors, 104; CGP queries about job for Lane, 124; and chartering of National Academy, 170

Bachhoffner, George, 24

Baconianism, as characterized by Pierre Duhem, 23

Bailey, Harriet. *See* Page, Harriet

Bailey, Marcellus, 177

Bain, Alexander, 72

Baird, Spencer, 1

Barlow, Peter, 139

Barton, Clara, 154, 155

Battery, 13, 16, 17, 18, 19, 20, 24, 25, 30, 62, 67-69, 82, 87, 88, 90, 100, 101, 102, 143; in CGP's locomotive, 96-97, 98, 99

Beach, Alfred E., 110, 111, 112, 113, 125. *See also Scientific American*

Beard, Charles and Mary, on American science, quoted, 26-27

Beardslee, George, details CGP's scientific attainments to Henry, 174

Becquerel, Antoine, 170

Beecher, Henry Ward, as student of Fitzgerald's, 58

Bell, Alexander Graham, 41; on CGP and genesis of electroacoustics, 18

Benton, Jessie. *See* Frémont, Jessie Benton

Benton, Thomas Hart, 45, 65, 165; sponsors appropriation for CGP's experiments, 84-95; concept of electric motor, 87; partisan of lead-mining interests, 87-88; and Central National Road, 88; proposes ship powered by electromagnetism, 90-91;

periments with magnetos and helices, 30; bolder about addressing matters beyond empirical verification, 31; sense of intimacy with electromagnetism, 31; temporarily retires from pursuit of science, 31, 39; Davenport refuses offer of partnership, 39; lacks sufficient income, 40, 44; practices medicine in northern Virginia, 44; joins National Institute, 44–45; becomes patent examiner (1842), 11, 46, 55; diversity of avocational pursuits, 46, 56; career marked by controversial episodes, 47; duties as patent examiner, 55–56; resumes electrical experimentation (1843), 56, 61–62; reviews first two years as examiner, 56–57; friendship with Ellsworth, 55, 60; workload grows, 61; begins experimenting with solenoid motors, 62; stages exhibition for Association of American Geologists and Naturalists (1844), 62; meets Priscilla Sewall Webster, 63; marriage and first children, 63; friendship with Daniel Webster, 65; steadfast Whig, 65; prime years, 66; becomes consultant to Morse, 58, 62, 67–69, 70; instrumental in formation of Magnetic Telegraph Company (1845), 70; testifies in Morse vs O'Reilly suit (1848), 71–72; terminates business relationship with Morse, 72; becomes Professor of Chemistry and Pharmacy at Columbian College, 72; helps establish National Medical College (1844), 62, 73; welcomes Henry to Washington, 74; corresponds with Henry on electrical science, 75–76; stages exhibitions at Washington Infirmary, 76; inquires about professorship at Princeton (1846), 77; inquires about professorship at University of Pennsylvania, 78; solicits letters of recommendation, 79–80; applies for professorship at Lawrence Scientific School, 80; decides to remain in Washington (1847), 81; demonstrates utility of solenoid motors, 81–82; seeks Congressional subsidy, 82; rejects theories of Joule and Helmholtz, 82–83; attracts allies, 83; cause taken up by Thomas Hart Benton, 84–85; demonstrates motors to special Senate committee, 85–86; expresses optimism about electric power, 86, 88–89; awarded $20,000 appropriation for further experi-

mentation (1849), 45, 87; outlines progress of experiments, 89; criticized by Davenport and Scientific American, 89–90, 105; son dies, 90; reports on experiments, 90, 91–92; Benton moves for second appropriation, 91; addresses AAAS meeting in New Haven (1850), 92, 105; leading scientists comment favorably, 92; concedes that electric power costs more than steam, 93; considers motors of alternative design, 93; constitutionality of appropriation disputed by Jefferson Davis, 94–95; attempt to secure House appropriation, 95–96; attacked by Andrew Johnson, 96; borrows money to complete locomotive, 96; trial run to Bladensburg and back (1851), 97–99; private investors not interested, 99; continues to uphold empiricism, 99–100, 101, 103; resumes public exhibitions, 100; denigrates "mathematical reasoning," 101, 103; involvement in science of galvanism, 101; importance in history of electromagnetism, 102; confronts tactical but not strategic problem, 102–103; interest of Ampère's son in locomotive, 103; turns to relatively unsophisticated sciences, 12, 103; publishes last significant paper on electromagnetism, 103; misapprehension about official sanction from Smithsonian, 104; requests investigation by Henry, Bache, and Johnson, 104; beginning of estrangement from Henry, 104–105, 107; rising status with inventors, 107; stays on as patent examiner, 108; warned by Burke about outside activities, 110; explains mounting backlog, 110, 111; attacked for being "illiberal," 113, 126; shifting views regarding novelty, 115–116, 126–127, 128; salary raised to $2500 (1848), 116; friendship with Lane, 117–118; distinguished colleagues (1849), 118; explains Buchanan's concern about politics of nominees, 123; queries Bache about job for Lane, 124; commended by St. Louis Reveille, 127; dilemma implied in "conversion," 128, 129, 131; estrangement from scientific community, 128–129, 130–131, 131–132; retains membership in AAAS until 1854, 130–131; publishes book exposing Fox sisters (1853), 131; ignored by Lazzaroni, 132, 141; disputes Henry's as-

Riley, Joshua, 45
Ritchie, Edward S., CGP charges coil copied by Ruhmkorff, 175-176
Rogers, H. D., 167, 181
Rogers, W. B., 181
Roget, Peter M., 75
Rostow, W. W., 53
Royal Agricultural School of Bavaria, 183
Royal Institution, 9
Royal Society Catalogue of Scientific Papers, CGP's citations in, 12
Ruggles, John, investigation of Patent Office, 49-50; reform bill of 1836, 49, 53, 120; on qualifications for examiner, 51, 55
Ruhmkorff, Heinrich D., 171-172, 173, 175; unveils first coil, 24; and Volta Prize, 171, 174, 180
Ruhmkorff coil, 28, 162, 172, 173, 174, 175, 176

St. Louis *Reveille,* commends CGP, 127
Salem, Massachusetts, 7, 8, 24, 42, 50; eminent sons of, 8-9; Essex Institute, 8, 13, 43; CGP leaves 9; milieu, 13, 41, 182; Athenæm, 13; English High School 14; CGP's office in, 14; Glee Club, 14; Light Infantry, 14; Lyceum, CGP lectures at, 14; opportunities for CGP, 41
Saxton, Joseph, 30, 67
Schaeffer, George C., 59, 155, 158, 164; Silliman, Jr., on, 150; attacked by *Scientific American,* 156; Lane on, 157; becomes agent, 160
Schoolcraft, Henry, 41-42
Science, American, 1, 3, 5, 11, 13, 30, 53, 61, 74, 117, 182, 186; CGP and Henry compared, 12, 22, 34-35; Henry on, 21, 47; Charles and Mary Beard on, 26-27; lack of patronage, 38-39; in federal government, 42; professionalization, 104, 105; *Scientific American* definition of, 112-113; Greeley's concept of, 130; CGP on quackery, 131; compared to European, 170; S. H. Wales on European ignorance of, 172; CGP on French ignorance of, 175; G. B. Goode on decade of 1830s, 181
Scientific American, 108, 139, 142; and CGP, 11, 68, 89-90, 100, 105, 126, 136, 171, 172; assumes leadership of patent lobby, 107; campaign to speed up patent examinations, 110-111, 113-115; circulation, 111;

and Smithsonian, 107, 111-112, 122, 130; upholds examiners, 115, 120; campaign for "liberalization," 119, 120, 125-126; serializes essay by Maher, 120-121; and Ewbank, 123, 124; and Renwick, 127; and Fitzgerald, 127-128, 135; and allocation of space in Patent Office, 134; patent agency, 137, 138-139, 147, 160; and Mason, 154; and Schaeffer, 156, 157; and Holt's removals, 156, 157, 158; and Everett, 157; and Thomas's Revising Board, 158-159; decries dismissals at outset of Lincoln Administration, 163
Scientific Club (Washington), 2, 164
Scoresby, William, 100
Seaton, W. W., 45
Self-induction, 15-16
Serrell, William, 53
Sewall, Thomas, 72, 73
Shelby College, 155
Shockley, William, 186
Silliman, Benjamin, 9, 10, 22, 29, 31, 48, 105, 128, 181; optimism about CGP's experiments, 92
Silliman, Benjamin, Jr., 145-146; on Schaeffer, 150
Silliman's Journal. See American Journal of Science
Singer, Isaac, 160, 170
Smith, F. O. J., 68, 70
Smith, John H., 54-55
Smithson, James, disposition of bequest, 10, 44, 96, 112, 130, 138
Smithsonian Institution, 1, 2, 116, 181, 182; CGP consultant to Building Committee, 12, 76; and CGP's telegraph magneto, 69, 131, 171; and Henry, 10, 22, 43, 74-75, 76, 112-113; fire of 1865, 69; archives, 74, 129; CGP demonstrates motors at, 82, 92; misconception about CGP's connection with, 104; and Lane, 106; criticized by *Scientific American,* 107, 112-113, 122, 130
Sprague, Charles, 64
Squier, E. G., 112, 113
Stanton, Frederick, proposes House appropriation for CGP, 95-96
Steinheil, Karl A., 71
Steinmetz, C. P., 119
Stephenson, Robert, 139
Stone, Henry, 45, 46
Stoughton, A. B., 160

227

091817